COMPLETE BOOK ON INDIAN ARMED FORCES

COMPLETE BOOK ON INDIAN ARMED FORCES

Rameshwar Prasad

CYBER TECH PUBLICATIONS
4264/3, Ansari Road, Daryaganj, New Delhi-110002 (India)
Ph.: 011-23244078, 011-43559448 Fax: 011-23280028
E-Mail: cyberpublicationsdelhi@yahoo.com
Website: www.cybertechpublications.com

COMPLETE BOOK ON INDIAN ARMED FORCES

Rameshwar Prasad

First Edition 2010

Reprint Edition 2024

Published by :

G.S. Rawat for **Cyber Tech Publications**
4264/3, Ansari Road, Daryaganj, New Delhi-110002 (India)
Ph.: 011-23244078, 011-43559448 Fax: 011-23280028
E-Mail: cyberpublicationsdelhi@yahoo.com
Website: www.cybertechpublications.com

Printed at: Asian Offset Printers, Delhi-53

Preface

The Indian Army is the world's second largest army in terms of military personnel, and the largest in terms of active manpower. It is a completely voluntary service, the military draft having never been imposed in India. The army has rich combat experience in diverse terrains, due to India's diverse geography, and also has a distinguished history of serving in United Nations peacekeeping operations.

The force is headed by the Chief of Army Staff of the Indian Army, currently Deepak Kapoor. The highest rank in the Indian Army is Field Marshal, but it is a largely ceremonial rank and appointments are made by the President of India, on the advice of the Union Cabinet of Ministers, only in exceptional circumstances. (See Field Marshal (India)). Late General S.H.F.J. Manekshaw and the late General K.M. Cariappa are the only two officers who have attained this rank.

The Indian Army has seen military action during the First Kashmir War, Operation Polo, the Sino-Indian War, the Second Kashmir War, the Indo-Pakistani War of 1971, the Sri Lankan Civil War and the Kargil War. Currently, the Indian army has dedicated one brigade of troops to the UN's standby arrangements. Through its large, sustained troop commitments India has come in for much praise for taking part in difficult operations for prolonged periods. The Indian Army has participated in several UN peacekeeping operations, including the ones in Cyprus, Lebanon, Congo, Angola, Cambodia, Vietnam, Namibia, El Salvador, Liberia, Mozambique and Somalia. The army also provided a paramedical unit to facilitate the withdrawal of the sick and wounded in Korea. So far, India has won the 1971 war against Pakistan and has defeated Pakistan's efforts during the Kargil war. The 1965 war resulted into a ceasefire mandated by the United Nations. However, it lost much territory in the Sino-Indian War which till date it has not managed to gain. The Indian army is considered one of the best armies in the world and is comparable to those of Russia, US and China. This book is all about the Indian Armed Forces and their functions and operations.

—Author

CONTENTS

1

Introduction

The Indian Armed Forces is the primary military organization responsible for the territorial security and defence of India. The President of India serves as the supreme commander of the armed forces, which are subordinate and responsible to the Government of India headed by the Prime Minister of India. The armed forces are administered by the Ministry of Defence and are composed of the Indian Army, the Indian Navy and the Indian Air Force. Auxiliary services include the Indian Coast Guard, the Paramilitary forces of India and the Strategic Forces Command.

All service personnel are volunteers although the government is empowered to undertake conscription if considered necessary for India's defence. However, India has never had conscription, even during the Indo-Pakistani Wars and the Sino-Indian War. The armed forces retain much of the organizational structure established by the British. However, the armed forces are an essential character of India's strategic importance, power and capabilities, which have increased after India became a declared nuclear weapons state.

ORGANIZATION AND COMMAND STRUCTURE

The headquarters of the Indian Armed Forces is in New Delhi, the capital city of India. The Indian armed force are split into different groups based on their region of operation. The Indian Army is administratively divided into 7 tactical commands, each under the control of different Lieutenant Generals.

STRUCTURE OF THE INDIAN ARMY

The Indian Army fields 34 divisions. Its headquarters is located in the Indian capital New Delhi and it is under the overall command of the Chief of Army Staff (COAS), currently General Deepak Kapoor.

The army has 6 commands and one training command known as ARTRAC. Each command is headed by General Officer Commanding-in-Chief with the rank of Lieutenant General. Each command is directly affiliated to the Army HQ in New Delhi.

There are 3 types of Corps in the Indian Army: Strike, Holding & Mixed. The Corps HQ is the largest field formation in the army. Other field formations include: Divisions, Brigades, Battalions, Companies, Platoons, and Sections.

These are several Battalions or Units under the same formation in a Regiment. The Gurkha Regiment, for instance, has several battalions. All formations under a Regiment are battalions of the same arms or Corps (i.e. Infantry, or Engineers). Regiments are not exactly field formations in the sense they mostly do not make a formation. For instance, all Regiments of the Gurkha's would not fight together as one formation, but can be dispersed over various Brigades or Corps or even Commands.

In addition, the Indian Army has 63 Armoured Regiments, see List of Armoured Regiments in the Indian Army.

The Regiment of Artillery constitutes a formidable operational arm of Indian Army. Historically, it takes its lineage from Moghul Emperor Babur, who is popularly credited with introduction of artillery to India in the Battle of Panipat in 1526. However, evidence of earlier use of guns by Bahmani Kings in the Battle of Adoni in 1368 and King Mohammed Shah of Gujrat in fifteenth century have been recorded.

RANK STRUCTURE

The highest ranking Commissioned Officer is the Field Marshal and only two have been awarded this rank so far. The rank of

General is held by the Chief of Army Staff, followed by Lieutenant-General, Major-General, Brigadier, Colonel, Lieutenant-Colonel, Major, Captain, and finally the Lieutenant. Among the Junior Commissioned Officers (JCOs), the ranks are organized from Honorary Captain (given to Outstanding JCO's Rank and pay of a Captain), Honorary Lieutenant (given to Outstanding JCO's Rank and pay of a Lieutenant), Subedar Major, Subedar to Naib Subedar.

Finally, among the Non-commissioned Officers (NCOs), the ranks are organized from Company Havildar Major, Company Quarter Master Havildar, Havildar, Naik, Lance Naik to the Sepoy.

Structure of the Indian Navy

The Indian Navy is organized into three main commands and one joint command.

- Eastern Naval Command at Visakhapatnam
- Western Naval Command at Mumbai
- Southern Naval Command at Kochi
- Far Eastern Naval Command (Joint command) at Port Blair in the Andaman & Nicobar Island chain

STRUCTURE OF THE INDIAN AIR-FORCE

Recruitment and Training

Recruitment is through three military related academies. These include the National Defence Academy, Indian Military Academy and Officers Training Academy. For entrance, one must display that they are both physically and mentally fit to be in the military by sitting examinations and undergoing medical checkups. The complete list of institutions training Indian army were listed in Military academies in India section.

Indian Army

Strength: During a conflict, the air-arm of the Indian army plays a crucial role in providing essential supplies and air cover to the ground forces. Shown here is the Indian Army's HAL Dhruv.

Indian Army Statistics

Active Troops	1,325,000 (2nd)
Artillery	7100
Battle Tanks	5010
Aircraft	52 squadrons of helicopters
Surface-to-air missiles	90,000+

The Indian Army is the world's second largest army in terms of military personnel (after China).

It is a completely voluntary service, the military draft having never been imposed in India. The army has rich combat experience in diverse terrains, due to India's diverse geography, and also has a distinguished history of serving in United Nations peacekeeping operations.

The force is headed by the Chief of Army Staff, currently General Deepak Kapoor.

The highest rank in the Indian Army is Field Marshal, but it is a largely ceremonial rank and appointments are made by the President of India, on the advice of the Union Cabinet of Ministers, only in exceptional circumstances. (See Field Marshal (India)). General S.H.F.J. Manekshaw and the late General K.M. Cariappa are the only two officers who have attained this rank.

The Indian Army has seen military action in the Indo-Pakistani War of 1947, the Indo-Pakistani War of 1965,the Indo-Pakistani War of 1971, and others such as Operation Polo in 1948, the Sino-Indian War in 1962 over the McMahon Line, and the Kargil War against Kashmiri insurgents and the Pakistan military personnel

Currently, the Indian army has dedicated one brigade of troops to the UN's standby arrangements. Through its large, sustained troop commitments India has come in for much praise for taking part in difficult operations for prolonged periods.

The Indian Army has participated in several UN peace-keeping operations, including the ones in Cyprus, Lebanon, Congo, Angola,

Cambodia, Vietnam, Namibia, El Salvador, Liberia, Mozambique and Somalia. The army also provided a paramedical unit to facilitate the withdrawal of the sick and wounded in Korea.

War Heroes

Major Som Nath Sharma	4th Battalion, Kumaon Regiment	November 3, 1947	Badgam, Kashmir, India
Lance Naik Karam Singh	1st Battalion, Sikh Regiment	October 13, 1948	Tithwal, Kashmir, India
Second Lieutenant Rama Raghoba Rane	Corps of Engineers	April 8, 1948	Naushera, Kashmir, India
Naik Jadu Nath Singh	1st Battalion, Rajput Regiment, now 4th Battalion, Brigade of the Guards (1st Rajput)	February 1948	Naushera, Kashmir, India
Company Havildar Major Piru Singh	6th Battalion, Rajputana Rifles	July 17/18, 1948	Tithwal, Kashmir, India
Captain Gurbachan Singh Salaria	3rd Battalion, 1st Gorkha Rifles (The Malaun Regiment)	December 5, 1961	Elizabethville, Katanga, Congo
Major Dhan Singh Thapa	1st Battalion, 8th Gorkha Rifles	October 20, 1962	Ladakh, India
Subedar Joginder Singh	1st Battalion, Sikh Regiment	October 23, 1962	Tongpen La, Northeast Frontier Agency, India
Major Shaitan Singh	13th Battalion, Kumaon Regiment	November 18, 1962	Rezang La
Company Quarter Master Havildar Abdul Hamid	4th Battalion, The Grenadiers	September 10, 1965	Chima, Khem Karan Sector
Lieutenant-Colonel Ardeshir Burzorji Tarapore	17th Poona Horse	October 15, 1965	Phillora, Sialkot Sector, Pakistan
Lance Naik Albert Ekka	14th Battalion, Brigade of the Guards	December 3, 1971	Gangasagar

2/Lieutenant Arun Khetarpal	17th Poona Horse	December 16, 1971	Jarpal, Shakargarh Sector
Major Hoshiar Singh	3rd Battalion, The Grenadiers	December 17, 1971	Basantar River, Shakargarh Sector
Naib Subedar Bana Singh	8th Battalion, Jammu and Kashmir Light Infantry	June 23, 1987	Siachen Glacier, Jammu and Kashmir
Major Ramaswamy Parmeshwaran	8th Battalion, Mahar Regiment	November 25, 1987	Sri Lanka
Captain Vikram Batra	13th Battalion, Jammu and Kashmir Rifles	July 6, 1999	Point 5140, Point 4875, Kargil Area
Captain Manoj Kumar Pandey	1st Battalion, 11th Gorkha Rifles	July 3, 1999	Khaluber/Juber Top, Batalik sector, Kargil area, Jammu and Kashmir
Grenadier Yogendra Singh Yadav	18th Battalion, The Grenadiers	July 4, 1999	Tiger Hill, Kargil area
Lance Naik Ghulam Mohammed Khan	12 Jammu and Kashmir Light Infantry	July 1999	Kargil area
Rifleman Sanjay Kumar	13th Battalion, Jammu and Kashmir Rifles	July 5, 1999	Area Flat Top, Kargil Area
Captain Haneef uddin	11 Rajputana Rifles	July 1999	Turtuk, Kargil area

- Lt. Nawang Kapadia
- Major Navneet Vats
- Major Rajesh Singh Adhikari, MVC
- Lance Naik Ahmed Ali
- Lieutenant Kieshing Clifford Nongrum

INDIAN NAVY

The Indian Navy is the naval branch of the armed forces of India. With 55,000 men and women, including 5,000 naval aviation personnel and 2,000 Marine Commandos (MARCOS), it is the world's fifth largest navy. The Indian Navy currently operates more than 155 vessels, including the aircraft carrier INS Viraat.

The navy is considered to have blue-water capabilities. It is fairly advanced in terms of technology and is in control of one of two Asian aircraft carriers. Two more aircraft carriers are on order and will be joining the Indian Navy. The ships of the Indian Navy are of Indian and foreign origin.

In its maritime doctrine, the Indian Navy establishes its role in providing support to maritime neighbours during natural disasters. This was demonstrated during the Asian tsunami crisis during which the Indian Navy sent 35 ships to support relief efforts in neighbouring countries.

The Indian navy has taken part in UN missions in the coast of Somalia and has provided security to an African Union summit held in Mozambique. India uses its navy to enhance its international relations through joint exercises, port visits, and humanitarian missions, including disaster relief. The Indian Navy is increasing its capabilities as a true blue-water navy; the Indian Navy's doctrine states that this is for the collective good of nations.

INDIAN AIR FORCE

The Indian Air Force is the fourth largest air force in the world. In its history, it has generally relied on Soviet technology to support its growth. However, in recent times, India has begun building its own original aircraft, including the HAL Tejas, which is a 4.5 generation fighter.

Also India and Russia are currently building a 5th generation stealth aircraft jointly. India has also developed UAV called Nishant and HAL Dhruv, an advanced light helicopter. Recently it has completed a test of long range BVR air to air missile named Astra and also conducted a successful test of Anti ballistic missile defense system and hence became the 4th country after US,Russia and Israel to do so.

PARAMILITARY FORCES OF INDIA

Indian Nuclear Power

It is estimated that India possesses around 200-250 nuclear warheads which could be deployed at short notice.

Nuclear Doctrine: The Indian military possesses nuclear weapons and sufficient means — by means of missiles and aircraft— to deliver anything over long distances.

However, India has a *nuclear no-first-use* and no use against non-nuclear weapons state policy. It also maintains a non-nuclear doctrine based on *credible minimum deterrence.* India is not a signatory to the Nuclear Non-proliferation Treaty (NPT), arguing that it unfairly favours the established nuclear powers: While the treaty places restrictions on the non-nuclear weapons states, it does little to curb the modernization and expansion of the nuclear arsenals of the nuclear weapons states; it provides no provision for complete nuclear disarmament.

Gallantry Awards: The highest wartime gallantry award given by the Military of India is the Param Vir Chakra (PVC), followed by the Maha Vir Chakra (MVC) and the Vir Chakra (VrC). Its peacetime equivalent is the Ashoka Chakra. The highest decoration for meritorious service is the Param Vishisht Seva Medal.

Future: Several reports have mentioned that the Indian military will be an even greater force to reckon with in the future given the twin advantage of economic growth and an increasing population. Analyses of the Central Intelligence Agency indicates that India is projected to possess the fourth most capable concentration of power by 2015. According to a report published by the US Congress, India is the developing world's leading arms purchaser.

ARMY

The army numbers about one million personnel and fields 34 divisions. Designed primarily to defend the country's frontiers, the army has become heavily committed to internal security duties in Kashmir and the Northeast.

In 2002 the Indian Army had 980,000 active troops, along with an Army Reserve consisting of: 300,000 first line troops (those within five years of full time service), and another 500,000 second line troops (subject to recall to service until 50 years of age). The Territorial Army numbered 40,000 first line troops (and 160,000 second line troops). In 1994 the army had approximately 940,000 men and women on active duty, and another 36,000 in the Territorial Army. As of 1998 the Army had a sanctioned troop strength of 1,045,000, but there was a shortage of about 59,000 troops.

At the beginning of World War II there were 170,000 soldiers in the Indian Army all regulars, but by June of 1948 there were 2,000,000. This was the reason British Officers were needed to help train and form new units. Each Battalion needed eight British Officers to take command, as all the lower ranks were manned by Indian Viceroy Commissioned Officers, and NCOs.

The army is headquartered in New Delhi and is under the direction of the chief of the army staff, always a full general. The chief of the army staff is assisted by a vice chief, two deputy chiefs, a military secretary, and the heads of four main staff divisions: the adjutant general, the quartermaster general, the master general of ordnance, and the engineer in chief.

The Army consists of a number of arms and services. These are: Armoured Corps, Regiment of Artillery, Corps of Engineers, Corps of Signals, Mechanised Infantry, Infantry, Army Service Corps, Military Nursing Service, Army Medical Corps, Army Dental Corps, Army Ordnance Corps, Corps of Electrical and Mechanical Engineers, Remount and Veterinary Corps, Military Farms Service, Army Education Corps, Intelligence Corps, Corps of Military Police, Judge Advocate General Department, Army Physical Training Corps, Pioneer Corps, Army Postal Service Corps and Defence Security Corps. In addition, the Army has its own Recruiting Organisation, Record Offices, Depots, Boys Establishments and Selection Centers and training institutions. These units are organized in twelve corps-level formations.

The army has five tactical area commands: the Northern Command headquartered at Udhampur in Jammu and Kashmir, the Western Command headquartered at Chandimandir in Chandigarh, the Central Command headquartered at Lucknow in Uttar Pradesh, the Eastern Command headquartered at Calcutta, and the Southern Command headquartered at Pune in Maharashtra. Each command is headed by a lieutenant general.

In the Indian context, Command Headquarter can be likened to a Field Army or even an Army Group Headquarter with a General Officer Commanding-in-Chief presiding over matters in the rank of a (three-star) Lieutenant General. Next the line are the Corps Headquarters, which are Field Army Headquarters elsewhere. The Indian Army's combat formations are now grouped and tailored under many such Corps Headquarters (with some forces being retained under static Area Commands). As with the American Army, all Corps have numerical designations. They also have names, by which they are more commonly known. These names may derive from the city in which they are headquartered [XVI Corps / Nagrota Corps], or they may be evocative [IV Corps is Gajraj Corps, meaning "King Elephant."

The field force is grouped into Corps. Some of these are defensively oriented and have, over the years, acquired an unofficial-'Holding'. The others are called reserve or, unofficially again, 'Strike' Corps. The former is really a misnomer since these contain ample offensive potential. Corps Headquarters are designed to. handle an all-arms field army-of three to five divisions or their equivalents. Army Headquarters reserves could be mammoth-size or small, but powerful in either case. Heavy-tracked-Corps are an instance of the former, and the three parachute commandos (battalion-size units), which perform special forces duties, of the latter. Airborne, Air Assault or Parachute troops are usually held centralized. The mounts', in all cases, are provided by the Indian Air Force.

The Division and Independent Brigade Group are the lowest (or the highest, depending on the viewpoint) individual formations. They integrate in themselves all arms and services for sustained independent operations. There is great flexibility in their force mix, and in 'grouping for tasks'. Brigade (regiment in some armies) size combined-arms groups can be shed or added on at will. Standard Tables of Organization and Equipment do exist, but these are taken lightly for accounting purposes only. Divisions and independent brigade groups are designated by function, terrain of operation, or by their equipment mix.

The Army has in its Order of Battle, mountain divisions, infantry divisions, armoured divisions (in which tank units predominate) and mechanized divisions (in which mechanized infantry units predominate). An Infantry Division typically has about 15,500 combat troops, with 8,000 support elements (artillery, engineers, etc).

It consists of 3 to 5 Infantry Brigades, an Armoured Regiment and an Artillery Brigade. A Brigade is commanded by a Brigadier, and an Infantary Brigade consists of three Infantry Battalions. A regiment can be a type of battalion (eg. in the Artillery/Engineers) or a grouping of a number of battalions of the same type (eg. The Rajput Regiment). The approximate strength of an infantry battalion, commanded by a Colonel, may be taken as 900-1,000 personnel. A battalion may consist of three to four companies, and may be commanded by a Lieutenant Colonel or a Colonel. A company normally consists of 100-120 men and is commanded by a Major.

Independent brigade groups, as the name suggests, are vested with limited capability to carry out an independent mission. Independent brigade groups or independent brigade-sized formations may be armoured, mechanized, air defence (missile or gun), parachute, engineer, field artillery, electronic warfare or even standard infantry and mountain. These form 'Corps/Army troops', that is, they are held at Corps and Army levels for balancing out missions and task forces. At these levels, one would find heavy logistic support units in terms of supply, transport, field ordnance depots, and medical facilities.

An extensive body of schools and centers supports army operations. The officer corps is largely drawn from the National

Defence Academy at Khadakvasla, Maharashtra, a joint services training institution that provides educational equivalents to the bachelor of arts or bachelor of science degrees to cadets for all three service arms.

Cadets spend their first three years at the National Defence Academy and then are sent to their respective service academies for further training before being commissioned in the armed forces. A preparatory school, the Rashtriya Indian Military College, at Dehra Dun, Uttar Pradesh, provides education to candidates for the National Defence Academy.

After completing their studies at the National Defence Academy, army cadets are sent to the Indian Military Academy at Dehra Dun. Other Indian Military Academy cadets are graduates of the Army Cadet College or are direct-entry students who have qualified by passing the Union Public Service Commission Examination. They spend between twelve and twenty-four months at the Indian Military Academy before being commissioned in the army as second lieutenants. Still other officer training occurs at the Officers' Training Academy in Madras, Tamil Nadu, where a forty-four-week session is offered to university graduates seeking a short-service commission.

In addition to the Indian Military Academy, the army runs a number of military education establishments. The more prominent ones include the College of Combat at Mhow, Madhya Pradesh; the High Altitude Warfare School at Gulmarg, Jammu and Kashmir; and the Counter-Insurgency and Jungle Warfare School at Vairengte, Mizoram.

The army also operates the Defence Services Staff College at Wellington in the Nilgiri Hills in Tamil Nadu, which provides master of science-level joint-service training for mid-level staff appointments and promotes interservice cooperation.

In 1994 it was reported that there were 200 women in the armed forces. In the army, which employs women as physicians and nurses, the participation of women is small but growing. The Indian Military Nursing Service was formed in 1926 and has eight nursing schools (five army, two navy, and one air force) and one nursing college in Pune. Bachelor of science graduates are commissioned as lieutenants in the Medical Nursing Service and attached to the various components of the armed forces.

Ranks as high as colonel can be attained by career officers. In the mid-1990s, a small but increasing number of women officers were being assigned to nonmedical services. In 1994, there were fifty women nonmedical army officers and another twenty-five in training. They are university graduates who have been put through rigorous training and are reported to be eager for combat unit assignments.

2

A Historical Overview of the Army

INTRODUCTION

The origin of the Indian Army goes back to the beginning of the British rule over India. During the last 250 years, it has undergone many changes, accomplished many feats and fought countless battles at home and abroad on different continents. It has been a unique organisation, vastly different in its ethos and traditions from the other armies of the world. Winston Churchill referred to the over two million strong Indian Army during the World War-II, as the largest volunteer army known to history. Even today at around 1.2 million personnel, the Indian Army it is one of the largest volunteer armies in the world. Like the caste system, which permeates our society, the theory of martial races has influenced the composition of the Indian Army. Though this theory has long been officially discarded it continues to survive, albeit on a gradually reducing scale. The regimental ethos based on regional and class affinity often reinforced by heredity, has always been a strong motivating factor for the soldiers of this army. This was an important ingredient of their high morale at a time when they did not have a nationalistic cause to serve.

This Army, while greatly influencing the course of political developments in its own country, has never participated in politics. It is one of the few apolitical armies in the world to not have a

Cromwell or a Napoleon trying to acquire political power. Raised by a foreign power to serve its commercial and imperial interests, the Indian Army did not have a nationalistic cause to serve for the first 200 years, but it was never a mercenary army. Its soldiers did not enlist for money to sell their loyalty to the highest bidder. They joined the Army, because they considered fighting an honourable profession and they fought for their honour which included that of the family, community, region and regiment.

The concept of nationhood was non-existent in 18th Century India. Thus many Indians enlisted in the Army of a foreign power and had no hesitation in fighting under their flag against their own countrymen and contributing to the establishment of British Imperial rule over India. However this duty got compensated by the action of many of them in the Great Revolution of 1857. The first spark of nationalism in the country in the modern period under British rule was lit by the Indian soldier. The revolution was thus essentially an affair of the Army. Even though the revolution failed, it became a source of inspiration for the subsequent generations in the freedom struggle. It is noteworthy that notwithstanding the Jallianwala Bagh incident, the Army was sparingly used against the freedom fighters. Terrorism or the non-violent struggle for freedom were mostly contained by the civil administration, using police for the purpose.

When the Army had to be called out, it was more like the British Army in India than the Indian Army. In 1930, the Garhwalis refused to open fire on the Red Shirts during the non-cooperation movement. They were court-martialled for mutiny but their action was applauded by the nation. Indian soldiers served all over the world during the British regime. They fought from China in the East to France and Africa in the West. They fought bravely during during the First and Second World Wars. The tales of their valour have been spread worldwide. The secret of success of the Indian Army has been its unflinching sense of duty, discipline and traditions of valour. During the Second World War, the emergence of the Indian National Army (INA) from the ranks of Indian Army prisoners with the Japanese, under the leadership of Netaji Subhash Chandra

Bose, to fight for Indian independence became a major development. In military terms, the contribution of the Indian National Army was limited but its political and psychological impact was tremendous.

After the war, the mutinies of the Army, Navy and Air Force at Bombay, Jabalpur and Karachi respectively, convinced a militarily and economically exhausted Britain that she could not rely on the Indian Army to uphold her imperial rule on India. This became an important factor in influencing her decision to quit. Thus the Indian Army, made a silent but significant contribution to the independence of India. Lord Wavell, the Viceroy of India, in his farewell speech on 21 March 1947, five months before Independence, said, "I believe that the stability of the Indian Army may perhaps be a deciding factor in the future of India." Later events more than justified this belief. At the time of Independence, the Indian Army had to undergo a major surgical operation with many Muslim Officers leaving for the newly created state of Pakistan. The senior ranks in the Army were all held by the British Officers and they left for home.

They were replaced by Indian Army Officers with much less experience. Besides there were other problems too. Most of the Army personnel were from North-India and the families of many had been uprooted from their homes a result of partition and were living in refugee camps. Their pay was slashed considerably just before independence and they accepted these cuts in a most disciplined manner. There were no representations nor any case was filed in any court of law. It was against this background that the Army was called upon to tackle the unprecedented carnage and the movement of millions of refugees in Punjab. The civil administration had collapsed. The Army was the only credible instrument available with the State to restore order. Within a couple of months after independence, normalcy was restored in riot-ravaged Punjab.

No sooner has this been done, the Army was called upon to defend J&K against an armed invasion first from Phatan rebels in October 1947 and then in 1948 from the Pakistan Army. Military operations in Jammu & Kashmir, in the most difficult terrain and at forbidding heights raged from October 1947 to January 1949, ended in a proud victory for the Indian Army and Pakistan failed to achieve its objectives. However, a cease-fire was accepted by India which enabled Pakistan to hold portions of Jammu & Kashmir state. These areas under Pakistan's occupation are called Pak-occupied Kashmir (PoK). In the wake of independence the question of integrating over 500 Indian States into the Union of India posed a major problem. The Army constituted the final sanction behind Sardar Vallabhai Patel's moves for integration. Where, this could not be achieved through diplomatic negotiations, the Indian Army had to be employed to enforce the nation's will, as happened in Junagarh, Hyderabad and Goa.

On 15 January 1948, General K.M. Cariappa became the first Indian Commander-in-Chief of the Indian Army. January 15, is now celebrated every year in India, as Army Day. On this occasion the Chief of the Army Staff (COAS) takes the salute at the Army Day Parade in the Delhi cantonment. The first decade or more after independence was an era in which India's moral authority stood very high in all chanceries of the world. The Indian Army was employed on tasks to promote international peace in Korea, Gaza, Lebanon and Congo on behalf of the United Nations and earned great honour for the country. China's belligerence in 1962 shook the nation. This was defeat, pure and simple, born of short-sightedness and bad decision. India was outclassed and outsmarted by masters of real geopolitik. This rude awakening in the Himalayas, caused the failure of the political & military leadership and brought about a great national humiliation.

The Army however soon recovered from this trauma. The glorified battles of the war with Pakistan three years later in 1965, helped partly to heal wounds. But honour was not really restored till the resounding victory in the 1971 Indo-Pak war, with tales of impossible victories won in places like Longewala with scores of Pakistani tanks destroyed. A decisive victory like this, had not taken place in centuries. Today India is at the cross-roads. In some spheres we have creditable progress, but in many others there has been alarming deterioration and are facing mounting crisis. Divisive and secessionist forces have been increasingly asserting themselves. Various contradictions in our society not only persist but have accentuated. The Army cannot remain totally isolated from these developments. The Sikh problem had its repercussions in the mutiny of some Sikh soldiers. The Gorkhaland problem may have ramifications amongst the Gorkha soldiers, if proper care is not taken. The Sikhs and the Gorkhas have been our finest soldiers and their record of loyalty and gallantry should not be allowed to get tarnished.

The Army also has certain organisational and functional problems which must be suitably resolved. Notwithstanding all the difficulties we face as a nation and problems faced by the Army, we can rely on the Indian Army to continue to serve the nation loyally and with a high standard of professionalism and gallantry. This may help the nation in proceeding along the desired path from the present cross-roads. A code of honour has come down to the Jawans from the great commanders and soldiers of the past eras. It is a matter of great pride that whenever India has been attacked, the Army stood by this code of valour, fidelity and honour. The tradition never to surrender has remained ingrained in our fighting men and the Army always has resolute soldiers who are ever ready to do their duty unto death without hesitation.

ETHOS OF THE INDIAN ARMY

- The safety, honour and welfare of your country comes first, always and every time.
- The honour, welfare and comfort of the men you command come next.
- Your own ease, comfort and safety come last, always and every time.

Characteristics of the Indian Army

- *Valour.* Fearlessness in combat, in the face of the enemy even when fighting at a great disadvantage or facing sure death.

- *Non-discrimination.* On account of caste, creed or religion. Total impartiality in performance of duty.
- *Comradeship and brotherhood of the brave.* Within the Army regardless of caste, creed or religion.
- *Discipline and integrity.* Patriotism, honesty and courage under all circumstances.
- *Spirit of selfless sacrifice.* The tradition never to question but to do or die.
- *Fairness and honesty.* Even towards the enemy, prisoners or wounded.
- *Fidelity, honour and courage.* Stand out as an example to others.
- *Dogged determination.* Even in defeat or adverse situations.

DEFENDING SARAGARHI, 12 SEPTEMBER 1897

Saragarhi is the incredible story of 21 men of the 36th Sikh Regiment (currently the 4th Sikh Regiment) who gave up their lives in devotion to their duty. In keeping with the tradition of the Indian Army, they fought to the death rather than surrender. The Battle at Saragarhi is one of eight stories of collective bravery published by UNESCO (United Nations Educational, Scientific and Cultural Organization). It has been mentioned as one of the five most significant events of its kind in the world which includes the Saga of Thermoplyae associated with the heroic stand of a small Greek force against the mighty Persian Army of Xerxes in 480 B.C.

THE BATTLE

The British colonial rulers had constructed a series of forts to control the NWFP (North West Frontier Province-today a state in Pakistan) and to provide security to troops against marauding tribesmen and their *lashkars* (large body of troops). Most of these forts had initially been built by Maharaja Ranjit Singh as part of the consolidation of the Sikh empire in Punjab and the British added some more. The British had only partially succeeded in gaining control over this region, consequently, skirmishes and sometimes serious fights with the tribals were a frequent occurrence. However, the NWFP was a good training ground for the Indian Army to hone its skills and techniques.

Two such forts on the Samana ridge of the Hindukush & Sulaiman ranges that is Fort Lockhart and Fort Gulistan were a few miles apart. Since these forts were not inter-visible, a signalling relay post called Saragarhi was located mid-way on a bluff to provide heliographic communications between them. This post or picket had been fortified to provide safety and protection to the signalling detachment.

In 1897 there was a general uprising in the NWFP engineered by Afghans as part of their policy, which came to be known as the 'prickly heat policy' to direct the wrath of the tribals against the British. In this uprising, *Mullahs* (Muslim religious leaders) played a prominent role. It was the duty of the 36th Sikh to occupy Gulistan and Lockhart forts. On 3rd and 9th September 1897, Orakazai and Afridi *lashkars* attacked Fort Gulistan. On both occasion the attacks were beaten back. A relief column was sent from the fort to assist in beating back these attacks.

The relief column from Lockhart on the return trip reinforced the signalling detachment at Saragarhi making its strength to 1 NCO (Non-Commissioned Officer) and 20 ORs (Other Ranks). In a renewed effort, on 12 September 1897, hordes of tribesmen laid siege to Fort Lockhart and Saragarhi, with the aim of overrunning the latter and at the same time preventing any help from the former.

The Commanding Officer of 36th Sikh, Lt. Col. Haughton, was at Fort Lockhart and was in communication with the Saragarhi post through helicograph. The defenders of Saragarhi under the indomitable and inspiring leadership of their detachment commander, Havildar Ishar Singh, resolved to defend their post in the best tradition of their race and regiment. They were not there to hand over the post to the enemy and seek safety elsewhere. Havildar Singh and his men knew well that the post would fall, because a handful of men in that make-shift fort of stones & mud walls with a wooden door could not stand the onslaught of thousands of tribesmen. These plucky men knew that they will go down but they had resolved to do so fighting to the last.

From Fort Lockhart, troops and the Commanding Officer could count at least 14 standards and that gave an idea of the number of tribes and their massed strength against the Saragarhi relay post (estimated at between 10,000 to 12,000 tribals). From early morning the tribals started battering the fort. The Sikhs fought back valiantly. Charge after charge was repulsed by the men of the 36th Sikh. The tribal leaders started to make tempting promises so that the Sikhs would surrender. But Havildar Singh and his men ignored them. For quite some time, the troops held their own against the determined and repeated attacks by the wild and ferocious hordes. A few attempts were made to send a relief column from Fort Lockhart but these were foiled by the tribals.

At Saragarhi, the enemy made two determined attempts to rush the gate of the post and on both occasions the defenders repulsed the assault. While the enemy suffered heavy casualties, the ranks of the defenders too kept dwindling as the fire from the attackers took its toll and their ammunition stocks were depleting. Unmindful of his safety, Sepoy Gurmukh Singh kept signalling a minute-to-minute account of the battle from the signal tower in the post to Battalion HQs. The battle lasted the better part of the day. When repeated attacks failed, the enemy set fire to the surrounding bushes & shrubs and two of the tribesmen under cover of smoke, managed to close in with the post's boundary wall in an area blind to the defender's observation and rifle fire from the post holes. They succeeded in making a breach in the wall. This development could be seen from Fort Lockhart and was flashed to the post.

A few men from those defending the approaches to the gate were dispatched to deal with the breach in the wall. This diversion by the enemy and the defenders' reaction resulted in weakening of the fire covering the gate. The enemy now rushed the gate as well as the breach. Thereafter, one of the fiercest hand-to-hand fights followed. One of the Havildar Singh's men, who was seriously wounded and was profusely bleeding, had taken charge of the guardroom. He shot four of the enemy as they tried to approach his charge. All this time, Sepoy Gurmukh Singh continued flashing the details of the action at the post. Beside this the Commanding Officer of 36th Sikh and others at Lockhart Fort also saw his unique saga of heroism and valour unfold at Saragarhi. The battle had come too close for Sepoy Gurmukh Singh's comfort, so he asked Battalion HQs for permission to shut down the heliograph and take up his rifle. Permission was flashed back. He dismounted his heliograph equipment, packed it in a leather bag, fixed bayonet on his rifle and joined the fight. From this vantage point in the tower he wrought havoc on the intruders in the post. He died fighting, but took 20 of the enemy with him.

The tribals set fire to the post, while the brave garrison lay dead or dying with their ammunition exhausted. Next morning the relief column reached the post and the tell tale marks of the epic fight were there for all to see. The tribals later admitted to figure of 180 dead and many more wounded. This episode when narrated in the British Parliament, drew from the members a standing ovation in the memory of the defenders of Saragarhi. The story of the heroic deeds of these men was also placed before Queen Victoria. The account was received all over the world with awe and admiration. All the 21 valiant men of this epic battle were awarded the Indian Order of Merit Class III (posthumously) which at the time was one of the highest gallantry awards given to Indian troops and is considered equivalent to the present-day Vir Chakra. All dependants of the Saragarhi heroes were awarded 50 acres of land and 500 Rupees. Never before or since has a body of troops-that is, all of them won gallantry awards in a single action. It is indeed a singularly unique action in the annals of Indian military history.

A tablet erected in the memory of these brave men. The tablet reads;

'The Government of India have caused this tablet to be erected to the memory of the twenty one non-commissioned officers and men of

the 36 Sikh Regiment of the Bengal Infantry whose names are engraved below as a perpetual record of the heroism shown by these gallant soldiers who died at their posts in the defence of the fort of Saragarhi, on the 12 September 1897, fighting against overwhelming numbers, thus proving their loyalty and devotion to their sovereign, the Queen Empress of India, and gloriously maintaining the reputation of the Sikhs for unflinching courage on the field of battle."

165 Havildar Ishar Singh

332 Naik Lal Singh	834 Sepoy Narayan Singh
546 Lance Naik Chanda Singh	814 Sepoy Gurmukh Singh
1321 Sepoy Sundar Singh	871 Sepoy Jivan Singh
287 Sepoy Ram Singh	1733 Sepoy Gurmukh Singh
492 Sepoy Uttar Singh	163 Sepoy Ram Singh
182 Sepoy Sahib Singh	1257 Sepoy Bhagwan Singh
359 Sepoy Hira Singh	1265 Sepoy Bhagwan Singh
687 Sepoy Daya Singh	1556 Sepoy Buta Singh
760 Sepoy Jivan Singh	1651 Sepoy Jivan Singh
791 Sepoy Bhola Singh	1221 Sepoy Nand Singh

HARI SINGH NALWA AND THE BATTLE OF NAUSHERA

India has had to face foreign invaders many more times than most other nations. The majority of these came through the Khyber pass in the North West of India. These invaders were lured either by riches of India, zeal to convert people to their beliefs or world domination through force. Th Afghans were among the last to come across the Khyber. By the late 1700s Afghans has set up small city states all over Punjab and North West. Rohillas of Awadh (UP), Tipu Sultan of Mysore, Nawab of Malerkotla, Multan, Kashmir all were ultimately descended from the invaders. The Afghans wrecked havoc on local population in their territories. Rapes and forced conversions were commonplace in the Afghan ruled territories. Children born out of forceful marriages and rapes were given a special caste of "Ranghars". And Ranghars were specially targeted by Maulavis to fill them a zeal of Islam, in order to make them fighters of Islam.

The Sikhs opposed these Afghan landlords and were able eventually to wrest control of the biggest city in Punjab, named Lahore, under the leadership of Maharaja Ranjit Singh Sandhu. In an attempt to bring the North West under their rule the Sikhs sought to sweep away isolated pockets of Afghan power. In his enterprise Maharaja Ranjit Singh Sandhu was helped by his many generals. Hari Singh Nalwa was the most illustrious of them all.

Hari Singh Nalwa

Sardar Hari Singh Nalwa was born to Gurdial Singh Uppal and Dharam Kaur at Gujranwala (now in Pakistan) in the year 1791. Gurdial Singh was an officer in Ranjit Singh 's army. He died during a campaign fighting Afghans in 1798, when Hari Singh was only seven years of age.

Hari Singh eventually assumed the responsibility of supervising the affairs of his father's lands. Hari Singh presented himself before Maharaja Ranjit Singh in his open Durbar. The Maharaja was so impressed by the feats of chivalry shown by him that he was taken in the royal service as a personal *khidmatgar* or an attendant.

Maharaja commissioned him into the army in 1804 by granted him a command of a cavalry of 700 men and horses with the honor of Sardar. Hari Singh Nalwa named his regiment 'Sher-Dil-Rajman'. Hari Singh earned a reputation for bravery quite early on. During the course of hunting expedition he happened to be a victim of a sudden attack of a tiger. The attack was so subtle and unexpected that he did not gain time to pull out his sword.

Sardar Hari Singh Nalwa faced the crucial situation with such boldness that he managed to catch hold of the jaw of the beast forcefully with his hands and pushed it away with the prowess of arms arranging thus to kill it with his sword. Baron Charles Hugel says he was called Nalwa for 'having cloven the head of a tiger who had already seized him as its prey'.

The Sikhs passing established themselves as the pre-eminent power in Punjab following their defeat of Ahmad Shah Abdali's governor at Lahore in 1765. But their mode of fighting then was hardly suited to the requirements of a well organized state. Maharaja Ranjit Singh out of these Sikhs became leader of whole Khalsa (Sarbat Khalsa). He built up a strong, centralized and efficient military system by drawing the best elements in foreign with the best elements found in the indigenous fighting systems.

After some major campaigns of Multan and Kasur where Hari Singh Nalwa's regiment fought with distinction, Maharaja turned towards Kashmir. Hari Singh Nalwa's regiment "Sher-Dil-Rajman' was in forefront in campaign to get back Shah Shuja from the Governor of Kashmir, Shah Shuja's wife Wafa Begum had promised Kohinoor Diamond for Maharaja if her husband was to be freed from prison of Kashmir. In 1814 A.D., Hari Singh routed the Kashmiri forces. Shah Shuja gave Ranjit Singh kohinoor Diamond, from that day on till his death Maharaja Ranjit Singh wore that Diamond on his right shoulder. Meanwhile, through political means, Ranjit Singh installed his own governor (Jahan Dad Khan) in Peshawar.

In 1821, Dost Mohammed Khan and Yar Mohammed Khan, two Afghans were able to expel the Maharaja's nominee Jahan Dad Khan from Peshawar and thus an expedition was undertaken by Ranjit Singh's Army. A large army under illustrious commanders was dispatched to rectify the situation in Peshawar (Cavalry commanded by Sardar Hari Singh Nalwa, Infantry by Dhanna Singh Malwai, and Jagat Singh Attariwala, Artillery by Mian Ghaus Khan). Dost Mohammed Khan managed to reconcile by paying a handsome nazarana to Maharaja and by accepting the submission to Khalsa kingdom rather than to kingdom of Kabul.

Battle of Naushera

Ranjit Singh's forces at this time were divided into regular and irregular infantry, regular and irregular cavalry and artillery. Regular forces were directly under Lahore Sultanate of Ranjit Singh, irregular forces were supplied by allies or by those kingdoms that were bound by treaties. Artillery was completely under state control and was led by Mian Ghaus Khan and General Allard. Ranjit Singh employed several foreigners in his military services. Famous ones were General Allard leading an artillery regiment and General Ventura leading a regiment made up of Poorbia (Bihar, Bengali, and UP) soldiers. Both Allard and Ventura had earlier fought in the armies of Napoleon Bonaparte of France. Ranjit Singh's motive to include foreigners in his army was to modernize his forces.

In 1822 Fakir Azizudeen, Maharaja Ranjit Singh's "foreign officer" was sent to Peshawar to collect annual tribute. He was well received by Yar Mohammed, who ordered the city to be illuminated in the Fakir's honor. Yar Mohammed paid the tribute in cash and horses. Then Fakir Azizuddin returned to Lahore well satisfied with his mission. This incident lowered the prestige of Yar Mohammed Khan among his people.

Mohammed Azim Khan who then ruled Kabul taunted Yar Mohammed for paying tribute to Sikh infidels. Azim Khan marched out of Kabul and the cry of jihad echoed at Khyber. Over forty-five thousand Khattaks and Yusufzai tribesmen under the leadership of Syed Akbar Shah of Balmer volunteered to fight. Yar Mohammed abandoned Peshawar and went into hiding. And once more Maharaja Ranjit Singh ordered his army to move north towards Peshawar.

Prince Sher Singh, Misr Dewan Chand and General Ventura were led the battalions of infantry. Hari Singh Nalwa, Phula Singh, Fateh Singh Ahluwalia, Desa Singh Majithia and Attar Singh Sandhawalia led the cavalry, while artillery was commanded by Mian Ghaus Khan and General Allard. Recently trained and incorporated battalions of Purbia (Bihari soldiers) and Gurkha Soldiers were also sent. These were led by General Ventura and General Balbhadra (Gurkha General). A grand total of about 25,000 men moved to defend the Sikh kingdom.

In December 1822 orders were given to march out of Lahore and Prince Sher Singh, younger son of Maharaja Ranjit Singh led the march with his battalions of Cavalry and Infantry. Hari Singh Nalwa whose Sher-e-Dil Rajaman battalion was replenished by additional soldiers making it the largest Cavalry regiment of about 5000 men and horses in the Lahore Darbar's army closely followed Prince Sher Singh. These advance columns of Lahore Durbar reached Attock river a month ahead of other forces.

They crossed the Attock river using a pontoon bridge and occupied the Sikh fort of Jehangiria. Mohammed Azim Khan and his Afghani Jihadis soon surrounded the fort of Jehangiria. Other men helping Mohammed Azim to lead their 45,000 forces of Mujahdeen were his brothers, Dost Mohammed (who had more than once paid tribute to Lahore), Sayyid Akbar Shah and Jabbar Khan, the ex-governor of Kashmir. They destroyed the pontoon bridge over river Attock so that Sikh forces could not cross and started pounding the fort with their guns. Hari Singh Nalwa and Prince Sher Singh with much grit and determination held the fort with their total of less then 10,000 men. Since this fort was right on the banks of a river, there was no shortage of water or other supplies. Hari Singh Nalwa led his cavalry in numerous sorties outside fort destroying two of the invaluable guns of Afghanis.

Meanwhile, Maharaja Ranjit Singh and rest of the Khalsa force which was following his advance columns leisurely arrived in January to find the only pontoon bridge across the river destroyed. To make matters worse next day there was a heavy snowfall. The Maharaja was being informed through his network of intelligence of the rapidly rising force of the enemy but decided to wait for his heavy guns to arrive which were due by mid-day (March 14, 1823) But, that morning Sikh a Gurmata (Resolution) was passed that the Afghans would be attacked before their forces could gather greater strength and irrespective of whether the heavy guns arrived or not. Fortunately, the artillery also arrived in time for the attack.

Hari Singh Nalwa and Prince Sher Singh had already taken on the enemy earlier crossing the river before the bridge was destroyed and capturing the fort of Jehangiria. They were exerting powerful pressure on the enemy but badly needed reinforcements which had arrived on the other side of that river, but could not wait for the bridge to be constructed under the threat of enemy fire. Ranjit Singh one early morning leading himself riding on his white horse he dipped in the freezing water to cross the river. Whole force followed but in this exercise much of the equipment was lost, that included much needed guns. Akali Phoola Singh's suicide squad who was following Ranjit Singh, now took the lead, and, without a moment's thought, plunged their horses in the swollen and turbulent river. How could the others stay behind ? Every one followed suit, but before they crossed over, the enemy had taken flight from Jehangiria leaving even their dead or dying in the battle-field and saying in despair:— " Toba, Toba,Khuda Khud Khalsa shud." (God forbid, but it appears, God himself has turned a Khalsa !)." It was believed that no one could cross the river at its full fury.

Thus catching the enemy by surprise Ranjit Singh and his forces broke open the cordon massacring more than 1,000 Afghans. The Afghanas who were from the Khattak and Yusufzai tribes, fled and entrenched themselves nearby a city then called Pir Sabak (this later became the British cantonment of Naushera, which is currently one of the major bases of Pakistan Army). This put a gap between the main Afghan force under Azim Khan's brothers and the column of tribal Jihadis. A small but swift stream called Landai put a further obstacle between the two Afghan armies. And he Sikhs were determined to maintain the initiative.

Consequently, whatever was left of Sikh artillery was sent to the bank of the Landai to forestall any attempts by the two Afghan columns to link up. Meanwhile when news of the disaster reached Azim Khan he made a dash from Peshawar to join his brothers on the bank of the Landai river. They could not cross the stream because of constant firing by Durbar guns. Azim Khan and his brothers then decided to launch an attack early morning when Punjabi guns were being rested. However, the Sikh Army decided to wipe out the tribal column before Azim Kahn could strike. As a result, the Gurkha and Purbia battalions were dispatched to deal with Pir Sabak Hill where tribal mujahids were resting. And though the Tribal column fought desperately they were overwhelmed by the Gurkhas and Purbias. General Balbhadra of Gurkha Infantry lost his life during this action in the midst of some of the fiercest to hand-to-hand fighting.

Meanwhile, seeing their comrades getting killed all Afghanis came together in a desperate effort to hold the attack by Darbar's army. Darbar's forces surrounded them from all sides. Both Hari Singh Nalwa and Akali Phula Singh from one end lead the cavalry charge while Gurkhas who were leaderless after martyrdom of General Balbhadra and Purbias under General Ventura and Punjabi soldiers under General Dewan Misr Chand holding their positions. Hari Singh Nalwa pressed on his cavalry deploying with precision and raising war cries of *Bole So Nihal Sat Sri Akal* from time to time, Hari Singh Nalwa and his disciplined soldiers emptied their muskets on Jihadis. A wave of about 50 soldiers on their horses would charge at Jihadis, firing their muskets and then sending more to meet their creator through their bayonets as they gallop across the battlefield. Hari Singh Nalwa and Akali Phula Singh with their cavalry regiment of Sher-Dil-Rajman and Nihangs as Khushwant Singh succinctly puts it gave them "coup de grace." They drove the Khattaks and Yusufzais from Pir Sabak Hill. Heavy artillery on the land surrounded the Jihadis and opened up a barrage to complete the slaughter.

While Hari Singh was leading his Sher-Dil-Rajman attacking Jihadis from one end, from other side Akali Phula Singh and his Cavalry of Nihangs, or the "Crocodile Sikhs who fight till death" were performing similar feat. Jihadis were surrounded by Gurkha Infantry at one end, General Ventura soldiers at other end, while waves of Cavalry charges were attacking from the one side. Jihadis changed their tactics and decided to go for the leaders in order to demoralize the Khalsa forces.

General Bhalbhadra was shot, General Ventura was injured and Akali Phula Singh's horse was shot. This angered Akali Phula Singh and he made a grave mistake by getting on an elephant. Now Akali Phula Singh's towering torso was seen from all over the battlefield. Ghazi Jihadis saw the Khalsa General on top of an elephant and immediately trained their muskets on him. Akali Phula Singh's body was riddled with bullets, he collapsed in his howdah exhorting the Nihang Sikhs to not to give way. Akali Phula Singh through his dashing feats had inspired other Sikh commanders his martyrdom renewed the vigor to fight.

Mohammed Azim Khan watched the massacre from the other side of the stream without being able to help his tribesmen brother. He did not had the will to fight till death. By the day's end, Four thousand tribesmen were left dead on the field. Probably two times that number were injured and left dying at the battlefield. It was a crushing defeat for Afghanis. Hari Singh Nalwa whose ideal was Akali Phula Singh, chased the remaining Afghans deep into their territory killing hundreds more.

Mohammed Azim was too ashamed to face the people of Peshawar and he returned to Afghanistan, where he died in couple of months. This battle proved the effectiveness of organized military. Death of a General Akali Phula Singh at this battle was the biggest loss of the campaign for Maharaja Ranjit Singh. Azim Khan's Jihadis had lost heart and abandoned their zeal for Jihad in complete disorder. 14 large and 18 small guns were captured by the Sikhs.

It showed them the effectiveness of organized artillery and cavalry regiments as well as old tactics of Guerilla warfare. In this battle not all of Ranjit Singh's forces took part, some regiments just waited for their turn which never came. General Allard and Ventura's participation in this battle with their divisions and trained army of Lahore kingdom with Akali division of the army had absolutely no match for untrained militia who although surpassed in sheer numbers, Afghans after a great massacre submitted and Naushera was captured. Albeit, the Lahore troops lost an indispensable commander. Hari Singh Nalwa played a conspicuous role first by inflicting a crushing defeat upon the enemy and secondly by pursuing the enemy after the defeat in order to be sure about the victory of the Lahore troops. The battle of Naushera made it evident to the frontier tribesmen that the Afghan militia was weaker than those of Lahore troops. This battle sealed the further prospects of Muhammad Azim of Kabul and established the Sikh supremacy over Peshawar.

"Akali Phula Singh's memorial still stands intact there. For Ranjit Singh as much as for others, the joy of a superb victory was marred by this sad and heart-rending event. This monument (now situated in the Frontier Province of Pakistan) on the bank of the river Kabul was endowed wish a Jagir by Ranjit Singh and a Gurdwara was also built on the site. Sardar Gurbaksh Singh. well-known Punjabi writer and editor of Preet Lari", settled there in early thirties of this century. and tilled the farm attached to this monument. The place is still called Samadh Akali Phoola Singh."

"Three days later the Maharaja entered Peshawar the head of his victorious troops. The citizens welcomed him and paid him homage with nazarana (gifts). The Maharajah's sojourn was, however, not a peaceful one. what the tribesmen could not achieve in open combat, they tried to gain by the cold-blooded murder of Punjabi soldiers under cover of darkness."

Ranjit Singh knew about the tactics of these tribesmen. A few days later both Yar Mohammed and Dost Mohammed presented themselves at court and sought the Maharajah's pardon. He forgave them readily and accepted their tribute of presents and horses. Yar Mohammed was reinvested governor of Peshawar on promising an increased annual revenue of Rs.1,000,000 to the Lahore Durbar.

This was first time that Afghanis were totally beaten and humiliated in their own country by their former subjects. Ranjit Singh made this possible through his able generals and brilliant military tactics. So huge was this victory that it caused apprehensions in British circles. British realized that sooner or later showdown with Ranjit Singh was inevitable. In particular, they realized that the Durbar's conquests had reached the furthest geographical limits of the Punjab in the north and north-west. Beyond were impassable mountains and inhospitable, unprofitable regions. In order to pacify his new conquests Ranjit Singh ordered Hari Singh Nalwa and Prince Sher Singh to remain in North West Frontier province at the end his campaign. He also ordered them to construct series of small forts all along the highway leading to Khyber pass. He correctly had assessed the importance of Khyber pass, and thus organized the defenses of his frontier around Kabul.

DEFENDING KASHMIR

Why did Pakistan invade Kashmir in the first place? First, Kashmir being a Muslim-dominant state was considered a natural part of Pakistan, which had made Islam the basis of its modern nationality. Second, Khan Abdul Gaffar Khan's Pathanistan Movement was gaining momentum and Kashmir was held out as a bait for luring the poor tribals away. The internal conditions of Jammu & Kashmir with religious passions aflame, lawlessness rampant and authority paralysed offered the right mix for the raiders to strike.

Operation Gulmarg

The Army Headquarters of Pakistan planned the main invasion plan, code-named Operation Gulmarg. Conclusive proof of this came through two different sources-Major Onkar Singh Kalkat, then serving as the Brigade Major at HQ Bannu Frontier Brigade Group, and GK Reddy, a journalist. Both happened to stumble upon the plan by chance. The invasion was planned meticulously with considerable strategic and tactical insight. According to Operation Gulmarg, as described by Major Kalkat, every Pathan tribe was required to enlist at least one Lashkar of 1,000 tribesmen.

These Lashkars were to be concentrated at Baftnu, Wana, Peshawar, Kohat, Thal and Nowshera by the first week of September 1947. The Brigade Commanders at these places were to issue them arms, ammunition and some essential clothing items. Each Lashkar was also to be provided with a Major, a Captain and ten JCOs of the regular Pakistan Army. The entire force was to be commanded by Major General Akbar Khan, who was given the code name Tariq.

All Lashkars were to meet at Abbottabad by October 18th. According to the plan, six Lashkars were to advance along the main road from Muzaffarabad to Srinagar via Domel, Uri and Baramula, with the specific task of capturing the aerodrome and subsequently advancing to the Banihal Pass. Two Lashkars were to advance from the Haji Pir Pass direct on to Gulmarg, thereby securing the right flank of the main force advancing from Muzaffarabad. Another two Lashkars were to advance from Tithwal through the Nastachhun Pass for capturing Sopore, Handwara and Bandipur. And 10 other Lashkars were to operate in the Poonch, Bhimbar and Rawalkot area with the intention of capturing Poonch and Rajauri before advancing to Jammu. Arrangements were also made for detailing of guides/informers from the so-called Azad Army, to all these tribal Lashkars. Major General Khan was also given the task of organising the Azad Army, the major portion of which was to come from the Muslim element of the J&K State forces. Dumps of arms, ammunition, supplies and clothing were to be established forward of Abbottabad by October 15th. These were to be subsequently moved to Muzaffarabad and Domel after the D-day. Pakistan's 7 Infantry Division was to concentrate the Murree-Abbottabad area by October 21st and was ordered to be ready to move immediately into J&K territory to back up the tribal Lashkars and consolidate their hold on the Valley. One infantry brigade was also held in readiness at Sialkot to move on to Jammu. The D-day for Operation Gulmarg was fixed as 22 October 1947, on which date the various Lashkars were to cross into J&K territory. The invasion plan was tactically sound and, in the beginning, brilliantly executed. The main attack had by necessity to be launched frontally along the motor road. Apart from rifles, the standard weapon of the raiders, the main force was also equipped with a few light machine guns and traveled in about 300 civilian lorries.

Fall of Domel and Baramula

The main strength of the defenders was at Domel where the two approach roads from Murree and Abbottabad met before leading towards Srinagar along the Jhelum gorge. Its two out posts Lohar Gali and Ramkot were the key to the whole defence and were guarded by the 4th Kashmir Infantry, which had a mix of Muslim and Dogra soldiers.

When the raiders struck in the morning of October 22nd, traitors within the 4th Kashmir Infantry joined the raiders and gave them complete information about the strength and disposition of the defending troops and helped them send sufficient force against each piquet of defenders. That proved to be the beginning of a series of successes for the raiders before they were ultimately held, and subsequently thrown back, by Indian reinforcements over the next two weeks or so.

Between October 22nd and 26th, the raiders had run over Domel, Muzaffarabad, Uri and Baramula. Yet in their success lay the seeds of their doom. For on their way, they took to looting and raping, and the ultimate goal of the 'Holy War' was forgotten. Each man tried to grab as much wealth or as many girls as he could, and the 'infidel' Maharaja at Srinagar or the 'liberation of the oppressed Muslims' of Kashmir was last on his mind.

The advance on Srinagar was held up for a few days, and that proved crucial. In Delhi, hundreds of kilometres from stricken Baramula, it had at last been decided to save Kashmir in its hour of peril. Even as the barbaric raiders were satisfying their greed and lust in Baramula, transport planes full of Indian troops were winging their way through the azure autumn skies: Destination Srinagar.

Smashing of the J&K Siege

When the first wave of tribal warriors from Pakistan invaded the Kashmir Valley on 22 October 1947, the kingdom of Jammu & Kashmir had not acceded to either Pakistan or India. Therefore, taking the plea that it was an internal matter, India refused to send in its troops to the Valley. However, when Maharaja Hari Singh signed the Instrument of Accession with the Indian Government on the evening of 26 October 1947, Jammu & Kashmir became an integral part of the Indian Dominion legally, morally and constitutionally. Now was the time to react to the tribal invasion, which India did commendably, considering the short notice given to its military commanders.

The first troops were flown to Srinagar with hardly a couple of days planning and preparation. The liberation of the Valley in early November 1947 was a splendid feat of arms by the 161 Brigade, fighting against hordes of raiders. This single brigade managed to hold its own throughout the long winter of 1947-48 when its only line of communication was blocked by snow.

Large areas in the Tithwal, Naushahra and Rajouri sectors were liberated from the invaders, and were held against repeated attacks by a vastly superior enemy. Naturally, the Indian Army also suffered setbacks, minor and major, at several places such as Jhangar, Pandu, Kargil and Skardu. But the situation was fully restored at Jhangar and Kargil. The long siege of Poonch was finally broken and Gurais & Dras areas were successfully recaptured against tremendous odds. The Army won five Param Vir Chakras (PVCs), 47 Maha Vir Chakras (MVCs) and not less than 284 Vir Chakras (VrCs), including three twin-awards of VrCs, during the J&K Operations of 1947-48.

During the long campaign, the Indian Army lost 76 officers, 31 JCOs and 996 men of other ranks. The wounded totalled 3152, including 81 officers and 107 JCOs. Apart from these casualties, J&K State Forces lost approximately 1990 officers and men.

The small Royal Indian Air Force (RIAF) lost 32 personnel, including 9 officers. The enemy casualties were definitely many times the total of Indian Army and RIAF casualties. By one estimate the enemy suffered 20,000 casualties, including 6000 killed. The gallantry and skill of all ranks of the Indian Army are amply borne out in the various accounts of these operations. But the exploits and the vital role of the RIAF deserve special mention here. Its contribution to the success of the J&K operations cannot be over emphasized, and it was the one weapon to which the enemy had no answer, as the Pakistan Air Force wisely desisted from joining the fray.

Only the impromptu airlift to Srinagar in October 1947 saved the Kashmir Valley. A hundred planes landed every day on the improvised airfield at Srinagar, bringing in troops, ammunition and supplies and evacuating casualties and the refugees. The RIAF and civilian pilots of these Dakotas defied the mountains, the weather, and fatigue, to continue the airlift till the Valley was saved. Giving invaluable support to these were the fearless fighter pilots who accurately and repeatedly attacked vital enemy positions at Gurais, Zoji La, Pindras and Rajouri.

Apart from the men in uniform, civilians played a crucial role in liberating the Valley. The dedication and skill of the civilian pilots who flew to Srinagar in October 1947 was no less than their counterparts in the RIAF. Very few know that a civilian washerman, Ram Chander, won a Maha Vir Chakra for rescuing an officer wounded during an ambush, shooting down several enemy troops in the process. It was this Indian spirit and valour that saved the Valley.

India to the Rescue

It was on 24 October 1947 that the Government of India first got news of the Kashmir invasion. By that time, Domel and Muzaffarabad had already fallen to the raiders, who were fast approaching Srinagar. The Maharaja of Kashmir sent an S.O.S. message to the Indian Government on the night of October 24th. After deliberations at the highest levels, it was decided that India couldn't send its troops till J&K formally acceded to India. Maharaja Hari Singh signed the Instrument of Accession in the evening of October 26th, which made J&K an integral part of India-legally, morally, and constitutionally. The Indian reaction, from then onwards, was swift, adverse ground conditions notwithstanding.

Operation Jak

The Indian rescue operation was beset with obvious difficulties from the very beginning. Srinagar was over 480 km from the nearest point on the Indian border. Troops in East Punjab were engaged in dealing with the refugees and maintaining law and order. Hence, air transport was the only way out. Worse still, the airport at Srinagar was hardly fit to land fully laden transport planes. But that was the only option available and it had to be taken. The rescue mission was code-named, Operation Jak. The first regiment to move in was 1 Sikh, stationed at Gurgaon at the time and commanded by Lt. Col. D.R. Rai. The troops were transported in four Dakota planes that took off from Delhi on October 27th and reached Srinagar early morning the same day. The first engagement with the enemy started on October 28th. Lt. Col. Rai was the first Indian officer to fall in the battle of liberation.

It was only after the first troops had landed at Srinagar that the gravity of the situation was realised. So, the Indian Army decided to throw its full weight to drive back the invaders. On October 28th, the Delhi and East Punjab Command was ordered to carry out Phase II of Operation Jak. It involved dispatching one Brigade Group to Jammu via Pathankot.

The next day, the Eastern Southern commands were asked to spare whatever troops they could for the operation. Airlifts were undertaken almost round-the-clock airlifts to increase the troop strength. On October 30th, two fighter aircraft of the RIAF were detailed to operate from the Srinagar airstrip to provide air-support to the ground troops. In the following days, many Harvards and Spitfires were based on that airfield and they gave invaluable support to the infantry.

Meanwhile, there had been some fierce engagements with the enemy on the ground, resulting in some casualties on the Indian side. But most importantly, the advance of the invaders had been checked.

The ground troops held the enemy. Transport planes took care of the supply of troops, equipment and ration. Interestingly, apart from three RIAF planes, 33 civil Dakotas were used in these sorties. Many of them even did a double trip to Srinagar on a single day- a tribute to the morale of the pilots and crew. By November 6th, the critical phase for Srinagar was over. The raiders had lost the initiative thanks to their looting at Baramula. About 3500 Indian troops had reached Srinagar by then. They threw a ring of machine guns and bayonets around Srinagar and the airfield. Although the invaders were only about 8 km away from the city at the nearest point, it was now impossible for them to penetrate the Indian positions and capture the capital, almost in their grasp. Having strengthened their position, the Indian Army was about to begin the liberation of the Kashmir valley.

The Liberation of the Valley

According to orders from the Defence Committee of the Cabinet, Baramula was to be recaptured from the enemy by November 17th, even if the Indian Army had to incur 500 casualties. The original plan was to launch the decisive battle on November 10th, but an unexpected attack on Indian positions at Shalateng on November 7th postponed the initiative.

In a masterly battle strategy, the Indian troops flanked the invaders from three sides and unleashed murderous firepower on them. The RIAF strafed them from the air. The Battle of Shalateng was over within 20 minutes. It put Srinagar and Kashmir Valley beyond the grasp of the invaders forever. There were encounters after that, but the enemy was being driven back steadily and surely. By the evening of November 13th, Uri was captured. With that the liberation of the Kashmir Valley was complete.

The Relief of Poonch

On 20 November 1947, a column for the relief of Poonch set out from Uri, but was halted at Kahuta, 13 km short of Poonch. The Poonch garrison held out for one full year before it was finally relieved. Operation Easy was aimed at establishing the final link-up with Poonch, which had proved to be difficult throughout most of 1948.

An attempt to link up with Poonch could be made either from the south, namely, via Thana Mandi or Rajouri, or from the north via the Haji Pir Pass. Lt. Gen. Cariappa (later Field Marshal and

Army Chief) gave the go-ahead for the link-up with Poonch via the south. Lt. Gen. Shrinagesh (later General and Army Chief), who had been appointed Corps Commander of J&K Forces on September 14th, ordered Major General Atma Singh to plan for a link-up accordingly.

Major General Atma Singh was further ordered to carry out Phase I (secure Pir Badesar) by October 8th; commence Phase II (demonstrate north of Thana Mandi) by October 10th; and concentrate in Rajouri the required force for Operation Easy by October 16th. On October 9th, Major General Atma Singh finalised his plan.

The force was to be under the command of Brigadier Yadunath Singh, Commander 19 Brigade, and was to consist of six infantry battalions plus one field battery and one mountain battery. It was to be divided into two columns, one column of three battalions under command of Brigadier Umrao Singh, Commander 5 Brigade, and the other column of three battalions under command of Lt. Col. Jagjit Singh Aurora (the same Lt. Gen. Jagjit Singh Aurora of 1971 War fame), Commander 1/2 Punjab. As a preliminary to the main operation, the deception plan was to be carried out about October 12 to secure Pir Badesar.

The main operation was to commence on about October 19th with 5 Brigade advancing from Rajouri and securing Pir Kalewa ridge. Lt. Col. Jagjit Singh's column was then to pass through, moving from south of Thana Mandi to secure a firm base in the area around Sangrot. Having secured the base, the intention was to advance to Potha with 5 Brigade and carry out operations from Potha for the link-up with Poonch.

Capture of Pir Badesar

Operation Ranjit: The task of carrying out Operation Ranjit for the capture of Pir Badesar was given to 268 Brigade, 1/2 Punjab, 1 (Para) Kumaon and 1/1 Gorkha Rifles concentrated south of Darhal on October 13th.

The brigade plan was for 1/1 Gorkha Rifles less one company and one platoon to lead the attack and secure Kater and the high ground north of Giran. Then 1/2 Punjab was to push on and capture Khalbahat Gala. 1 (Para) Kumaon was to take the lead next and capture Point 5432. At 2000 hours on October 14th, the brigade moved out, 1/1 Gorkha Rifles leading, and the first objective, Kater was secured without opposition. 1/2 Punjab captured Point 3978 at 0600 hours on October 15th. 1 (Para) Kumaon captured Pir Badesar by 1700 hours on the same day. Artillery played an important part in Operation Ranjit also. After the capture of Pir Badesar, there was an important modification in Operation Easy and it was decided that the link-up with Poonch should be made via Mendhar and not via Potha. An ad hoc formation named Durga Force under overall command of Brigadier Yadunath Singh was to undertake Operation Easy and was composed of 5 Infantry Brigade, 19 Infantry Brigade, and the Rajouri Garrison. To provide air support, the RIAF No.10 Squadron of Tempests and No.12 Squadron (Transport) of Dakotas and No.1 AOP Flight of Austers were made available. As per the plan, 5 Brigade secured the vital Pir Kalewa ridge at 1200 hours on October 28th. The next important features to be secured were Ramgarh Fort and Bhimbar Gali.

Poonch Finally Relieved

Major General Atma Singh now detailed 19 Brigade Group to capture Point 5732 with a view to exploit Jhhika Gali, an enemy stronghold barring the way to Mendhar. 5 Brigade Group was assigned the task of capturing Point 4394 and securing the right flank of the main column up to but excluding Point 3295. The plan was to capture Topa area with a view to linking up with 101 Brigade from Poonch. 19 Brigade less one battalion, supported by all available artillery was to commence attack on night of November 19/20th. 101 Brigade was to start operations on the night of November 19/20th to capture Point 6005 and Point 6876 (Pir Margot Ghazi). It was expected that the link-up with 101 Brigade would take place by the evening of November 20th. During the night of November

19/20th, 1/4 Gorkha Rifles and 5 Rajputana Rifles carried out a night march. Point 5982 was captured by 0730 hours on November 20th without much opposition. Meanwhile, the leading company of 1/4 Gorkha Rifles had also captured its objective at 0620 hours. Then exploitation began. One platoon 1/4 Gorkha Rifles was sent to Point 6793 and met the troops of 101 Brigade at 1200 hours. 1/2 Punjab passed through the positions of 5 Rajputana Rifles and captured Topa at 1500 hours on November 20th. The link-up with Poonch in November 1948 was a notable performance. The enemy ring round Poonch was broken and attempts to force the Poonch garrison to surrender were finally frustrated.

The Battle of Naushera

The capture of Jhangar on 24 December 1947 gave the enemy a tremendous advantage. It was, hence, vital to Indian strategy to recapture Jhangar. The battle of Naushahra on 06 February 1948 was decisive in this context and paved the way for the recapture of Jhangar later on. Lt. Col. R.G. Naidu, CO of 2 Jat, was put in command of Operation Satyanas for clearing the enemy from the area around Beri Pattan. The troops occupied Tung on January 23rd and crossed the Thandapaniwali Tawi the next morning. In the early hours of January 25th, as they advanced to attack Siot and Pt. 2502, they came under heavy enemy fire and had to make a retreat, but not before inflicting heavy casualties on the enemy, estimated to be 100 dead and wounded.

To weaken and disrupt the enemy's offensive, a mobile force known as 'Cheeta Force' was formed. It consisted of Stuart tanks from 7 Light Cavalry. Orders were given to this mobile force on January 24th. The plan was simple. Two small detachments of mixed armour and infantry were to be established at Amberala and Chordhaki to guard the rear; the rest of the mobile column was to push right up to area Assar-Kadala-Bhimbar to destroy the enemy base. The mobile force launched its operation at 0530 hours on January 25th. Despite earlier reverses, it was able to inflict heavy losses on the enemy at Amberala, Chordhaki, and Assar/Kadala.

Operation Kipper

Intelligence reports revealed that a strong enemy build-up was taking place at Kot. Situated about 9 km north-east of Naushahra on the highest point, Kot allowed observation over the Rajouri road to a point near Merian. It was therefore, planned to attack and capture this strong enemy position, which was a serious threat to Naushahra. Other important enemy bases in the area were at Uparla Dandesar and Pathradi. The enemy strength here was estimated to be one battalion, about 500 strong, equipped with 3" mortars, medium machine guns, light machine guns and about 400 rifles.

On January 30th, Brigadier Usman issued instructions for Operation Kipper, the code name for dislodging the enemy from Kot-Pathradi-Uparla Dandesar area and to establish a permanent picket in Kot.

The responsibility fell on 50 Para Brigade Group which included 2/2 Punjab, 3 (Para) Mahratta Light Infantry, 1 Rajput (A Coy), 3 (Para) Rajput (B Coy), 7 Cavalry (B Sqn), 1 Mahar (MMG) (Y Coy), among others. The plan was to attack Kot and Pathradi on a two-battalion front. On the left was 2/2 Punjab with objective Pt. 3227 and Kot; on the right 3 MLI with objectives Pt. 3284, Pathradi and Uparla Dandesar. The assault was timed for 0630 hours on February 1st and it was to be a silent dawn attack. The RIAF was to support the ground attack by softening the strong enemy positions.

As per a deception plan the enemy was made to believe that an advance towards Jhangar was imminent. Meanwhile, 3 MLI moved from Naushahra camp at 1915 hours on January 31st to area Pt. 2300. Enemy opposition was liquidated and Pathradi was captured by 0710 hours on February 1st. Meanwhile, 2/2 Punjab too had secured its objectives. But, the enemy launched a counter offensive almost immediately and recaptured Kot. It was after a fierce fighting that Kot was finally recovered at 1010 hours. Capture of Kot area had a significant bearing on future operations, as it was from this base that the enemy used to operate its successful efforts to cut the supply route to Naushahra. The occupation of Pathradi and Kot by the enemy would have rendered matters critical in the major attack on Naushahra that followed on February 6th.

Victory at Naushahra

Stung by the loss of Kot, the enemy launched the expected all-out attack on Naushahra on 06 February 1948. The pickets at Kot and Tain Dhar were heavily mortared between 0640 and 0715 hours. Picket No. 2 at Tain Dhar bore the brunt of the attack but they fought to the last man.

At about 0715 hours, Brigadier Usman realising the gravity of the situation sent a company of 3 (Para) Rajput to reinforce the main picket. It was the turning point of the whole battle. At Kot, fighting continued throughout the day and night of February 6/7th. Indian troops held the onslaught and beat off the enemy attacks. The estimated enemy casualties at Kot and Tain Dhar were 400 killed and 250 wounded.

The enemy also attacked the Kangota picket. This picket was heavily mortared and attacked at about 0700 hours. About a 1000-strong enemy force surrounded the picket and tried to rush it, but was beaten back in hand-to-hand fighting. Simultaneously, the enemy, approximately 5000 strong, attacked other pickets from the west and south-west.

To meet this serious threat to the Naushahra valley, Brigadier Usman decided to take the offensive and send his small reserve to attack the enemy concentration southwest of Naushahra. The valley was cleared of the hostiles by 1500 hours. In the annals of military warfare, the battle of Naushahra was par excellence a gunners battle.

The Recapture of Jhangar

Operation Bharatpur: After the victory at Naushahra on 06 February 1948, the stage was set for the recapture of Jhangar. For that it was essential to dislodge the enemy who was still holding Ambli Dhar and Kaman Gosha Gala. The responsibility to push back the enemy from Ambli Dhar fell on the 2 Jat through Operation Bharatpur, which was launched on 28 February 1948.

The plan was to launch a surprise attack at dawn after an approach march. A deceptive attack was launched in the east towards Bhata Village to mislead the enemy. The decoy worked and the enemy did not realise the threat of the main advance until 2 Jat was half way up for the attack on Ambli Dhar. Soon, Pt. 3319 on Ambli Dhar was captured and the enemy was forced to retreat to lower positions. After an hour's lull, however, there was a counter offensive by the enemy in which one Junior Commissioned Officer (JCO) and two men were killed and seven wounded. Eighty raiders were also wounded in the return fire.

Operation Vijay: By March 5th, Ambli Dhar was secured and the enemy had been cleared from Kaman Gosha Gala as well. It was now time for the final assault on Jhangar. Operation Vijay was to be completed in two phases.

In the first phase, the 19 Independent Brigade, consisting of 1 Rajput, 4 Dogra, 1 Kumaon Rifles and ancillary units, was to secure Pt. 3327 and 3283. In phase two, the 50 Para Brigade Group, consisting of 3 (Para) Maratha Light Infantry, 3 (Para) Rajput, 1 Patiala and ancillary units, was to secure Pt. 2701, Jhangar, Pt.3399 and Pt. 3374. Unknown even to the Indian troops, a squadron of the 7 Cavalry was also pushed into the operation.

The tanks arrived from Naushera camouflaged with wooden covers at night. The secret plan to push in tanks paid off, as the enemy was completely surprised by their arrival. One of the vital strategic points on the way to Jhangar was Pir Thil held by the enemy.

On March 15th, 3 MLI was sent on offensive reconnaissance to locate the enemy position in the area, but it was resisted with strength. It was now confirmed that there was an equivalent of one enemy brigade, six medium machine guns, a couple of light machine guns and two 3" mortars.

Based on the information, Brigadier Usman modified his plan and decided to attack two places on the Pir Thil feature about 360 metres apart with two battalions-the 3 MLI on the right and the 1 Patiala on the left. By March 17th, the 50 Para Brigade had captured Pir Thil Nakka and the way was now clear for the final attack on Jhangar.

The offensive started on March 18th. That day, the 3 (Para) Rajput captured Pt. 3477, following which the 50 Para Brigade, the 3 MLI and the 1 Patiala concentrated at this feature. The plan was to attack with two forward battalions-the 1 Patiala, on the right, was to secure objective ring contour and the 3 MLI, on the left, was to secure Pt. 3399 and Pt. 3574. Both the objectives were secured the same day.

The enemy fled towards Mirpur, leaving behind 46 dead and a cache of ammunition. Meanwhile, the Stuart tanks of 7 Cavalry (C Sqn), were already on their way. Brushing aside minor opposition, which resulted in the loss of one tank, the squadron along with one company of the 1 Rajput entered Jhangar at 1400 hours that day.

With the recapture of Jhangar on March 18th, the main land route leading into the Naushahra Valley was secured and the enemy's supply line was disrupted. Operation Vijay thus ended in Vijay, i.e. Victory.

The Fall of Skardu

The northern front of the Kashmir campaign included the sectors of Gurais, Skardu, Dras and Kargil, and Leh. From November 1947 to August 1948, the enemy achieved impressive successes in the region.

But equally impressive was the valour of the Indian troops who held their positions against all odds. Of particular importance was the siege of Skardu. It was at Skardu that the true spirit of a typical Indian soldier was first demonstrated. After the fall of Gilgit to the enemy in November 1947, it fell on Lt. Col. Sher Jung Thapa and his men of 6 J&K Infantry to defend Skardu.

The troops reached Skardu on December 03rd and positioned themselves inside a fort. With a total strength of about 285 men, Lt. Col. Thapa was to defend his picket against a 600-strong enemy who was equipped with modern rifles, 2" and 3" mortars and was led by professional fighters. The enemy attacked on February 11th. From that day till August 13th, when Skardu finally fell to the enemy, it was a saga of defiance, gallantry and determination. Lt. Col. Thapa and his men repulsed waves after waves of enemy attacks. To make matters worse, the fort had hundreds of refugees men, women and children who had trusted Lt. Col. Thapa with their lives against the raiders.

The brave men held the siege for more than six months fighting not only the relentless enemy, but also ration and ammunition shortage. A major attempt to send reinforcements to the besieged men had ended in failure. There came a stage when there was just enough food to feed 70-80 mouths, but the garrison and the refugees numbered 600! Meanwhile, Kargil had fallen to the enemy.

The priority of the headquarters shifted to recapturing Kargil to establish the crucial line of communications. Lt. Col. Thapa and his men were literally forgotten. Reinforcements were few and scarce. Lt. Col. Thapa sent his last message to his commanders at 0800 hours on August 13th. That day, after holding out for six months against overwhelming odds, Skardu finally capitulated.

Offensives in the Uri Area

Uri was of great strategic importance since it commanded the routes to Domel, Poonch and Srinagar. Hence, the main objective of major offensives carried out in the Uri area was only to establish a firm base there in order to prevent the raiders from entering the Kashmir valley. Uri had its first heavy snowfall about the middle of January 1948, resulting in this front getting more or less frozen for the time being. Activity on both sides was, therefore, confined to local patrolling only. Intelligence reports, however, showed that an enemy build-up was taking place in Uri and Mahura in order to destroy the powerhouse and to cut off the line of communication between Rampur and Uri.

By the first week of April, enemy reinforcements in this area had swelled manifolds. The Indian response had been somewhat similar and 161 Infantry Brigade-responsible for holding the area-was suitably reorganized and reinforced. Till the first week of April, both the sides were mostly involved in small raids and counter raids owing to heavy snow. With the onset of spring, vigorous offensives were launched. From the Indian perspective, the first major offensive was directed at capturing Kopra. 4 Kumaon regiment secured the objective on April 15th and Indian pickets were established there. Another major achievement during this period was the capture of Point 9062. The Indian troops launched an attack in heavy rain. Despite slippery and steep slopes, the offensive was successful and the enemy was driven out of what was supposed to be a very strong defensive base. The threat to Mahura was finally ended when 3 Royal Garhwal secured Zambur Pattan on April 21st.

Meanwhile, a threat was developing at Kaurali where enemy in large numbers had infiltrated from Poonch. In one of the most tragic ambushes, the enemy annihilated the entire patrol party of 1 Madras, including its commander Lt. Col. Menon. A sole survivor who had escaped by hiding under a waterfall for more than three hours conveyed the tragic news to the base. The Indian troops during this period repulsed many enemy raids on various pickets. Of special significance was the fight at Nalwa-the picket described as 'Uri ka Morcha' due to its strategic importance to safeguard Uri. Jemadar Sanwal Ram who was commanding this post was awarded the Vir Chakra for successfully defending it against severe enemy onslaught.

Failure to force the Haji Pir Pass

The Haji Pir Pass, situated 22 km south of Uri along the Uri-Poonch road, was dominated on either side by high ridges, both of which were held by the enemy who was two-battalion strong and equipped with 12 medium machine guns. Despite bold attempts by the 2 (Para) Madras to evict the enemy from the ridges and break through the Pass, the objective was not secured. Overall, the strenuous efforts on the Indian forces in the Uri area met with limited success. Domel remained out of reach and Haji Pir Pass couldn't be broken through.

Operations in the Jammu Division

Operation Ranjit and Capture of Rajouri: One of the tasks assigned to Major General Kulwant Singh by Lt. Gen. Cariappa on 06 April 1948 was to carry out Operation Ranjit (earlier called Operation Mumtaz) for capturing Rajouri. The 48-km road that the Indian troops had to traverse to capture Rajouri was thickly wooded and well defended by enemy armed with machine guns and mortars.

The operation was to be completed in two phases. The first phase involved capturing Chingas, while the second phase was to capture Rajouri. The task was assigned to 19 Brigade.

To secure Chingas, it was essential to push out the enemy from the Barwali ridge. Despite heavy shelling from mortars, the enemy was forced out of his position. It was during this offensive that Captain J.N. Jatar received the Maha Vir Chakra for showing exemplary courage and presence of mind. Meanwhile, troops had also secured other objective en-route to Chingas without much opposition.

Chingas was captured on 11 April 1948. Of special mention during this period was the work done by 2nd Lt. R.R. Rane who was in-charge of clearing the road of landmines. Despite losing two of his men, and himself being wounded, he completed his task fearlessly amidst incessant enemy fire and enabled the tanks to reach Chingas. He was awarded the Param Vir Chakra for the most conspicuous gallantry.

The enemy resistance simply collapsed after the capture of Chingas. But the tanks and men had to wade across the river Tawi in water one and a half metre deep to reach Rajouri, which was captured on 12 April 1948.

Total enemy losses were estimated at 500 killed and an equal number wounded. The enemy also blew up his ammunition dump though the Indian troops captured clothing and ration stores. Three big pits around the town were full of dead bodies as a result of atrocities committed by the enemy.

In a well-conceived strategy to facilitate the capture of Rajouri, two brigades were to carry out diversionary operations. While 50 Para Brigade carried out its Operation Hathi successfully at a place 5 kilometre north of Jhangar, 80 Brigade did so in the Beri Pattan area. Enemy reaction to the loss of Rajouri was to launch coordinated attacks on Jhangar and Naushera. But all these attacks were successfully repulsed by Indian troops.

Operation Birbal: While other Indian troops were busy consolidating their positions and probing enemy positions around Rajouri, 19 Brigade was planning to launch Operation Birbal to capture Thana Mandi. As per the plan, Thana Mandi was to be attacked after first capturing the feature east of Sain Samut. In a fierce battle that lasted for two and a half hours, the feature was secured but at the cost of 4 killed and 19 wounded. Thana Mandi was captured the next day, i.e. 02 May 1948 without any resistance.

3

CHIEFS OF THE INDIAN ARMY

-Field Marshal Kodandera Madappa Cariappa, OBE

Commanders-in-Chief from Inception to Independence			
Sir Robert Lockhart	Sir Roy Bucher	K.M. Cariappa	K.S. Rajendrasinhji
S.M. Shrinagesh	K.S. Thimayya	P.N. Thapar	J.N. Chaudhuri
P.P. Kumaramangalam	S.H.F.J. Manekshaw	G.G. Bewoor	T.N. Raina
O.P. Malhotra	K.V. Krishna Rao	A.S. Vaidya	K. Sundarji
V.N. Sharma	S.F. Rodrigues	B.C. Joshi	S. Roychowdhury
/V.P. Malik	S. Padmanabhan	N.C. Vij	J.J. Singh
Deepak Kapoor			

GENERAL SIR ROBERT LOCKHART, KCB, CIE, MC

C-in-C, 15 Aug 1947-31 Dec 1947
Infantry, 51 Sikhs Frontier Force

Born on 23 June 1893, Sir Robert McGregor Macdonald Lockhart was commissioned in the British Indian Army and joined 51st Sikhs Frontier Force on 08 March 1914. He served as Military Attaché in Kabul, Afghanistan from March 1934 to December 1935. He was then appointed as the Deputy Director of Staff Duties, India in December 1939 and then took over as the Director of Staff Duties, India from 1940 and held that appointment till December 1941. He was subsequently selected to serve as the Secretary of Military Department, Indian Office and held that post from 1941 to 1943. In April 1945, he was posted to the Southern Army as the General Officer Commanding-in-Chief and served in that capacity till June 1947. He was appointed as the Commander-in-Chief of the Indian Army from 15 August 1947 and served till 31 December 1947.

After the Second World War, he served on the World Scout Committee of the World Organisition of the Scout movement from 1953 to 1959. He was awarded the Bronze Wolf Award, the only distinction of the World Organisition of the Scout Movement, awarded by the World Scout Committee for exceptional services to world scouting, in 1961. He passed away in 1981.

GENERAL SIR ROY BUCHER, CB, OBE, MC
C-in-C, 31 Dec 1947-15 Jan 1949
Infantry

Born on 31 August 1895, Sir Francis Robert Roy Bucher was commissioned into the British Army on 15 August 1914 and took part in World War I with the Cameronians (Scottish Rifles) in France from 1914 to 1915.

He then joined the 55th Coke's Rifles (Frontier Force) in India in 1915 and subsequently the 31st Duke of Connaught's Own Lancers in 1916. He served with the Mahsud-a Pashtun tribe in Waziristan, Pakistan-in 1917. He attended Staff College, Camberley from 1926 to 1927 and then served as the Deputy Assistant Adjutant General in India's Deccan District from 1930 to 1932.

In 1937, he joined the 13th Duke of Connaught's Own Lancers as its Commanding Officer. He was the Commandant of Sam Browne's Cavalry (12th Frontier Force) from 1939 to 1940; the Assistant Commandant of the Indian Cavalry Training Center, India in 1940; the Assistant Adjutant General at General Headquarters from January 1941 to June 1941; the Assistant Quartermaster General at Iraq from June 1941 to March 1942; Chief Administration Officer at Southern Command, India from 1942 to 1945; the General Officer Commanding Bengal and Assam Area, India in 1946; the General Officer Commanding-in-Chief, Eastern Command,

India from 1946 to 1947; the Chief of General Staff, Army Headquarters, India 1947 and finally culminating in the Commander-in-Chief and Chief of General Staff, Indian Army from 31 December 1947 to 15 January 1949. He passed away in 1980.

FIELD MARSHAL K.M. CARIAPPA, OBE
C-in-C, 15 Jan 1949-14 Jan 1953
Infantry, Rajput Regiment

Kodandera Madappa Cariappa was born on 28 January 1899 at Shanivarsanthe in erstwhile Coorg, which was centrally administered by the British. Cariappa, known as Chimma to his relatives, had his formal education in the Central High School at Madikeri, after which he pursued his college education at Presidency College, Madras. At the College, he grew up equally attached to books and plays under the guidance of renowned academicians. He was an active sportsman and played with vigour and brilliance, games like hockey and tennis. In addition to this, he loved music and had fondness for a sleight of hand tricks. When World War I had concluded in 1918, Indian politicians of the time raised a demand to sanction Indians to the King's Commission. After strict screening, Cariappa was one among the privileged few who was selected for the first batch, which underwent rigorous pre-commission. He joined the first batch of KCIOs (King's Commissioned Indian Officers) at the Daly Cadet College in Indore and was commissioned in the Carnatic Infantry at Bombay.

Cariappa saw active service with the 37 (Prince of Wales) Dogra in Mesopotamia (present-day Iraq) and was later posted to the 2nd Rajput Light Infantry (Queen Victoria's Own) which became his permanent regimental home. He was the first Indian officer to undergo the course at Staff College, Quetta in 1933. In 1946, he was promoted as the Brigadier of the Frontier Brigade Group. It was during this time that Colonel Ayub Khan-later Field Marshal and President of Pakistan, 1962-1969-served under him.

Cariappa served in Iraq, Syria and Iran from 1941-1942 and then in Burma in 1943-1944. He spent many of his soldiering years in Wagiristan. He earned his Mentioned-in-Despatches' as DAA and QMG of General (later Field Marshal) Slim's 10th Division. He was the first Indian Officer to be given command of a unit in 1942. After command he volunteered to serve in 26 Division engaged in clearing the Japanese from Burma, where he was awarded the Order of the British Empire (OBE).

In 1947, Cariappa was the first Indian who was selected to undergo a training course at Imperial Defence College, Camberly, UK on the higher directions of war. During the traumatic period of partition, he handled the division of the Indian Army and sharing of its assets between Pakistan and India, in a most amicable, just and orderly manner. He was then the Indian officer in-charge to oversee the transition.

Post-Independence, Cariappa was appointed as the Deputy Chief of General Staff with the rank of Major General. On promotion to Lieutenant General he became the Eastern Army Commander.

On outbreak of war with Pakistan in 1947, he was moved as General Officer Commanding-in-Chief, Western Command and directed operations for the recapture of Zojila, Dras and Kargil and re-established a linkup with Leh. In all this, he showed tremendous energy in moving troops, against heavy odds and finally ensuring success. On being appointed as the first Commander-in-Chief of an independent Indian Army on 15 January 1949, he was instrumental in;

- Integration of troops and turning an imperial army into a national army.
- Raised the Brigade of the Guards and the Parachute Regiments on an all-India caste composition.
- Raised the National Cadet Corps (NCC) and Territorial Army (TA) using troops from the Regular Army.

His career in the Army during which he had the rare distinction of being first in many spheres is a continuous tale of upward progress;

- The first Indian to be commissioned at the age of 19.
- The first Indian cadet to be commissioned from Daly Cadet College, Indore.
- The first Indian Brigadier.
- The first Indian to enter Imperial Defence College in England.
- The first Indian Officer to enter Staff College, Quetta.
- The first Indian Major General in 1947.
- The first Indian Chief of Staff.

Cariappa held no truck on commission in the Indian Army and in picturesque, forthright language remarked after the partition, "I don't care a damn if a man is a Hindu, Muslim, Sikh, Parsi or Christian as long as he plays the game to serve our country well.

This is all that matters to me." His association with the Indian Army is spread over an unbroken period of more than 29 years, during which he had wide experience of staff and command work. He lived and remained, as he said, "an Indian and to the last breath would remain an Indian. To me there is only two Sthans-Hindusthan (India) and Foujisthan (the Army)." After his retirement from Indian Army in 1953, he served as the High Commissioner to Australia and New Zealand till 1956.

Cariappa settled down amidst greenery and nature, in his own Roshanara at Madikeri after his retirement from public service. He loved the environment and the flora & fauna around him. He lived a life of simplicity and dignity, which was the hallmark of a man. He spent a lot of his leisure time educating people about cleanliness, pollution control and other essential issues.

During the 1962, the 1965 and the 1971 wars, he visited the front lines to talk to the troops and keep their morale up. Every Jawan of the Indian Army was inspired by his words. He always said, "An officer is nothing without the soldiers." He gave the following credo to the Indian officers, which remains even now the guiding spirit. He insisted that every officer carried in his breast pocket the red booklet, 'A Code of Conduct For Officers' and he would not hesitate to check accordingly. He insisted on small details, knowing full well that attention to minor matters would lead to a good future for the Army.

Apart from being a military man, Cariappa had insight about the status of the country. He is quoted as saying, "In modern warfare, a large army is not sufficient, it needs industrial potential behind it. If the army is the first line of defence, the industry is the second."

Cariappa had even said that "soldiers know the facility of wars to solve the internal problems. We ought to be ashamed that today they had more peace in war than peace in peace." Such insight has placed him above many in this field. "Army is there to serve the Government of the day, and we should make sure that it does not get mixed up with party politics. A soldier is above politics and should not believe in caste or creed," was another insight of this soldier.

He was affectionately known as Kipper and as the story goes, a British officer's wife found it difficult to pronounce Cariappa and shortened it to a convenient Kipper. The name stuck. In the years that followed, his colleagues, and others who knew him well, continued to call him Kipper. Cariappa had great concern for the nation and saw himself as an Indian first and only then as an officer of high rank, which is one of the reasons why he is still held in high esteem by his fellow men in his native Coorg and the rest of the country.

Cariappa took active part in the reorganisation of armed forces in many foreign countries. He was a much traveled man and visited parts of China, Japan, United States, Great Britain, Canada and most of the European countries. He was conferred with 'Order of the Chief Commander of the Legion of Merit' by American President, Harry S. Truman. As a token of heartfelt gratitude of the nation for the exemplary service rendered by him, the Government of India conferred the rank of Field Marshal on Cariappa in 1983. If there is one man whom the Kodavas can identify with reverence and respect it is undoubtedly Cariappa. Field Marshal K.M. Cariappa is an unforgettable name in the history of Indian Army. Old soldiers never die, they just fade away and he has proved this proverb. He has been a legend in his lifetime and he has left an indelible impression that would inspire the people of India, for a long time to come. He was the first and the last Commander-in-Chief of the Indian Army and was a man of great discipline and integrity. He breathed his last at Bangalore at a ripe age of 94, on 15 May 1993. The legendary hero of this great country who professed duty, discipline and loyalty to the nation is now history.

In 1953, General Kodandera Madappa Cariappa became India's third High Commissioner to Australia. He was 53 and had recently stepped down from his demanding role as the first Commander-in-Chief of the Army of Independent India. He did not particularly want to go to Australia, but Prime Minister Nehru had insisted and that, of course, settled the matter. Cariappa was an intriguing choice as High Commissioner.

He was a revered figure, admired for his substantial accomplishments and the high character that distinguished his army career. As India's pre-eminent soldier, he had worked and fought alongside the British and was comfortable in their company. Although adept at the silky arts of persuasion, Cariappa was a soldier who spoke his mind. He was not a diplomat by training or by inclination.

Cariappa (Kipper to his army colleagues and Carry to the world at large) was a lively conversationalist and a generous companion. An Australian novelist described him as a "tall, striking man still capable of playing a couple of useful chukkas of polo...in some ways more British than the British, but with a good deal more elasticity and charm." There was certainly elasticity, but also discipline and pride. Our novelist judged that the General had gone down well in Australia. No other High Commissioner in Canberra at the time had travelled more extensively or was better known. He visited many small country towns, places far removed from Canberra's cocktail circuit and the brittle tinkle of polite conversation. Cariappa had come to like Australia and Australians, although he had his reservations.

The Immigration Issue

In March 1956, one month before the end of his Australian mission, "Kipper" received a letter from an old army friend and India hand, Field Marshal Sir Claude Auchinleck. The "Auk" remarked on how foolishly provocative it was to allow so much of Australia to remain "empty" when land-hungry Asia was at the doorstep. Cariappa had a better understanding of the limits to population growth in Australia. He was well aware that vast deserts and unpredictable rainfall imposed severe limits on settlement.

Cariappa did not think Australia was the answer to India's over-population, but he resented the White Australia policy that restricted immigration to Europeans and he certainly made his feelings known in private. It was a time when Australia was receptive to some fresh thinking about immigration.

Throughout the 1950s domestic criticism of the White Australia policy gained support in progressive circles. There were even whispers of dissent in External Affairs where some people recognised that the rigid application of immigration policy was doing Australia damage throughout Asia, not the least in India.

The only thing many Asians knew about post-war Australia was that it did not want them as immigrants no matter what their gifts or talents. Cariappa felt the insult keenly. The Indian Army had tied the Japanese down in Burma, a crucial contribution to Australian security during the war. Many of his ex-army colleagues from these campaigns would make excellent settlers, but rather than accept them Australia had thrown open its doors to European immigrants, including Italians and others from former enemy countries. These were welcomed, but no Indians need apply.

The policy was particularly galling because Cariappa was frequently told of Australia's new appreciation of its Asian neighbours. In the 1950s, strenuous efforts were made to show that Australia was Asia-friendly. Government ministers readily claimed that Colombo Plan students studying in Australian universities experienced no racial intolerance and no "colour bar".

Australia's Future Lay in Asia

Richard Casey, the Minister for External Affairs, took charge of the hospitality offensive. A former Governor of Bengal, Casey was committed to the White Australia policy intellectually and pragmatically. He believed in racial homogeneity and knew that the quickest way to end a political career in Australia was to criticise restrictive immigration. However, Casey also recognised that Australia's future lay in Asia. He used neighbourly allusions to describe the Commonwealth as a family, exchanging confidences, sharing a joke and speaking frankly when required, a grouping drawn together by shared experiences.

The irony was that at Independence Lord Louis Mountbatten had been required to use all his persuasive powers to keep India within the Commonwealth family. It is less well known that he also attempted to secure some relaxation of the White Australia policy on India's behalf. Had they known of it, ordinary Australians would have condemned this strategy. It was precisely the kind of trade-off that made them suspicious of the titled elite who, they believed, ran the Empire. They suspected the top people didn't think much either of the White Australia policy or of white Australians for sticking to it so vehemently. A suspicion developed that Cariappa was working hand in glove with those who wanted to see an end to the restrictive immigration programme.

Conspiracy theories do not require much nourishment in order to flourish. From the late 19th Century some Australians suspected that Britain would put the commercial interests of its "polyglot" Empire before the Australian ideal of a racially pure continent set aside for the development of the "higher races". One prominent zealot declared that it was Australia's "sacred duty" to breed "a pure race in a clean continent". This seemed an ideal that Britain did not understand and would not want to defend.

The Shadow of Suspicion

That Cariappa moved freely among people like Claude Auchinleck and Viscount William Slim, Australia's Governor General, fuelled suspicion. He was also a great hit among titled Australians and particularly, so it seems, among titled women. This set more raw nerves quivering. In the demonology of the time, there is no more a menacing figure than the suave "oriental" with an impressive command of English. We encounter one of the worst (or finest) examples of the type in Madge Peterson's The Lure of the Little Drum, set in India just before the First World War. The villain is the sinister Ishaq Khan. He is tall, handsome, accomplished and, most worrying of all, Oxford educated. Beautifully shaped sentences roll from his tongue and, inevitably, the exquisite but susceptible Esther falls for his charms. The harem and an early and humiliating death await her. Khan (unaccountably) is not interested in Esther's shapely profile. His purpose is to degrade "what we white men hold so dear, our women".

Cariappa may well have thought that being a handsome, accomplished and beautifully spoken member of the Commonwealth would be well-received in Australia and proof that educated Indians could make a positive contribution to Australian development. He may have hoped that he could win over public opinion. Cariappa's charms certainly worked wonders in some quarters, but this may have deepened suspicions in others. The Ishaq Khan principle reveals that certain accomplishments were considered threatening. Cariappa was a dangerously seductive figure. He was a war hero and a thinker deeply versed in British and in Indian traditions. He could expound the Upanishads and execute a perfect fox trot. If the occasion required, he could do both simultaneously. He was witty and charming over drinks and could be wonderfully theatrical as he flourished his personally monogrammed Sobranie black Russian cigarettes (ordered in batches of 1,000 from London). And he was unattached.

Australian upper class ladies, some with titles, began to fall at his feet. Edith, a resident of one of Sydney's best suburbs, explained to "Dear Carry" that she was studying international affairs, paying particular attention to Australia's Asian neighbours. By "close study and personal associations" she hoped to banish English prejudice from her system. Some weeks later she writes again. Somehow the Marabar Caves had found their way to Australia. Edith appealed to Cariappa to overlook a recent episode in which she had behaved as a "silly ass" for "intimating any undue personal feelings towards you". We do not know how Cariappa responded to being the object of Edith's bold experiment in self-improvement.

In some eyes these may have been suspicious conquests, part of a cleverly laid plan to turn susceptible British Australians like Edith against the White Australia policy and have Australia opened up to immigration from India. Here was another potent apprehension, deeply embedded in Australia's white history: the flood from the north, the obliterating "yellow wave" sweeping an insecure white Australia right off the map.

The contradictory pressures shaping the post-war world and the now multiracial British Commonwealth were not easily contained. Cariappa quickly discovered this when in June in 1954 he visited northern Queensland. This was a voyage into tropical Australia and the famous "empty north", a part of Australia acutely sensitive to its lack of population. Public opinion in Queensland was stridently opposed to Asian immigration of any kind. After a long and tiring trip Cariappa returned to Brisbane where he agreed to grant an interview to the Brisbane *Courier Mail.*

The Brisbane Controversy

What Cariappa said is now difficult to ascertain. He was reported to have said that Australia's restrictive immigration policies might drive India and Pakistan out of the Commonwealth and into the hands of the communist powers. He added that Australians were more interested in the colour of a person's skin (tapping the back of his hand for effect) than in their hearts and minds. He rejected the fond talk about the Commonwealth family when it was clear that Australia preferred any white immigrant to the Commonwealth's coloured ex-servicemen. The *Courier Mail* story was soon picked up nationally and reported overseas, including in India. For white Australia diehards, Cariappa's statement was all the proof they needed that secret plans were being hatched to do away with the White Australia policy.

Yet although Cariappa was always prepared to make it clear in private discussions that the White Australia policy was repugnant and offensive, there is no evidence that he or the Indian government ever wanted to force the issue. Although Cariappa was roundly condemned in some quarters, to his supporters his Brisbane comments seemed to state an obvious truth: all the efforts to win over the neighbours and create a friendly image in the region were negated by the White Australia policy. It could not be explained away, no matter how hard Casey and others tried.

Cariappa was shaken and angered by the Brisbane controversy. He thought of returning to India, but believed this might be interpreted as an official rebuke and a recall. The old soldier in him refused to surrender. He would not give his Australian critics this comfort. Cariappa also found more indirect means of making his case about the Commonwealth family. He was instrumental in founding the Commonwealth Club in Canberra and as he travelled Australia he made a point of visiting war memorials. In the small town of Gundagai, Cariappa and his Sikh driver found the local memorial overgrown with weeds. These two spectacular figures got to work and soon had the memorial looking ship-shape.

The story found its way into the papers and became another part of the Cariappa mythology. No one could reasonably object to a soldier paying his respects to fallen colleagues, but few could have missed his point that India had been a loyal friend in the Second World War. Cariappa's impact is not easy to assess, but he gave heart to those agitating for immigration reform and consistently drew attention to the logic of Australia seeing itself as part of Asia. In simply being who he was he made white Australia re-consider its embarrassingly insular and offensive prejudices. And more than any other figure in Australia at the time, he spoke out for and embodied the newly independent India.

GENERAL MAHARAJ K.S. RAJENDRASINHJI, DSO
C-in-C, 14 Jan 1953-31 March 1955
COAS, 01 April 1955-14 May 1955
Armoured Corps, 2 Lancers

General Maharaj Kumar Shri Rajendrasinhji (also known as Maharaj Shri Ranjitsinhji and Rajendrasinhji Jadeja) assumed charge of the Indian Army, as the 2nd Chief of Army Staff, on 14 January 1953. Born on 15 June 1899, he attended Rajkumar College at Rajkot in Gujarat and then joined the Royal Military Academy (RMA) at Sandhurst on 10 September 1919. Commissioned into the Indian Army in 1921, he joined the 2nd Royal Lancers in 1922 as a Second Lieutenant.

He held various ranks and offices in the British Indian Army and served with distinction during the Second World War. He was also deputed to serve as Military Attaché in Washington D.C. in 1945-46. He took over as the Commander-in-Chief of the Indian Army on 14 January 1953, a post he held until 31 March 1955. Since the President of India was appointed as the Commander-in-Chief of the Indian Armed Forces, his designation was changed to the Chief of Army Staff on 01 April 1955.

In 1941 he went to North Africa, to serve as a squadron commander in his regiment. Early in that year the 3rd Indian Motor Brigade, of which the 2nd Royal Lancers was a part, was surrounded at Mechili by vastly superior German and Italian forces. As a last desperate measure the encircled regiments decided to force their way through the enemy and into the desert.

The then-Major Maharaj Rajendrasinhji, with two squadrons of his regiment, were acting as rearguard and had to wait for their divisional headquarters to move out. Most of his regiment was overwhelmed by a German tank attack, although his own squadron was not seriously involved. It was then that he charged with his men straight into the enemy, crashing through their battery of guns. After shaking off pursuit, they hid themselves in the hills for the rest of the day. Moving out once more at night they eventually reached the place of safety, but not before having a couple of skirmishes with the enemy. His squadron fought the actions successfully and brought back 60 prisoners. For his courageous leadership and determined action he was awarded the DSO (Distinguished Service Order), the first Indian to be honoured with such an award in World War II.

The Independence of India in 1947 caused an upheaval in both the security situation and the dynamics of the Indian Army. The partition of India meant the division of the Indian Army, which was concurrently called upon to deal with several critical security situations arising from the partition of the country and the integration of the princely states. Also during this period, British officers who held most of the senior ranks in the Indian Army were gradually disengaged, being replaced with Indian officers. During this critical period, Rajendrasinhji was called upon to shoulder many onerous responsibilities and received rapid promotion in rank commensurately. He was made Brigadier in 1946, Major General in 1947 and Lieutenant General in 1948. He served successively as General Officer Commanding (GOC) of Delhi and East Punjab (1947-48), GOC Eastern Command (1948) and GOC Southern Command (1948-53). Operation Polo, which resulted in the integration of Hyderabad State with India, was executed during his term in office as GOC Southern Command.

Addressing a passing-out parade at the National Defence Academy in Dehra Dun on 09 June 1953, General Maharaj Rajendrasinhji advised the newly-commissioned Army officers to remember that loyalty, duty, discipline, physical & mental fitness and a thorough knowledge of their military profession were the most important attributes expected of an officer and their achievements will require really hard work through their Army career. He also said, "To-day you are on the threshold of your careers as officers of the Indian Army. Tomorrow you will become members of a brotherhood that has a code of honour and sense of duty unequalled in any other profession in the world. See to it that your responsibilities and obligations to this brotherhood do not find you lacking in spirit or energy. Your loyalty to your country and the Army must be the dominating factor. Keep abreast of your profession, and ensure that you keep pace with new weapons and their effects in applied military science.

The men who respect your professional knowledge, and have confidence in your leadership will follow you anywhere. You must be the leader of your men and cannot afford to lag behind being out of condition. Go out shooting, trekking, mountaineering, go in for games that develop sound judgment, decision-making and team work, because these are the qualities that will make your career a success."

General Rajendrasinhji served in the Indian Army with distinction for 34 years till his retirement on 14 May 1955. Married to Maya Kunwarba in 1928, he had three children. He passed away on 01 January 1964.

General Rajendrasinhji's Medals & Decorations

- First Indian commissioned officer to be awarded the DSO during World War II
- India General Service Medal (1941)
- Africa & Burma stars
- Defence & War medals (1945)
- Officer of the Legion of Merit of the USA (1948)
- Indian Independence Medal (1947)
- George V Silver Jubilee Medal (1935)
- George VI Coronation Medal (1937)

GENERAL S.M. SHRINAGESH
COAS, 14 May 1955-07 May 1957
Infantry, Kumaon Regiment

General Satyawant Mallannah Shrinagesh assumed charge of the Indian Army, as the 3rd Chief of Army Staff, on 14 May 1955.

He was the eldest son of Dr Shrinagesh Mallannah, who was the personal physician to the Nizam of Hyderabad. Born in 1903 at Kolhapur, Maharashtra he went to a public school in England and entered Cambridge University in 1921.

Among the earliest batches of Indians to be nominated for the Sandhurst Military Academy in the U.K., he won the Quetta Cup for the best man at arms entering the Indian Army in 1923. He was subsequently commissioned into the 19th Hyderabad Regiment (presently known as the Kumaon Regiment) on 30 August 1923. After a brief association with the North Staffordshire Regiment, he was posted to the 2/1 Madras Pioneers with which he served mostly in Burma until it was disbanded. In 1933, he joined the 4/19th Hyderabad Regiment and served in Singapore as its adjutant. In December 1939, he was posted as an Instructor at the Indian Military Academy, Dehra Dun.

From 17 December 1942 till 28 August 1945, he was the Commanding Officer of the 6/19th Hyderabad Regiment (now 6th Kumaon). He then officiated as the Brigade Commander of the 64th Indian Infantry Brigade of the 19th Indian (Dagger) Division in Burma from August 1945. He was then appointed as the first Indian Commandant of the Kumaon Regimental Centre in Agra on 02 October 1946 and served in that capacity till 12 December 1946. He was then chosen to lead the 268th Infantry Brigade British Commonwealth Occupation Force (BCOF) in post World War II Japan and served in that post till 1947. He was also Brigade Commander of the famous Lushai Brigade in Burma in 1947. He was selected to go to Germany as Deputy Chief of the Indian Military Mission in November 1945. In that capacity, he also worked as the Economic Adviser & Consul looking after the interests of Indian nationals in Germany and locating missing Prisoners of War (POWs).

On his return from Japan, he was promoted to Major General and was appointed the General Officer Commanding of the Madras Area. From January 1948, he was appointed as the Adjutant General at the Army Headquarters and held that post till August of the same year. He also commanded the 5th Corps (later designated as 15th Corps). He was appointed the overall commander of all troops in Jammu & Kashmir during the 1947-48 Indo-Pak War and held this command till the ceasefire on 01 January 1949. Promoted to the rank of Lieutenant General in 1950, he was chosen as the GOC-in-C Western Command on 15 January 1949. He was then appointed as the GOC-in-C Southern Command and held that post, till he assumed charge as the Army Chief on 14 May 1955.

General Shrinagesh retired on 07 May 1957, completing 34 years of distinguished military service. Post retirement, he served as the Governor of Assam from 1959 to 1962, then as the Governor of Andhra Pradesh from 1962 to 1964 and finally as Governor of Mysore (now Karnataka) from 1964 to 1965. From 1959 to 1957, he also served as the Principal of the Administrative Staff College in Hyderabad. He passed away on 27 December 1977.

GENERAL K.S. THIMAYYA
Padma Vibushan, DSO, MD, ADC
COAS, 07 May 1957-07 May 1961
Infantry, Kumaon Regiment

General Kodandera Subayya Thimayya assumed charge of the Indian Army, as the 4th Chief of Army Staff, on 07 May 1957. Timmy, as he was better known, was a graduate of the Royal Indian Military College in Dehra Dun, a necessary stepping stone for a commission in the Indian Army. He was commissioned into the Army in 1926 and was attached to the Highland Light Infantry. He was soon posted to the 4/19th Hyderabad (the name changed to Kumaon in 1946) Regiment. He cut his soldiering skills on that famous training ground in the Northwest Frontier (present-day Pakistan), battling recalcitrant Pathan tribals.

Timmy's merits were soon recognized and just before World War II he was posted as an Adjutant at the University Training Corps in Madras, as a fitting example for young Indian undergraduates interested in joining the Indian Army, of what a good soldier should be. Due to an illness he was evacuated to India in 1939, just as World War II broke out, and was posted as the Second-in-Command of the Hyderabad Regimental Centre. He did however serve during the war and his record as a company commander, battalion commander and brigade commander came to the fore in operations against the tenacious Japanese in Burma.

He did his Staff College in Quetta and was posted to the 26th Infantry Division as a Grade II Staff Officer. His infantry division was conducting jungle warfare training and was preparing to go into Burma to face the Japanese Army during World War II. In Burma, he was posted to his old battalion as a Commanding Officer, which he led with outstanding success in battle. For a short while the battalion was under the command of the 3rd Command Brigade, with Brigadier C R Hardy at the helm, who during the height of a battle presented a trophy to the 8/19th Hyderabad. It was a green beret-the command's head dress-with a little typed message on a card, "We cannot buy anything here but we would like you to accept this as a token of our great admiration for the bravery and achievement of your battalion." He was also promoted to the rank of Brigadier in the field! For his outstanding service in battle, he was awarded the much coveted Distinguished Service Order (DSO) and also Mention-in-Despatches.

His innate talents of professional soldiering and leadership were soon recognized by Field Marshal Sir Claude Auchinleck, the Commander-in-Chief of the Indian Army. He was specially selected to lead the 268th Indian Infantry Brigade as part of the British Commonwealth Occupation Force in Japan after World War II. He got this assignment due to his outstanding battle experience as a Brigadier and being the only Indian to command a battle formation in the field. As an independent brigade, the 268th had done excellent work in the Burma Campaign and it had to represent, in Japan, the might & valour of the Indian Army. India made great contributions in stopping and later defeating the Axis forces and had raised the greatest volunteer fighting force in all of history, with more than two million men. More than two-thirds of the Allied land forces in South-East Asia were men of the Indian Army and among them were the original battalions of the 268th Brigade. It was now to be commanded by Timmy, who had won great honour and renown in the fighting against Japan.

Timmy proved to be an outstanding commander and his diplomatic skills emerged as he had to deal with General Douglas MacArthur, the Supreme Allied Commander of the Southwest Pacific Theatre, the other Allies and the vanquished Japanese. His popularity was to be seen to be believed and he was most suited by his personality, charm of manners and unassailable reputation, to impress on the Japanese the calibre of Indian commanders. He represented the country during the surrender of the Japanese in Singapore, followed by the surrender of the Japanese in the Philippines. At the ceremony of Japanese surrender in Singapore, Timmy signed on behalf of India. He was awarded the 'Keys to Manila' when he was sent to the Philippines. As Indian Independence approached, he was recalled to India by Field Marshal Sir Auchinleck for greater things.

He returned to India in 1947, during the Partition, as member of the committee to agree to the allotment of weapons, equipment and regiments that were to remain in India, or to be allotted to Pakistan. Soon after the commission was completed, he was promoted to the rank of Major General and was then assigned the command of the Fourth Infantry Division and also to take over the Punjab Boundary Force, dealing with the exodus and intake of refugees fleeing to their respective countries. His next appointment was command of the 19th Infantry Division in Jammu & Kashmir to drive the raiders and the Pakistan Army out of the Kashmir Valley. He succeeded in driving them beyond Uri and he ordered Stuart Light Tanks of the 7th Light Cavalry to the dizzy heights of the Zoji La Pass, to drive out the entrenched raiders and Pakistan Army regulars from the dominating heights.

He established the best of relations with Sheikh Abdullah and Bakshi Ghulam Mohammad and even Prime Minister Nehru, but his pleas to give him three more months to drive the raiders back to Muzzarfarabad fell on deaf ears and instead, Prime Minister Nehru went to the United Nations (UN). The rest is history.

Thereafter, Timmy served as the Commandant of the prestigious Indian Military Academy, Dehra Dun. The experience gained by him in Japan stood him in good stead when he was specially selected by the United Nations to head the Neutral Nations Repatriation Commission in Korea. It was a very sensitive and delicate task dealing with unruly Chinese and Korean prisoners. Here again, through sheer charisma, impartiality, firmness and diplomacy, he completed this task to the satisfaction of the world body. He returned to India and served as the Chief of the Southern Command and took over the reins of the Indian Army on 07 May 1957.

In 1959, he handed his resignation in protest to Prime Minister Nehru due to Defence Minister V.K. Krishna Menon's blatant interference in purely Army matters. Fortunately for the Indian Army, and the nation, Prime Minister Nehru persuaded him to withdraw his resignation and he continued as the Army Chief till his retirement on 07 May 1961, completing 35 years of distinguished military service.

After retirement from the Indian Army, the UN sought his services yet once again when he was appointed as the Commander of UN Forces in Cyprus (UNFICYP) in July 1964. He carried out this ticklish issue with consummate diplomatic skill earning the confidence of both parties. Alas, he passed away during his tenure as UNFICYP in December 1965 and his mortal remains were flown to Bangalore for the last rites. Of all the eulogies for him, the late Lieutenant General Premindra Singh Bhagat, VC (Retd.) summed it up best, "A General Thimayya is not born in every generation. The likes of him there will seldom be a soldier. The General is a man's man, the Army his soul and his soul the Army."

General Thimayya or Timmy, also more familiarly known by us as Dubbu, were old family friends. When he visited us, he used to come roaring into the colony, in his Ford car, with a couple of piglets strapped to the carrier of his car. In the evenings, he would drive my younger sister Bolly, my younger brother Bunny and myself at great speed and go around a huge tree located near Sivasamudram's famous landmark, twin waterfalls. On Christmas Day in 1926, there was a big party at the local club and we all left for the party including Dubbu. At the party, when everybody were enjoying themselves, one of the persons got up to sing. However his voice sounded a little better than a fog horn. Dubbu, in his enthusiasm to silence the singer, threw a potato at him which landed straight in his open mouth. There were roars of laughter amongst the revellers.

In 1926, after his commission as an officer in the Indian Army, he was posted to the Highland Light Infantry, then based at Bangalore. As the champion athlete of his Regiment, his fellow British officers wanted him to be a member of the Bangalore Club. However the recommendation of the British Officers were turned down by the Club's Committee, as at that time, no Indian could be a member. In protest, his fellow British Officers all resigned en-bloc from the club. In 1935, he married my elder sister Nina, who had returned to India after her education in France. In May 1935, his battalion was located at Quetta (present-day Pakistan) which suffered a devastating earthquake and Nina helped in comforting the homeless refugees of the earthquake. She was awarded the KAISER-I-HIND medal for her social work at the tender age of nineteen, the youngest to do so.

In 1941, I served as a Sepoy in the Regiment of Artillery at Muttra (today known as Mathura), a short distance from Agra. In 1942, I was selected for an Officers' Commission and did my training at the Royal Indian Military Academy, Dehra Dun and was then later commissioned into the 19th Hyderabad Regimental Centre at Agra. Dubbu's younger brother Freddy (later killed in action in Jammu & Kashmir), a very great friend of mine, was also posted to Agra. We young officers were billeted in a huge house which had a large drawing cum dining room surrounded by four large bed rooms and bathrooms. Freddy and I stayed in one of those rooms and we had local servants who polished our shoes, saw to the upkeep of our uniforms and the washing of our linen. However the food in the officers' mess was insipid and we were getting fed up of eating it all the time.

We young officers decided to have a party. There were ten of us. On a Saturday night, we went to the mess, nibbled at the food, said goodnight to Colonel Campbell who was surprised at our sudden departure. Our civilian bearers were told that they had to lay out a sumptuous meal of biryani, chicken, parotas, veggies and dancing girls (for which Agra was famous) for all of us, including the musicians as well. All of us, including the lovely dancing girls who were from Jaisalmer, the musicians, food and drink, and our bearers to act as servers, were having one whale of a time when at about 11 o'clock at night, Colonel Campbell and the Second-in-Command, Major Thimayya appeared.

Everything came to a standstill. The girls stopped singing and shaking their hips. The musicians were paralysed and we were frozen and thought to ourselves, "Now we have had it." Women were strictly forbidden to enter any Army bachelor quarters. Colonel Campbell asked as to why we were so silent, but there was not a single peep from any of us. He turned around to Dubbu and said, "Don't you think we should join them?" and Dubbu, ever ready for fun, agreed whole heartedly. We were so relieved and all of us had a blast that night, with the Colonel and the Major joining in, shaking their legs or dancing with the beautiful girls. The party got over at 2 o'clock in the morning, with Colonel Campbell and Dubbu having to stagger home, but not before we put them both in a tonga. The next time Dubbu and I met was in Rangoon, when he was on his way to Singapore to represent the Indian Army for the surrender of the Japanese. He was then a Brigadier with a DSO and a Mention-in-Despatches. From the surrender at Singapore, he went on to Manila, where he received the keys to the city. Later on, he was to command the 268th Indian Infantry Brigade as part of the British Commonwealth Occupation Force in Japan after the Second World War.

Dubbu was called back to India in 1947, as the partition of India was in progress, and was promoted to the rank of Major General. I too landed in India from Burma, whilst the partition riots were in full ferocity. I had to report to Army HQ in New Delhi for my posting orders, and was told that I was to report to Dubbu as his ADC in Jalandhar. Upon reaching Jalandhar, I stayed at the Officers Mess and waited for four days to report for duty. I was getting impatient doing nothing, and was longing to report back to my unit.

On the fifth day, I received a message ordering me to report to Major General Thimayya at his residence immediately. A truck was waiting to collect me and I quickly hopped in and reported to the General. I saluted him and said, "Captain Cariappa reporting for duty as ADC Sir!" He then asked, "Who sent you as my ADC?" I replied, "Sir, I did not want to be an ADC. I am too senior for the job, and I should be with my battalion at this time with all the disturbances going in due to the massive flow of refugees from Pakistan and those also moving in great hordes from India." He then told me that I had to be his ADC for the moment and until he found a suitable replacement, I had to stay put. The official interview ended and then we sat down and chatted about our home affairs. During my stay as his ADC, nobody at the Divisional Headquarters knew we were related. It was always "Yes Sir" and "No Sir" with Dubbu and at my farewell party (after finding my replacement) where everyone knew the rest of my family, they were surprised to know that we were related.

Dubbu had two responsibilities. He was the GOC 4th Infantry Division and also of the Punjab Boundary Force, and he maintained direct, personal contact with his counterpart in Pakistan. He made frequent official visits of the border areas and led huge Muslim refugee columns to Pakistan and did the same with Indian refugee columns, by having them follow his vehicle along the route. He was tremendously popular and well respected on both sides, but that still did not stop the carnage between the citizens of India and Pakistan.

The route was lined by the most ghastly sights and the stench of rotting human flesh in the thousands was unbearable. After completing that task in true 'Thimayya' fashion, he was posted as the Commandant of the Indian Military Academy and then later on as Quarter Master General (QMG) at Army HQ in New Delhi. In that post, he sorted out the 'Baniya System' that was prevalent in all units whereby the local contractor supplied all wants of the men in the matter of food, drink, cigarettes and civilian clothing. He stopped all contractors and units were made to run their own canteens with profits going to the unit itself. Today, it has become a very big organisation called the Canteen Department and is headed by a Major General, with all canteen items sold at a very cheap rate, the profits going to all units every year, some of which is used to finance officers, jawans and families who are in need of financial assistance and medical treatment.

In 1953, the United Nations appointed him as the Chairman of the Neutral Nations Repatriation Commission in Korea to solve the problem of the North and South Korean POWs. He was awarded the Padma Vibushan for his services rendered during his UN tenure, was promoted to the rank of Lieutenant General and took over as the GOC Western Command and later on as the GOC Southern Command. After his retirement from the Indian Army, he was appointed as Commander of UN Forces in Cyprus (UNFICYP) in July 1964. His old regiment, the Highland Light Infantry, was under his command and the young officers of the regiment were surprised when he went around mentioning the names of the soldiers he knew, as many of them were the sons of soldiers who had served with him early on in his army career.

During his tenure as Commander of UNFICYP, he was called on by President Dr Sarvepalli Radhakrishnan and was told that he would be reinstated into the Indian Army and would be appointed as Chairman, Chiefs of Staff Committee. Unfortunately, he passed away before it could come into effect. Back in 1947, he was recommended by Admiral Lord Mountbatten, the then Governor General and by Prime Minister Nehru to take over as the Army

Chief, but Defence Minister Gopalaswamy Iyengar opposed it, as he said that Dubbu was very young (in his early forties) and his talent would be wasted if he had to retire after doing his tenure as Army Chief. On his death at Cyprus, the regiment that did the Honour Guard and sounded the last post was the Highland Light Infantry, the regiment that he first served in. The Government of Cyprus, named a road after him in their nation and published a stamp in his name.

The late Lieutenant General Harbaksh Singh, PVSM, VC (Retd.) who served under Dubbu in several military operations and as his staff officer later on, had this to say about Dubbu, "I had an exceptional opportunity to study General Thimayya not only as a soldier on the battlefield in Jammu & Kashmir, but also during peace time as his Principal Staff Officer, when he was Army Commander, Western Command. I was able to see him both as a military leader as well as a man. In his official dealings, he would not let his personal interests or prejudices weigh with him. Yet whether in office or outside, he was always relaxed, jovial, friendly and freely exuding goodwill and bonhomie.

People were generally fond of him as a man. He was fond of the nicer things of life and was often seen enjoying himself in five-star hotels and restaurants in the metropolis of Delhi. He once told me, when he was COAS in Delhi, that one morning Panditji (Prime Minister Nehru) sent for him in his office, and obviously tutored by Intelligence Staff, suggested that he should not be seen at public places late at nights as it created a bad impression. To this he humorously replied, 'Panditji isn't that better than planning a coup in the middle of the night?' Panditji, I believe, laughed it off-such was his confidence in the General's integrity."

Dubbu's death was a great loss to our country and his achievements are sadly not lauded by our countrymen. Our people have not realised what an outstanding soldier and diplomat he was. A person who was loved by his soldiers and greatly respected in international circles. He always set a very high example of courage and steadfastness under the most dangerous conditions in the battlefield and that is why he was so loved and respected by all ranks under his command. He was undoubtedly a born leader of men, if there was one. He instantly won the confidence of his subordinates through his forthrightness, practical approach to problems and an even handed attitude to both his seniors and juniors alike.

He had the knack of getting the best out of those who served under him and soon established his relationship with them as their hero. His greatest quality as a military leader was that he never sought credit for himself, but always gave it is to his subordinates, and that is why they were ready to do their best for him. His human relationship was the epitome of his popularity and general acceptance among the public. He was by nature generous and forgiving and he never thought ill of any one, nor was any one inimically inclined towards him, barring one or two of his contemporaries who were victims of professional jealously. As the old saying goes and is still very much valid, "A prophet has no value in his own country."

GENERAL PRAN NATH THAPAR
COAS, 07 May 1961-19 Nov 1962
Infantry, Bengal Infantry & Punjab

General Pran Nath Thapar assumed charge of the Indian Army, as the 5th Chief of Army Staff, on 07 May 1961. Born on 08 May 1906, he was educated at Government College in Lahore and was commissioned into the 1st Punjab Regiment from the Royal Military Academy at Sandhurst in 1926. As a regimental officer, he spent nearly ten years with the 1st Punjab Regiment and later attended staff courses at Quetta (in present-day Pakistan) and at Minley-Manor in England.

During the Second World War, he saw service in Burma in 1941, followed by a tenure in 1943-44 in the Middle East and Italy. In 1945, he was appointed as the Assistant Military Secretary, General Headquarters in India. Later on, he was selected to serve on the Army Reorganization Committee. After victory over Japan in 1945, he commanded the 1st Battalion of his parent regiment in Indonesia during the national trouble in that country in 1946. Later he commanded the 161st Indian Infantry Brigade in East Bengal. On the advent of partition and during its first turbulent months, General Thapar served as the Director of Military Operations & Intelligence at Army Headquarters from August 1947 to December 1947. In November 1947, he was promoted to Major General and officiated for a few months as the Chief of General Staff and later appointed as the Military Secretary, a post he held till August 1949. This was followed by his appointment as the Master General of Ordnance from August 1949 to April 1950. He served as the Colonel of The Rajputana Rifles from 18 July 1949 to 20 July 1963.

General Thapar commanded an Infantry Division for about four years and was promoted to the rank of Lieutenant General in 1954 as Commander of a Corps. He held this appointment till December 1955 when he was selected to attend the Imperial Defence College in London from January to December 1956. On successful completion of the course, he was appointed as the General Officer Commanding-in-Chief, Southern Command and later took over as the General Officer Commanding-in-Chief, Western Command on 25 May 1959.

He hails from a distinguished family and brought to his high office a wealth of experience & knowledge gained on various fronts during his 35 years of service. He was forced to resign from the Indian Army on 19 November 1962, after the debacle of the 1962 Indo-China War. A keen tennis and golf player, he was at one time the Defence Services' tennis champion. After retirement, he was appointed as Indian Ambassador to Afghanistan from August 1964 and held that appointment till 01 January 1969. He passed away on 23 January 1975, at the age of 69.

GENERAL J.N. CHAUDHURI, OBE
COAS, 19 Nov 1962-07 June 1966
Armoured Corps, 16 CAV and 7 LC

General Joyanto Nath Chaudhuri assumed charge of the Indian Army, as the 6th Chief of Army Staff, on 19 November 1962. Born on 10 June 1908, he received his early education at St. Xavier's College in Calcutta and later at Highgate School in London. Obtaining a nomination to the Royal Military College at Sandhurst in 1926, he was commissioned into the Indian Army in February 1928 and subsequently joined the 7th Light Cavalry. In 1940, he went overseas with the 5th Indian Division and saw service in Sudan, Eritrea, Abyssinia (present-day Ethiopia) and the western deserts of Africa. He rose from the rank of Captain to Lieutenant Colonel within a span of two years. He was present at the capitulation of the Italian Forces in Italian-controlled East Africa. For his services he was awarded the Order of the British Empire (OBE) and was thrice Mentioned in Dispatches.

Recalled to India, he was appointed as the Senior Instructor at the British Staff College in Quetta (in present day Pakistan) and in 1941 led a regiment of the Indian Armoured Corps on a trek of 3,000 miles to join the fighting in Burma. The regiment, which then went on to lead the allied march to Rangoon, won great renown for its part in the fighting. At the end of the Burma campaign, he saw service in French Indo-China with his regiment in Java, Indonesia. In 1946, he was promoted to the rank of Brigadier in Malaya (a part of Malaysia which lies on the Malay Peninsula) and in the same year was selected to command the Indian Victory Contingent to London. Following a course at the Imperial Defence College at England in 1947, he returned to India and was appointed Director of Military Operations & Intelligence at Army Headquarters in New Delhi.

In February 1948, he was promoted to the rank of Major General and became the officiating Chief of the General Staff. In May 1948, he took over command of the 1st Armoured Division which played a major role in the 1948 Hyderabad Operations. Following Operation Polo in 1948, **he** was appointed as the Military Governor of Hyderabad State and from where he also functioned as Chancellor of Osmania University and Chairman of Deccan Airways. In the years following, he occupied important military posts and led an Indian Military Delegation to China.

In 1949, he was appointed as the first Colonel Commandant of the Electrical & Mechanical Engineers. In January 1952, he was appointed as the Adjutant General, Army HQ and in January 1953, he again took over as the Chief of the General Staff. On 19 November 1962, he was promoted to the rank of General and took over as the Chief of Army Staff (COAS). A facet of his talents and interests was demonstrated during his term as COAS, where he founded and was first president of the Delhi Symphony Society-an organization designed to promote Western music in New Delhi. He retired on 07 June 1966, after completing 38 years of distinguished military service. For his services to the nation, he was presented with the Padma Vibhushan-India's second highest civilian honour-by the President of India.

Six weeks after his retirement from the Indian Army, he was appointed as the Indian High Commissioner to Canada on 19 July 1966. He was married and had two children. In addition to being a distinguished military man, he displayed notable talent as a writer and literary critic. He wrote two books on military themes and was also the military correspondent and literary reviewer for one of India's leading newspapers. He passed away on 06 April 1983, at the age of 75.

OPERATION POLO: THE 100-HOUR WAR

The State of Hyderabad comprised most of the Deccan Plateau. Having risen from the ruins of the Mughal Empire it like many other states was a Hindu majority state with a Muslim ruler called the Nizam. Established in the 18th century by Nizam-ul-Mulk Asaf Jha, it came under British protection as per the Subsidiary Alliance of Wellesley. In 1947 the Nizam of Hyderabad was Nawab Mir Osman Ali Khan, a man of vast wealth. Dreaming of an independent state he sought Dominion status from the British only to rebuffed by Lord Mountbatten. The Indian Government was averse to a forced takeover and agreed to conclude a Standstill Agreement. It was hoped that this would open negotiations and the eventual peaceful accession of the state. However this only emboldened the Razakars a militant organization led by Kasim Razvi. Helped by the manipulations of the Nizam and his men, the Razakars aided by the communists let loose an orgy of violence,

THE INITIAL SKIRMISHES

The Razakars went on a recruiting spree including many from outside the state. There was an orgy of political murders and Hindu villages were razed. By the spring of 1948, they become bold enough to raid the Union territory. On September 6th, a police post near Chillakallu village came under heavy fire from Razakar units. A squadron of Poona Horse and a company of 2/5 Gorkha Rifles were sent to investigate.

They too came under fire. The tanks then chased the Razakars to Kodar, in Hyderabad territory. Here they were opposed by the armoured cars of 1 Hyderabad Lancers. In a brief action the Poona Horse destroyed one armoured car and forced the surrender of the state garrison at Kodar. Since the trouble began the Razakars had attacked about 70 villages in the state, 150 attacks outside the state, killing, raping and looting. The Nizam was given a last warning to rein in the Razakars.

LAST DITCH EFFORTS

The Nizam instead continued to insist that the conditions were normal and that his own troops were capable of maintaining law and order. Then hoping to get the UN to intervene, a delegation of his advisors left for UN headquarters via Karachi. This raised the possibility of the same power politics that plagued the case of Jammu & Kashmir. It was time for decisive action.

The first plans for a military operation were outlined by Lieutenant General E N Goddard, GOC-in-C Southern Army Command. This envisaged the capture of Hyderabad the state capital with a dual thrust by 1st Armoured Division, from Vijayawada in the East a distance of 250 km and Sholapur in the West, a distance of 300 km while small units will pin down the Nizam forces on the border.

The ORDER OF BATTLE

Hyderabad had a large army, with a tradition of hiring mercenary forces. This included Arabs, Rohillas, Pathans and Uttar Pradesh Muslims. The State Army consisted of 3 armoured regiments, a horsed cavalry regiment, 11 infantry battalions and artillery. There were supplemented by irregular units with a horse cavalry, four infantry battalions (Saraf-i-Khas, Paigah, Arab and Refugee) and a garrison battalion for a total of 22,000 men. Finally there were the Home Guards and Razakars. They were commanded by Major General El Edroos-an Arab.

The Razakars totalled about 200,000 although only 25% were armed with modern small arms and the rest with muzzle loaders and swords. The final plan for Operation Polo was based on the Goddard Plan. It envisaged two major thrusts: a western thrust through the Sholapur-Hyderabad axis and an eastern thrust along the Vijaywada-Hyderabad axis. Smaller thrust were to be made from the South to protect the railway lines of communications and from the North in the Jalna area. The Indian Task force, commanded by Major General J N Chaudhuri (later General and Chief of Army Staff) for the thrust from Sholapur, consisted of four operational groups:

Strike Force:

9th Dogra-Lt. Col. Ram Singh

Skinner's Horse minus one squadron (Stuart tanks)-Lt. Col. Kamla Nand

1 Troop Div HQ Squadron (Shermans)

Battery 1st Field Regiment (self-propelled)

1 Forward Air Control team

Smash Force:

1st Armoured Brigade (Brigadier S D Verma)

3rd Cavalry minus one squadron (Shermans)-Lt. Col. DC Basapa

17th Horse minus one squadron (Shermans)-Lt. Col. K Jangshamsher Singh

One troop-Skinner's Horse

1st Field Regiment less one battery (self-propelled)

2nd Battery-40 Medium Regiment

One Company-9th Dogra

Engineer and Administrative

Kill Force:

7th Infantry Brigade (Brigadier Gurbachan Singh)

2nd Sikh

3rd Grenadiers

14th Rajput

9th Para Field Regiment

Engineer and Administrative

Vir Force:

9th Infantry Brigade (Brigadier Apji Randhir Singh)

3rd Punjab

2/1 Gorkha Rifles

34th Anti-Tank Regiment

Engineer and Administrative

The advance from the Vijaywada was led by Major General A A Rudra and consisted of:

2/5 Gorkha Rifles

1 Squadron minus a troop of 17th Horse

1 troop from 19th Field battery + Engineers and ancillary units

Besides these forces four infantry battalions were to neutralise and protect lines of communication. Two squadrons of Tempest aircraft were available from Pune to provide air support. The overall control was in the hands of Lieutenant General Rajendrasinghji, DSO (later C-in-C and COAS, IA). The date was fixed for September 13th and all foreign governments especially the US, British, Canadians and Australians were asked to evacuate their national embassies. At

0500 hrs on the morning of the 13th, the Pakistan Army was informed about the decision.

Last Minute Discussions

It is interesting to note that General Sir Roy Bucher (C-in-C, IA) was opposed to the military action, and if agreeable was for an attack from the south, even though Lt. Gen. Rajendrasinhji was in favour of the western approach. A cabinet meeting was organised for September 12th to take a final decision. Among those who attended were Prime Minister Nehru, Home Minister Patel, Defence Minister Baldev Singh, Gopalswamy Iyengar, General Bucher, Lt. Gen. (later Field Marshal and C-in-C, IA) K M Cariappa and Air Marshal Sir Thomas W. Elmhirst (C-in-C, IAF).

As the decision was being finalised, Gen. Bucher stood up and said, "Gentlemen, you have taken a decision in a difficult matter. I must give you my warning. We are also committed in Kashmir. We cannot say how long it will take so we will end up having two operations on our hands. This is not advisable, so as your C-in-C I ask you not to start the operations." He further offered his resignation if his advice was not heeded.

There was a silence while a distressed and worried Nehru looked around. Patel replied, "You may resign General Bucher, but the police action will start tomorrow." A angry General Bucher stormed out, and coincidentally the next few days saw a rise in the Kashmir operations.

The War Begins-september 13

The first obstacle was the Naldurg fort which stood on the Sholapur-Secunderabad road about 19 km from the state border. Behind it was the Bori river with a bridge vital for the passage of Indian armour. The fort was defended by the 1 Hyderabad Infantry, some irregulars and a pair of 25 pounders. The task of capturing the bridge was given to 7th Brigade consisting of 2 Sikh, 3 Grenadiers and a battery from 34th anti tank regiment, a detachment from armoured reconnaissance and some Engineers. It started on the night of 12th Sept and moved to an area 23 km South of Naldrug in Indian territory.

Here the column split with one going for the bridge and the other for the guns. Achieving complete surprise the bridge was secured intact. The main column set of at 0400 hours. Led by 1 Armoured Brigade it consisted of 3 Cavalry less 2 squadrons, 17 horse less a squadron, 1 Field regiment less a battery, 7 Field Company, 14th Rajput, 4 Gwalior and a company of Dogras. Brushing aside the odd sniping and the occasional 25 pounder it linked up with the 7th Brigade. Meanwhile 2 Sikh made a dash for Jalkot 8 km east of Naldurg. Havildar Bachittar Singh commanding a platoon saw 2 vehicles coming from Naldurg. In spite of the withering fire he ran forward and succeeded in capturing the vehicles with their escorts. Latter during the day an entrenched Hyderabadi position opened up with Bren guns. Havildar Bachittar Singh led a skilful charge. 25 metres from the post he was hit on the thigh. Still he crawled forward and silenced the post with 2 grenades. Refusing to allow any medical help he kept encouraging his men till the end. He was awarded the Ashok Chakra.

The armoured columns of 1 Armoured brigade now reached Jalkot around 0900 hours. Chaudhari now asked the 3rd column to pass through and continue advancing. Under Lt Col Ram Singh this column consisted of 1 Horse (less a squadron), 1 battery of 1 field regiment, 1 battery of 40 medium regiment, an Engineer detachment, 9 Dogra less a company and some ancillary units. Brushing aside the resistance they made it to Umarge, 61 km inside Hyderabad, by 1515 hours. The Razakars in the town resisted but were quickly overpowered.

The 4th column was in charge of clearing the Northern flank of the main advance. Under 9th Brigade it consisted a squadron of 3rd Cavalry, a troop from 18th cavalry, a troop from 9 Para field regiment, 10 Field company engineers, 3/2 Punjab Regiment, 2/1 Gorkhs Rifles, 1 Mewar Infantry and ancillary units. Its task was to capture Tuljapur, 34 km NW of Naldurg.

This straddled the Sholapur Osmanabad road and connected to Naldurg by road. A battalion group consisting 2/1 Gorkha rifles, a battery of 9 Field regiment, a squadron of 3rd cavalry and a detachment of engineers advanced from Barsi and crossed the border at 2000 hours. By dawn they had isolated Tuljapur by stationing a company each on the Tuljapur-Osmanabad road and the Tuljapur-Naldurg road. A ridge commanding the plateau below was held by 200 Razakars and 1 Hyderabad infantry. There was a stubborn resistance for two hours, even though the issue was never in doubt.

Another group of 9th Brigade consisting of 3/2 Punjab, Mewar Infantry, a troop of 18th Cavalry, a battery from 9 Field regiment and some Engineers advanced along the Sholapur-Tuljapur road. Though the tanks got bogged down, the Punjabis continued to lead the advance and linked up with the Gorkhas at 1530 hour. Further movement towards Lohara was given up due to the swollen nulla on the way. After the units linked the Mewar infantry was given the task of mopping and holding to Tuljapur. Thus ended the first day with the Indians battering the Hyderabad forces and inflicting heavy losses. A number of men were captured including a British mercenary tasked with blowing up the Naldurg bridge.

Meanwhile the column from Vijayawada leading the Eastern thrust was making good progress. The opposition was in the form of 2 armoured units of Humbers and Stagehounds. The task of neutralising it was given to 4 battalions: 9/2 Punjab, 3 Sikh LI, 6 Jat and 6 Kumaon. Some support was provided by 17 Poona Horse. The force was commanded by Lt Col Amrik Singh. The advance began at dawn on Sept 13 and by 0830 hours they had reached Kodar. Leaving the 9/2 Punjab to guard Kodar. Lt Col Singh pressed on to reach Mungala by afternoon.

On the Southern borders of Hyderabad, the Indian aim was to ensure the safety of the rail communications that passed through the area. The bridges at Kurnool, Tungabhadra and Hospet were the responsibility of units under Brigadier N V Bal. Headquartered in Guntakal he had the 5/5 Gorkha Rifles, 1 Mysore Infantry and Mysore Lancers (on horses). He had two armoured trains for patrolling. These units did not encounter much resistance except at Hospet, where a company of the Mysore Infantry ran into trouble.

A sugar factory by the bridge was occupied by a large number of Razakars and Pathans. Twice the company took over the factory only to be beaten back by large numbers of the defenders. A company of the 4th Rajputana rifles trying to aid the Mysoremen was itself in trouble when the train in which they were travelling got derailed. However the stubborn resistance could not hold out against determined Indian efforts.

A company of 5/5 Gorkha rifles left Guntakal for the Tungabhadra bridge in the early hours of 13th Sept. The bridge was guarded by a strong contingent of the Hyderabad forces, its flanks covered by Bren gun posts. A section led by Nail Narbahadur Thapa engaged the defenders. Under heavy fire he dashed across hundred yards of open ground between him and the Bren gun position and decapitated its crew with his khukri. With it all resistance collapsed. Naik Narbahadur Thapa got the Ashok Chakra.

Day 2-september 14

Maj Gen Chaudhuri's aim was to reach Rajasur, 48 km east of Umarga. However the road passed through an 8 km defile near Talmud. Here the hills on both sides of the road were covered with scrub. Furthermore the ground at the end of the defile rose sharply providing a good vantage point for artillery observers. Air recce had indicated well defended positions. The Indian Air Force was called in and a couple of strikes by IAF Tempests caused the Hyderabadis to abandon their positions. With Rajasur falling in the afternoon, a small detachment was sent to take care of Kalyani which was held by some Razakars.

Meanwhile in the Kodar area the Hyderabad army had dug an anti tank ditch. The ditch was filled up and as the advance continued heavy fire was encountered from some low hills 6 km short of Suriappet. The fire was coming from units of 1 Lancer and 5 Infantry but fight as well as they did they could not hold long against the veterans of the Burma campaign the 2/5 Gorkha rifles. The cost was 35 Hyderabadis dead and 49 captured for 2 Gorkha soldiers killed. Meanwhile a column of 3/11 Gorkha Rifles and a squadron of 8th cavalry advanced on to Osmanabad from the North. However its main defences were in the South and provided stiff resistance to a column from 9th Brigade which advanced from Tuljapur. Heavy street to street combat took place as the Razakars fought doggedly.

Major General D S Brar was given the task of taking Aurangabad. An important military and civil centre its early capture was essential. Major General Brar organised six columns for this purpose. A column comprising 3/5 Gorkha Rifles, 2 companies of 17th Sikh, a squadron of Stuarts and armored cars from Armoured Corps School, 20 Field Battery and Engineers and ancillary under Lt Col P S Thapa was tasked with taking the city. Moving along the Nangaon-Aurangabad axis, it brushed aside the odd opposition and entered Daulatabad fort by the afternoon. As the column reached the city outskirts the civil administration came out to surrender. A column consisting of 3 Sikh, a company of 2 Jodhpur infantry and some tanks from 18 Cavalry marched to Jalna. Here the Hyderabadi forces resisted stubbornly before giving up.

Day 3-september 15

The action here continued till early morning when the elements from 9th Brigade were joined in by 8th cavalry. The action left 75 Razakars killed and 84 taken prisoner. Once this was over a company of 3/11 Gorkhas were left behind with some tanks to hold the city while the rest of the forces moved to Latur. By afternoon they reached Mominabad. The 3 Golconda Lancers who held it, after some initial half hearted resistance threw in the towel.

Suriapet was strafed by the IAF in the morning, followed by a rapid advance by the 2/5 Gorkhas. The Hyderabadis had withdrawn but a few dozen Razakars were captured in mopping operations.

The retreating Hyderabadis partially destroyed the Musi Bridge. But they neglected to lay covering fire and it was repaired and the advance resumed. The only other action was at Narkatpalli where a Razakar battalion was decimated.

The column led by 1 Armoured was cautious as it approached Zahirabad and Bidar. This were well defended and the aim was to take over Homanabad and launch probing operrations towards Zahirabad and Bidar. Homanabad fell at 0800 hours with only sporadic resistance. Leaving the 9th Brigade to mop up, the armoured units moved towards Bidar but soon ran into a swollen nullah. The other column led by Ram Singh advanced about 16 km towards Zahirabad before halting for the day.

Day 4-september 16

Ram Singh's forces moved out towards Zahirabad in the early hours of the morning to capture the junction where the road from Bidar met the Sholapur-Hyderabad road. If that fell he was to turn north towards Bidar while the armoured column moved towards Zahirabad. The armoured columns was slowed down by a mine field which were cleared in due time. Ram Singh's forces encountered fire at the junction. Some time into the fighting the armoured column joined up and Ram Singh's units disengaged and moved north, leaving the fighting to the armoured column. All along the route there was sporadic resistance by Hyderabadi forces and by nightfall Ram Singh's men were a few kms short of Bidar. Meanwhile the armoured column met with determined resistance from the Razakars. Within the built up areas the Razakars enjoyed a brief advantage till the 75mm guns of the tanks were brought into play. By nightfall the forces had moved 15 kilometres beyond Zahirabad.

Day 5-september 17 the War Ends

On Sept 17 in the early hours the Indian Army entered Bidar. With the Nizam forces being routed from all directions, the Government resigned. The forces led by the 1 Armoured Regiment were at Chityal about 60 km from the capital. Another column took over Hingoli. With no escape route and no foreign aid coming, the Nizam went on the air and asked his remaining forces to cease fire by 1700 hours. He banned the Razakars and allowed Union troops into Secunderabad and Bolurum. The next day Major General Chaudhuri rode at the head of an armoured column to Secunderabad and at 1600 hours the Hyderabad Army represented by Major General El Edroos surrendered.

Major General Chaudhuri took over as Military Governor. Over the next few days mopping operations continued against the Razakars with their leader Razvi arrested on Sept 19. On November 24th, Major General Chaudhuri handed over control to a civilian Governor following the Nizam's accession to the Union. The Indian Army suffered 66 killed and 97 wounded. The Hyderabad State forces had 490 killed and 122 wounded. The Razakars suffered even more.

GENERAL P.P. KUMARAMANGALAM, DSO
COAS, 07 June 1966-07 June 1969
Regiment of Artillery

General Paramasiva Prabhakar **Kumaramangalam** assumed charge of the Indian Army, as the 7th Chief of Army Staff, on 07 June 1966. Born on 01 July 1913, he completed his early education at Eton College and graduated from Woolwich College in England. He was the last of the King's Commissioned Indian Officers trained at the Royal Military Academy, Sandhurst and was the second Indian Officer to be commissioned into the Regiment of Artillery on 19 August 1933.

During the Second World War, he participated in the operations in the Middle East and was awarded the Distinguished Service Order (DSO) as a Major for action in Libya on 27 May 1942. He was taken Prisoner of War (POW) in Italy in 1942, however he did not stay long and escaped. However his luck ran out and he was caught again and imprisoned, this time in Germany. At the end of the war in 1945, he returned to India and become a Brigadier in 1948.

General Kumaramangalam took over as the General Officer Commanding–in-Chief (GOC-in-C), Eastern Command in May 1963. In November 1964, he was appointed as the Deputy Chief of Army Staff (DCAS) and on 15 January 1965, he became the Vice Chief of Army Staff (VCAS). He also served as the Adjutant General and the Commandant of the Defence Services Staff College (DSSC) at Wellington, before becoming the Army Chief on 07 June 1966. General Kumaramangalam was the first gunner from the Regiment of Artillery, to serve as the Army Chief. His tenure as Army Chief was marked by an unpublicised, but exhaustive, re-organisation of the Indian Army which included up-gradation of weapons and training & tactics based on the lessons learned from the 1965 Indo-Pak War. He served in the Indian Army with distinction for 36 years till his retirement on 07 June 1969. For his services to the nation, he was presented with the Padma Vibhushan-India's second highest civilian honour-by the President of India in 1970.

General Kumaramangalam was an avid polo player and a keen cricketer. He was also a member of the Marylebone Cricket Club, a prestigious cricket club in England; the President of the Indian Polo Association and Equestrian Federation of India and a Fellow of the Royal Horticultural Society. He was the Senior Colonel Commandant of the Regiment of Artillery from 05 July 1959 to 04 July 1969 and the Honorary Colonel Commandant from 05 July 1969 to 30 June 1975. On retirement as Army Chief, he was elected President of the World Wildlife Fund-India during its formative stages. He passed away on 13 March 2000, following cardio respiratory failure, at the age of 87.

FIELD MARSHAL S.H.F.J. MANEKSHAW
Padma Vibhushan, Padma Bhushan, MC
COAS, 07 June 1969-15 Jan 1973
Infantry, 8 Gorkha Rifles

Field Marshal Sam Hormusji Framji Jamshedji Manekshaw assumed charge of the Indian Army, as the 8th Chief of Army Staff, on 07 June 1969. Born in Amritsar, Punjab on 03 April 1914, he completed his schooling in Amritsar and Sherwood College, Nainital. He then joined the first batch of 40 cadets at Indian Military Academy (IMA), Dehra Dun on 01 October 1932. He passed out of the IMA in December 1934 and was commissioned as a Second Lieutenant in the Indian Army. He held several regimental assignments and was first attached to the Royal Scouts and later to the 12 Frontier Force Rifles.

During World War II, he saw action in the Burma campaign on Sittang river and has the rare distinction of being honoured for his bravery on the battle front itself. During World War II, he was leading a counter-offensive against the invading Japanese Army in Burma.

As he charged forward with his men, a Japanese soldier suddenly emerged from the bushes and fired at him, wounding him seriously in the stomach. Fortunately, Major General D.T. Cowan spotted Manekshaw holding on to life and was aware of his valour in face of stiff resistance from the Japanese. Fearing the worst, Major General Cowan quickly pinned his own Military Cross ribbon on to Manekshaw saying, "A dead person cannot be awarded a Military Cross."

Having recovered from those near-fatal wounds in Burma, Manekshaw went for a course at Staff College, Quetta and later also served there as an instructor before being sent to join 12 Frontier Force Rifles in Burma under General (later Field Marshal) Slim's 14th Army. He was once again involved in a fierce battle with the Japanese, and was wounded for a second time. Towards the close of World War II, Manekshaw was sent as Staff Officer to General Daisy in Indo-China where, after the Japanese surrender, he helped rehabilitate over 10,000 POWs. He, then, went on a six-month lecture tour to Australia in 1946, and after his return served as a First Grade Staff Officer in the Military Operations Directorate at Army HQ in New Delhi.

Manekshaw showed acumen for planning and administration while handling the issues related to partition in 1947, and later put to use his battle skills during the 1947-48 Jammu & Kashmir Operations.

After command of an Infantry Brigade he was posted as the Commandant of the Infantry School and also became the Colonel of 8 Gorkha Rifles (his regimental home) and 61 Cavalry. He commanded a Division in Jammu & Kashmir and a Corps in the North East, with a tenure as Commandant of Defence Services Staff College (DSSC) in between. As GOC-in-C Eastern Command, he handled the tricky problem of insurgency in Nagaland and the grateful nation honoured him with a Padma Bhushan-India's third highest civilian honour-in 1968.

Manekshaw succeeded General Kumaramangalam as Chief of Army Staff (COAS) on 07 June 1969. His years of military experience were soon put to the test as thousands of refugees from the erstwhile East Pakistan started crossing over to India as a result of oppression unleashed from West Pakistan.

The volatile situation got worse, and soon erupted into a full-scale war in December 1971. During the military campaign, Manekshaw showed uncommon ability to motivate the forces, coupling it with a mature war strategy. The war ended with Pakistan's unconditional surrender, and the formation of Bangladesh. For his selfless service to the nation, he was awarded the Padma Vibhushan in 1972 and was conferred with the honorary rank of Field Marshal on 01 January 1973. He retired a fortnight later, on 15 January 1973, after completing nearly four decades of military service.

Some of his achievements as COAS are;

- Prepared the Army for a well-planned and a well executed operation against Pakistan in 1971, leading to the creation of Bangladesh.
- As Chairman of Chiefs of Staff Committee, he welded the Army, Navy and Air Force into a well-knit team.
- Taking of over 90,000 Pakistan POWs, thereby paving the way for favourable negotiations.

SAM BAHADHUR

The man eventually destined to be free India's first Field Marshal was born on 03 April 1914 at Amritsar. How did a Parsi couple settle for the holy city of the Sikhs? I once asked him and was told that in 1899, his father recently qualified as a doctor and just married, could make no professional headway in Bombay, and was advised to try his luck at Lahore in the Punjab. With his young wife, he set off by train for Lahore.

The long dusty and hot journey took five days and by the end of it, his young wife, who had never left the comforts and civilization of Bombay, was in hysterics and cried to go back. Poor Dr Manekshaw did all he could to comfort her, but as the train steamed into Amritsar, with her first sight of the Sikhs the young bride screamed her lungs out and refused to go any further. So they left the train at Amritsar, and there they stayed for forty-five years.

The Manekshaws had six children, four boys and two girls, and Sam was the fifth child. Sam had his schooling at Nainital's Sherwood College. After completing his schooling, he should have gone to England to pursue higher studies; this was the promise made to him by his father but, fortunately for the Indian Army, Dr Manekshaw felt that this particular son was far too young to be on his own in a foreign country, even with his two elder brothers already studying there. So he was admitted to the Hindu Sabha College, Amritsar. If he had gone abroad, he often reminisces, he would have become a doctor. "What doctor?" I queried, and was told "Gynaecologist."

After a stint in Hindu College, he applied for and was accepted for entry into the first batch of the newly opened Indian Military Academy at Dehradun for training Indians for commissioned rank in the British Indian Army. He received his commission on 04 February 1934 and, after an attachment as was the practice then with a British Infantry Battalion, the 2nd Battalion the Royal Scots, he joined the 4th Battalion, 12 Frontier Force Regiment, commonly called the 54th Sikhs. In 1937, at a social gathering in Lahore he met his future wife, Silloo Bode; they fell in love and were married on

22nd April 1939. Silloo is a graduate of Bombay's renowned Elphinstone College and also studied at the JJ (Jamsetjee Jeejeebhoy) School of Arts there. A voracious reader, a gifted painter and an extremely intelligent and interesting conversationalist, she has made an admirable wife and a wonderful mother.

The outbreak of the Second World War saw the 4/12 Frontier Force Regiment in action in Burma with the famed 17 Infantry Division. Sam was separated from his family for over three years and this separation was the cause of a celebrated example he was later to give while answering questions put to him in his capacity as Chief of the Army Staff by the Pay Commission. The question, which triggered off the reply was, why should the army continue to get separation allowance? This, to clarify, is a token sum every officer and enlisted man gets when his unit moves to a non-family station thus necessitating separation. I say 'token' because the name is a misnomer; whereas it is meant to cover the expenditure incurred in running two establishments, the amount paid is, in fact, a pittance. For example, an officer used to get just seventy rupees a month and the men an even smaller amount. The answer to explain the need was "After my marriage, I went off to war and didn't see my wife for three long years, and when I returned I found I had a brand-new daughter, and the only reason I am sure the child is mine is because she looks just like me." Needless to say, the Pay Commission broke up in laughter, but went away convinced. The separation allowance continues.

On 22 February 1942, occurred the much publicised event when Sam Manekshaw was wounded. The retreat through the Burma jungle ended abruptly for him on 22 February 1942, when seven bullets from a Japanese machine gun whipped through his body. The young captain who had just led two companies in the courageous capture of a vital hill was awarded the Military Cross. "We made an immediate recommendation," a senior officer explained, "Because you can't award a dead man the Military Cross." His orderly Sher Singh evacuated him to the Regimental Aid Post where the regimental medical officer, Captain G M Diwan, treated him overruling his protestations that the doctor treat other patients first. Sam was evacuated to the hospital at Pegu where he was operated upon, and then evacuated further to Rangoon, from where he sailed for India in one of the last ships to leave that port before it fell to the Japanese. He still carries the scars of this wound and I am not quite sure whether it is that or regular exercise that keeps his stomach in — to the envy of people much younger than he.

I was to see a great deal of Sher Singh during my tenure in Delhi. He and some other grizzled old veterans of the 4/12 Frontier Force Regiment were frequent visitors to Army House and South Block. The entire staff including all guards and sentries, had strict orders that if a man said he was from the 54th Sikhs he was to be led straight to the Chief, whatever the time or whatever the Chief happened to be doing. Consequently, these gentlemen would turn up whenever it suited them with a string of requests that ranged from wanting a bag of sugar for a daughter's marriage (easy to solve) to asking that a relative or friend's relative be given immediate out-of-turn promotion. When I patiently attempted to explained the impossibility of the latter request and others like it, the worthy would bristle and inform me: "In the British time if the Jangi Lat gave an order it was executed without question." No amount of explanation that times had changed and that such Nadirshahi orders would now invite representations which could not possibly be answered, would pacify them and they would go away and complain to the Chief about the incapable and unhelpful Colonel Sahib he had from the Gorkhas.

The war over, saw Sam working in the Military Operations Directorate at Army Headquarters, first as a General Staff Officer Grade I, and later as Director of Military Operations. It was from here that he oversaw the fighting that broke out between India and Pakistan, over Kashmir, the two nations that until so recently had been one. It was also under his direct supervision, when the cease-fire was declared, that the famous line called the Cease Fire Line was drawn. Many, many years later, by a strange coincidence, while he was Chief of the Army Staff, it was he whose brainchild it was to scrap the Cease Fire Line and call it the Line of Actual Control. Promotions followed in rapid succession and 1959 saw Sam as commandant of the Defence Services Staff College.

There his outspoken frankness got him into trouble with the Defence Minister, V K Krishna Menon, and his protégé of the time, the late Lieutenant General B M Kaul; a court of inquiry was ordered against him. Despite persistent questioning I have not been able to ascertain from him the reasons and the facts that led up to a situation where the Indian Army could have lost its most brilliant up-and-coming general officer: he just refuses to talk, calling the entire episode, just another phase. Be that as it may, the court of inquiry that was convened with the late Lieutenant General Daulet Singh, then Western Army commander, as presiding officer, exonerated Sam, but before a no case could be announced, fate intervened in the shape of the Chinese hordes that swept over what we had always considered the impregnable Himalayas.

The Indian Army, that proud, disciplined and distinguished force that had fought and triumphed in practically every battlefield of the world, was outmatched, out manoeuvred and outfought; its remnants streamed back dazed and humiliated leaving among the lush green mountains of the North Eastern Frontier Agency and the stark white to Ladakh its dead, its wounded and its pride.

The North Eastern Frontier Agency (NEFA), now called Arunachal Pradesh, was where we suffered our worst defeat, and it was to 4 Corps that providence ironically decreed and Army Headquarters ordered Sam Manekshaw to succeed Lieutenant General B M Kaul, the man who had almost ruined his professional career. He took over 4 Corps on 28th November 1962 on promotion to lieutenant general, and the same day addressed a conference of what must surely have been a very shaken group of staff officers. He entered the room with his usual jaunty step, looked as if he were meeting each eye trained on him and said, "Gentleman, I have arrived! There will be no more withdrawals in 4 Corps, Thank You," and walked out.

But the charisma that surrounds the man had preceded him and soldier and officer alike knew the 'chosen one' had arrived and henceforth all would be well. It was as if the dark and oppressive atmosphere had suddenly been lightened and Sam was the bearer of the light.

On 04 December 1963, Sam took over as Army Commander in the west, the second rung from the top. One of his Brigade Commanders was H S Yadav, the man who had been the principal prosecution witness in the case cooked up against him in 1961. At a party in an officers mess in Kashmir one evening, talk veered round to Yadav, and the senior brass, knowing the background and not averse to making a few points with the Army Commander, started on what each planned to do to catch or embarrass Yadav. The Army Commander heard this for some moments and then butted in ('before I got sick' as he told me later) with "Look chaps, professionally, Kim Yadav is head and shoulders above most of you, so forget about trying to catch him out. He just lacks character and there is nothing anyone of you can do about that."

At a meeting in Delhi a few months later, Chavan, then the Defence Minister, asked him his views on which army command Sam considered most important, challenging and threatened. Eastern, said Sam, as it had the Chinese in the North, East Pakistan in the South and on its flank insurgency rampant in Nagaland and the Mizo Hills and, if all that was not enough to fill the hands of the incumbent, the troubled state of West Bengal certainly would.

Chavan thought over the answer for a few moments and then asked if Sam would like to accept the challenge of taking over that command. He accepted immediately. Eastern Army had to keep one wary eye directed north on the Chinese; another eye had to be kept on erstwhile east Pakistan which lay in its gut, it had to fight insurgency in Nagaland which later spread to the Mizo Hills, and finally it had to watch over the politically volatile states of Assam and West Bengal. It was, therefore, no bed of roses, and the job of lower formations was not facilitated by the army commander's personally coming on the telephone every now and then and 'grilling' staff officers and commanders with endless questions about detail.

I remember an occasion in Shillong where I once asked the senior staff officer why he was looking a bit off-colour. He told me he had just finished a telephone conversation with the army commander who had wanted answers to so many questions that, 'I am now in orbit.' His mastery of detail was fantastic and, as I was to learn later, he could quote an answer given verbally or in writing months previously to correct someone who was saying something else.

A battalion employed in the Mizo Hills, paying perhaps a little more attention to the welfare of its troops and, in the process, a little less than desirable to the operational side received a rude reminder that 'someone up there' was watching, very keenly, every move that was made. A parcel of bangles was delivered to the Commanding Officer with the compliments of the Army Commander with a cryptic note: "If you are avoiding contact with the hostile give these to your men to wear." Needless to say, the next few weeks saw a flurry of activity by this battalion resulting in another, more soothing message: "Send the bangles back."

He was officiating as Army Chief in 1967 when the Chinese had their first clash with the Indian Army since 1962. This occurred at the 14,000 foot high pass, Natu La, in Sikkim where the Chinese learnt to their cost that the Indian Army of 1967 was a different kettle of fish from that of 1962. He was summoned to a meeting of the Cabinet where, as he recalled later, everyone present at the meeting was vying with the others to present to the Prime Minister his grasp of the situation and offering one suggestion after another as to what should be done. After hearing most of the speakers, the Prime Minister enquired whether the officiating army chief, until then a silent spectator, had something to say. "I am afraid they are enacting Hamlet without the Prince," he said. "I will now tell you exactly what has happened, and how I intend to deal with the situation." He then proceeded to do so.

Bengal in those days was a very troubled state where anarchy was prevalent, and law and order was almost on the way out. Sam was traveling to Dum Dum airport, Calcutta, once when he found the road blocked for traffic by a huge crowd being harangued by one person.

The outrider and the staff officer accompanying him both advised a detour, but this would have meant running away and would have been noticed by the locals. So he got out of his staff car instead, and started walking up to the speaker who, he discovered to his disquiet as he approached, was a 'huge fellow, well over six feet tall.' Anyway, hiding his mounting uneasiness, he put his hand out and announced, "I am Sam Manekshaw." This unsettled the other person somewhat as he had probably anticipated an argument. He too, put his hand out and mumbled his name. He was then asked to clear the road, as otherwise "I shall miss my plane." The speaker, by now completely confused, hastened to obey, and the last glimpse the Army Commander had of his latest acquaintance was of that worthy helping to clear the road.

By then Sam Manekshaw had become one of the most popular and well-known officers in the Indian Army. Stories of the many admirable qualities he possessed and did not hesitate to display were legion. Always an unconventional dresser, he once met Lieutenant General Kulwant Singh, at that time commanding Western Army and an awe-inspiring man, in a jacket that could best he described as a cross between a regulation shirt and bush shirt.

When the Army Commander pointed this out he was asked: "Have you come to see my formation or my dress?" While he could stand up to his superiors, he always stood by his subordinates. Service with him, it was rumoured, was certain to bring rewards in its wake. But, helpful as he was, he never consciously helped a subordinate at the cost of someone else. In other words, 'No throat was cut.' I once asked him if he was aware of the jealousy his so-called favourites aroused among others. He replied he was aware of this but as his 'favourites' were all competent officers he defied anyone to point a finger at them as far as their professional competence was concerned. On another occasion I asked him why he could not 'see through' the slick types who fawned and flattered him, and why he acceded to their requests. "Oh, I see through them all right," he replied. "I detest them, but I make use of them."

He was human and approachable to a fault. Once, so a story goes, while he was a Corps Commander, a junior officer on his staff asked for some leave, and the request was turned down by the officer's immediate superior.

The officer then tried the indirect approach and made his problem known to the Corps Commander who called the man's immediate superior the next day and said, 'Look, I have had a letter from this youngster's father asking that the boy be sent on a spot of leave as there is some family problem to sort out. I am sure we can spare the bugger for a few days, let him go, we won't miss him.' The officer got his leave; no feathers were ruffled and everyone was happy, which brings us to his next great quality, the ability to run a very happy and contented team. His professional qualities ensured that the team was also a competent one. He was believed to finish his own work in an hour and spend the remainder of the time walking from one office to another, sitting down with the harried junior staff and helping them sort out the problems they were working on.

They said he never raised his voice, but even a mild reproving look from him with a 'Sweetheart, this won't do,' was enough to shake the stoutest heart. Sharply critical, but always constructively so, there was nothing his eye ever missed or his fantastically retentive memory ever forgot. He forgave easily, being basically a kind man. While he was Chief of the Army Staff, at an 'at Home' he attended in Rashtrapati Bhavan, as the guests came out into the Mughal Gardens he found himself walking beside Mr V K Krishna Menon, of whom mention has been made earlier. Polite to a fault, he wished Mr Menon the time of day and also enquired how the latter was progressing health-wise. He then turned to Mrs Manekshaw, who was also walking in line, and asked her: "Darling, you remember, Mr Menon?" Mrs Manekshaw, not quite as forgiving as her spouse, at least on this occasion, replied brusquely: "No, I don't."

A Legend Turns 90

In the company of generals, children, politicians, journalists and illustrious members of the global Parsi community and with traditional Zoroastrian rituals, Field Marshal Sam Hormusji Framji Jamshedji Manekshaw, India's first and only living field marshal, celebrated his 90th birthday in New Delhi on 03 April 2003. Manekshaw, his legendary wit and charm intact, cut his birthday cake with a silver khukri, the favourite dagger of the legendary Gurkha soldiers, as the large gathering sang *Happy Birthday to You.* The hero of the 1971 war with Pakistan, which resulted in the birth of Bangladesh, made no speech at the evening function organised by the Parzor Foundation, a UNESCO-supported initiative for the preservation and promotion of Parsi Zoroastrian culture and heritage.

But he was visibly overwhelmed by the gathering and its affection. Defence Minister George Fernandes, Tourism Minister Jagmohan, the three Service Chiefs, numerous retired war heroes and several former service chiefs were present at the function. Defence Minister Fernandes pointed out that Field Marshal Manekshaw not only created history, but also created a nation. Everyone who knew Manekshaw had a tale or two to recollect, as the crowd gathered to share some delightful Parsi snacks. Field Marshal Manekshaw, who almost lost his life during World War II in Burma and won a Military Cross for bravery, was the first Indian officer to command the Gurkhas after Independence.

A documentary — In War and Peace: The Life of Field Marshal Sam Manekshaw, MC — was screened as the Parzor Foundation celebrated his life as a mark of the contribution of the Parsi community to India and a celebration of India's multiculturalism. The documentary, which has India's favourite soldier narrating his life to his grandson Jehan, details his legendary career. Delhi's military circles has been abuzz for the last week with anecdotes of the exploits of Sam Bahadur, as Manekshaw was known to his troops. In 1962, in the midst of the humiliating defeat against China, Manekshaw took over the Tezpur-based 4 Corps and famously told his troops, 'Gentlemen, there will be no more withdrawals.' In 1971, he prevailed upon Prime Minister Indira Gandhi to give him six months to wait out the monsoon and prepare for the invasion of East Pakistan, bulldozed the finance ministry to give the military extra funds, and skipped major cities to take Dacca, and create Bangladesh.

Despite his age, Manekshaw did not disappoint Delhi on this visit. On 02 April 2003, at the Battle Honours Mess, he was at his witty best as he quipped, "Officers, you have kept up the great tradition of the Indian Army... [pause] of having beautiful wives." When the wife of a former army chief asked Field Marshal Manekshaw how he managed to remember the first names of most army wives, he remarked there are two things no honourable man should forget: His wife's birthday and the first name of the women around him. The Field Marshal now lives in the Nilgiri Hills in south India, looked after by a loyal Gurkha family.

The Courage to Say No!

At the start of this year, a popular journal featured a leading article on prominent living Indians who, in the 20th century, had inspired India's younger generation. I have no comments about those listed but was disappointed to note the article did not include the name of Field Marshal Sam Hormusji Framji Jamshedji Manekshaw. Was this an unfortunate lapse?

Did the editor consider the soldier unworthy of inclusion? Was this another example of the tendency in democracies to only remember their military leaders in times of danger and forget them in peacetime? I'm not sure of the answers to these questions. Today, Sam Manekshaw celebrated his 90th birthday.

Senior Army officers celebrated the occasion in Delhi and many newspapers published summaries of the Field Marshal's distinguished career. I have no desire to add to this paean of praise.

However, one incident in Manekshaw's distinguished career bears repetition. Readers may recall that, on 25 March 1971, when political events in East Pakistan had taken a turn for the worse, the Pakistan Army cracked down on Bengali intellectuals and leaders, killing over 50,000 of them. Millions of refugees began fleeing into India to escape from this organised genocide. The exodus of refugees placed an unbearable financial burden on India and strained the fabric of social structure and political stability in eastern India.

Then Prime Minister Indira Gandhi toured the border in order to see for herself the unprecedented and desperate situation prevailing in the region. On her return from Calcutta, she drove straight to South Block and walked into the operations room of Army Headquarters. After giving her firsthand assessment of the situation in East Pakistan and the Indian border, she turned to Manekshaw and bluntly asked, "What can the Indian Army could do in this situation?" Manekshaw, in his inimitable cryptic style, replied, "Nothing." Gandhi's entourage, consisting of a few ministers and bureaucrats, were shocked at the General's abrupt answer. No one had ever dared to respond to the PM in this manner. The Army Chief went on to explain it took time to launch military operations and the Army was not ready. The PM said, "I want the army to launch an offensive into East Pakistan as early as possible. You should be prepared to attend a Cabinet meeting in two days' time and outline your plans."

Later, Manekshaw attended a Cabinet meeting where the PM repeated she wanted the armed forces to invade East Pakistan as quickly as possible so that a pro-Mujibur Rehman government could be installed and millions of refugees returned to their homes. The General explained there were over 90,000 Pakistani troops in East Bengal and he needed to move two army corps into the area, one into Bengal and the other into north-east India. These moves could not be completed in less than two months. The PM kept quiet but her ministers protested and said the economic and political situation in the states adjoining East Pakistan had become intolerable and he must act more quickly. Manekshaw ignored the protests. He turned to the PM and said, "Even when my troops are in position in June, I do not recommend we launch any operations for two reasons. Firstly, the monsoon would be raging at the time. Secondly, the Himalayan mountain passes would be open and I will not be able to withdraw troops from the northern borders for operations against East Pakistan. Moreover, India must guard against the prospect of fighting a war on two fronts. That would present me with problems far more complex than what had been the bane of the German general staff for more than 50 years across two world wars. It would be unwise to rely on diplomatic assurances that the Chinese would not react in support of Pakistan. We must wait for the snow to block the northern passes."

Manekshaw recommended the earliest India should launch military operations was in November. This statement was met with an uproar of indignant protests. The PM again kept quiet but her ministers said such a prolonged delay was unacceptable. Manekshaw told the Cabinet the monsoon in that region was very severe. He quietly explained how the whole area of Bengal, East Pakistan and northeast India becomes a virtual lake. All road transport would cease. If India launched operations in June, the results would be disastrous. He would rather resign than act against his professional judgement. The PM ordered the general to move his formations into position and be ready by June. Operations would then be launched depending on the circumstances. The Cabinet meeting was called to a close. Throughout the months that followed, a whispering campaign of calumny was mounted against Manekshaw.

His critics talked of the General having cold feet and no stomach for a fight (The fact that Manekshaw had won the Military Cross for bravery in Burma during World War II, where his stomach had taken a full burst of machine gun fire, meant nothing to these people). The army's state of un-preparedness became a cocktail circuit joke. Manekshaw's daughter faced continuous pinpricks from her friends (daughters of senior bureaucrats and police officials), who made fun of the army's lack of guts. They suggested if the army was not up to this task, the BSF should be allowed to clear up East Pakistan. Manekshaw was well aware of all that was being said against him. He kept his cool. While he managed the movement of troops, essential supplies and armaments to the east and dealt with the politicians in Delhi, he gave the Eastern Command a free hand to plan the operations in detail. Meanwhile, the armed forces built up the minimum required administrative and communication facilities around East Pakistan. The delay also enabled the arming and training of the Bengali guerrilla freedom fighters, the Mukti Bahini. The delay witnessed the establishment of a formal Bangladesh government in exile inside India, enabled the government of India to finalise a Treaty of Friendship with the Soviet Union and neutralise interference from both China and the US. By late October, as the intensity of the rains decreased, the media once again clamoured for military action. Armchair strategists had a field day publishing various tactical scenarios on how best to overcome Pakistan's defences. A late monsoon made cross-country movement difficult until the last week of November. By this time, the performance of the Bengali freedom fighters had gained momentum. They dominated the countryside in East Pakistan and had confined the Pakistani army into several garrison towns, cut off from Dacca. The morale of the Pakistan army in East Bengal was very low. On the other hand, thanks to thorough planning, our troops were properly located and well prepared. Thus, when the Pakistani air force carried out a pre-emptive strike on the Indian airfields on 03 December 1971, from West Pakistan, Indian forces around East Bengal were itching to go into action and were able to end the campaign in a fortnight and capture over 90,000 Prisoners of War.

Two historical events of far-reaching consequence, though widely separated by time and space, have striking similarities. General Manekshaw's refusal to be hustled into attacking East Pakistan during May and June 1971 bears a marked similarity to the refusal by Marshal Kutuzov, the Commander-in-Chief of Russian armies, to defend Moscow against Napoleon in 1812. Both came under increasing pressure from their governments — the czar in Kutuzov's case and Indira Gandhi in Sam's case. One refused to defend and the other declined to attack. By refusing to defend Moscow against Napoleon, Kutuzov saved the Russian armies and eventually saved Russia. By declining to attack East Pakistan in May-June, Manekshaw preserved India's honour.

Both resolutely held on to their professional assessments of the military situation and nothing could make them budge from that position. All are now agreed that had India attacked East Pakistan in June 1971 it would have been an unmitigated disaster for the Indian Army. Had it been a lesser army chief than Sam Manekshaw, the government would have stampeded him into on the offensive as it so easily did in the 1962 war against China, Operation Blue Star in Amritsar and the misadventure in Sri Lanka.

Indian troops won their last great victory against a foreign army of importance in 303 B.C. when Chandragupta Maurya's army defeated Seleucus Nicator. After 2300 years of unremitting defeats of Indian armies against every invading army, Sam Manekshaw made the country experience the glow of a stunning victory against the Pakistan army in what is now Bangladesh. That will remain Field Marshal Manekshaw's unique position in Indian military history.

Sunbeam Rapier

In fluent Nepalese, Sam Manekshaw, India's first Field Marshal, instructed Sule Bahadur, his trusted and loyal aide from his beloved Gurkha Regiment, to bring home his Sunbeam Rapier from the Staff College in Coonoor. It took an hour for Sule Bahadur to return but time flew by as the eloquent Manekshaw regaled us with stories of his illustrious life in the army. Manekshaw joined the army at a time when motorised transport was non-existent. "When I joined my regiment, we only had mules and horses and we began getting motorised three-tonners in 1936. The first time we used tanks was in 1948 when we opened the Zoji La Pass to get to Ladakh. I was then Director of Military Operations."

During his early years in the army, Manekshaw developed a fondness for driving and wanted a car that was more than just transport. So after his course in the Imperial Defence College in London, he returned with a Sunbeam Rapier which he bought for the princely sum of 600 pounds. It cost him another 100 pounds to ship the car to India and 6000 Rupees in customs duty. "In those days one pound was worth 12 or 13 Rupees, so the total cost to me was around 15,000 Rupees."

Manekshaw was posted all over the country but his Rapier followed him wherever he went. "Almost immediately after I got back from London, I was given the command of a division in Kashmir, so I drove the Rapier up there. It was wonderful driving it in the hills as I had enough power from its twin-carb engine. I would drive from Kashmir to Bombay regularly but with no air-conditioning, the summer heat would be scorching." When Manekshaw was posted back in the Nilgiris he would drive back to Bombay regularly for his holidays.

The Rapier went to the East as well when he was posted in Calcutta as Eastern Army Commandant. "It's given me excellent service and all it has required is normal maintenance from a regular garage. But when I came to Coonoor, I got TVS to do a really good job and get it into shape. It's a bit heavy on petrol in the hills but still runs without missing a beat."

The Rapier was driven mostly by Manekshaw himself, except for the last four to five years when he stopped driving. "My eyesight is not so good now and neither is my hearing. Besides I have a bad temper, so I've stopped driving altogether." Besides the occasional spin with Sule Bahadur in the Rapier, Manekshaw's regular transport is a Daewoo Cielo.

"Since I don't drive anymore I don't care what car I have, as long as it is comfortable and the air-conditioning works well." Manekshaw also has an old Maruti 800 which belonged to his late wife, Silloo. "That is my wife's car, which she used almost till the day she died. Now the Gurkhas use it for shopping and the odd errand. Occasionally I use it myself when I have go down to the market, which is pretty congested to take a big car."

Manekshaw loved bikes as well and bought a James motorcycle from a British Officer for 1600 Rupees in 1947. Just two days before partition, his good friend Major Yahya Khan, who went on to become President of Pakistan, begged Manekshaw to sell him the bike. "What will I use?" asked Manekshaw. To which Yahya replied, "Sir, you will get everything in India, we will get nothing in Pakistan." Manekshaw agreed to sell the bike for a Thousand Rupees and said, "Okay, Yahya take it!" Yahya looked at his superior and said, "Sir, I haven't got a thousand. I will send it to you." Manekshaw was never paid the thousand rupees but says, "Yahya made up for it by giving me the whole of East Pakistan!" Sule Bahadur was back with the Rapier, which meant it was time to end this interview and get on with the photography. I was amazed at the condition of the car. Original paint, original upholstery, not a bit of rust and the engine sounded crisp and healthy. The 1958 Sunbeam was remarkably well kept for its age. Just like the 90-year-old Field Marshal himself.

GENERAL G.G. BEWOOR, PVSM
COAS, 15 Jan 1973-31 May 1975
Infantry, 11 Gorkha Rifles and 2 Dogra

General Gopal Gurunath Bewoor assumed charge of the Indian Army, as the 9th Chief of Army Staff, on 15 January 1973. Born at Seoni, Madhya Pradesh on 11 August 1917, he is an alumnus of the Royal Indian Military College (RIMC) in Dehra Dun and was commissioned into the Indian Military Academy (IMA), Dehra Dun in July 1937. Whilst at the IMA, he was awarded the Gold Medal for being best all-round cadet and the coveted Sword of Honour. He was commissioned into the 2nd Green Howards Regiment on 15 July 1937 during operations in Waziristan (present-day Pakistan). He later joined the 5th Baluch Regiment and spent his World War II days in Burma, fighting the Japenese. He served with the 5th Baluch till July 1945. He attended Staff College, Quetta in 1945 and subsequently served as the Under-Secretary (Military) of the Viceroy's Co-ordination Council in 1946. He was the only Indian officer to be given this coveted appointment. He was the Secretary of the Army Partition Committee in 1947, which determined the allotment of weapons, equipment and regiments that were to remain in India or to be allotted to Pakistan. Since his parent regiment-the Baluch-went to Pakistan, he was transferred to the Dogra Regiment and promoted to Lieutenant Colonel in December 1947. Earlier, he took over command of 2 Dogra in October 1947. With a view to imparting basic military training to school and college students, he was appointed as the Director of the NCC (National Cadet Corps) in April 1948 as a Colonel.

On promotion to the rank of Brigadier in July 1951, he was initially appointed as Commander 'Chand Sector' and later as Commanding Officer of the 80th Infantry Brigade in Jammu & Kashmir. In August 1953 he served as the Director, Personnel Services at Army HQ. He was appointed as the first Chief of Staff at the Western Command HQ in Shimla in February 1959 and had the unique distinction of becoming the youngest Major General of the Indian Army at the age of 42 years and six months. He assumed the appointment of the Colonel of the 11 Gorkha Rifles on 25 May 1960. He was then appointed as the GOC of the 27th Infantry Division in February 1961 at Jalandhar. Later he moved this division to Kalimpong (West Bengal) in the wake of Chinese aggression during the 1962 Indo-China War. In June 1963, he was appointed as the Director of Military Training at Army HQ and remained there till November 1964.

He was promoted as General Officer Commanding 33 Corps at Siliguri in November 1964. He moved to Army HQ in May 1967, as the Deputy Chief of Army Staff (DCAS) and held that appointment till June 1969. As DCAS, he was awarded Param Vishist Seva Medal (PVSM) for his meritorious services. In July 1969, he assumed the appointment of General Officer Commanding–in–Chief, Southern Command. During the 1971 Indo-Pak War, he was awarded the Padma Bhushan-India's third highest civilian honour-for conducting successful operations in the Rajasthan Sector. He took over as Army Chief on 15 January 1973 and held that appointment for two years and four months till his retirement on 31 May 1975. He served as the Honorary Colonel of the Dogra Regiment up to 11 August 1979. After retirement, he served as the Indian Ambassador to Denmark, from February 1976 to March 1978. He served as a member of the Senate of the University of Pune, for two years from August 1979 onwards. He was also on the Board of Directors of Kirloskar Oil Engines & Vickers Sperry of Pune. Besides, he was often invited to give talks on leadership and military matters by various educational societies. He passed away on 24 October 1989.

GENERAL T.N. RAINA, MVC
COAS, 31 May 1975-31 May 1978
Infantry, Kumaon Regiment

General Tapishwar Narain Raina assumed charge of the Indian Army, as the 10th Chief of Army Staff, on 15 May 1975. His early education was done at Ludhiana, Punjab because his father-Pandit B.N. Raina-was posted there as a head postmaster. Commissioned into the Kumaon Regiment on 12 April 1942, he took part in the Burma Campaign of World War II and was Mentioned–in–Dispatches for gallantry. During his Burma campaign, he was injured a grenade accident which resulted in the loss of an eye. He had a glass eye in place for the rest of his career in the Indian Army.

He commanded the 14th Kumaon (now the 5th Mechanised Infantry) from September 1957 to September 1959. He then commanded the 114th Infantry Brigade from 1959 to 1962, during the Indo-China conflict of 1962 and was awarded the Maha Vir Chakra (MVC) for showing great courage and leadership qualities in organizing the defences of Chushul. He later became the Brigadier General Staff of the 33 Corps in Siliguri, West Bengal. He also served as the Deputy Adjutant General at Army Headquarters and as GOC of the 25th Infantry Division.

In 1971, he was the GOC II Corps in the Khulna sector. He was awarded the Padma Bhushan -India's third highest civilian honour-for his contributions during the 1971 Indo-Pak War. He was General Officer Commanding–in-Chief of Western Command from 1974 to 1975. He was the Chief of Army Staff from 01 June 1975 to 31 May 1978. He was the Colonel of the Kumaon Regiment and the Naga Regiment from 16 May 1971 to 31 May 1978.

During his tenure as Army Chief, the Central Government led by Prime Minister Indira Gandhi imposed national emergency in India. Before the imposition of the emergency, it is believed that Prime Minister Gandhi asked for the Indian Army's support in the venture, but General Raina told the Prime Minister that the Indian Army would not be used to further her ends but obey only those orders of a legally construed government. This was considered a crucial moment that kept the Indian Army out of politics at a critical juncture. He retired on 31 May 1978, after completing more than 36 years of service to the Indian Army and the nation. He was married to Marie Antoinette Raina, a French woman. He was appointed as the Indian High Commissioner to Canada in February 1979. He passed away on 19 May 1980 in Ottawa, Canada during his tenure as the Indian High Commissioner.

GENERAL O.P. MALHOTRA, PVSM
COAS, 31 May 1978-31 May 1981
Regiment of Artillery

General Om Prakash Malhotra assumed charge of the Indian Army, as the 11th Chief of Army Staff, on 31 May 1978. Born on 06 August 1922 in Srinagar, Kashmir he was commissioned into the Indian Army as a 2nd Lieutenant in the Regiment of Artillery, in November 1941, at the young age of 19. He quickly rose up the ranks, which led to commanding a number of artillery regiments between November 1950 and July 1961. Later on in his army career, he became an instructor at the Defence Services Staff College (DSSC), Wellington and also served as the Military Attaché at the Indian Embassy in Moscow, Russia for three years from June 1962 onwards. General Malhotra commanded an Artillery Brigade from August 1965 to January 1966 and then took over command of a

Mountain Brigade. After being promoted to Major General in September 1967, he commanded an Infantry Division for two years. He was then appointed as GOC 4 Corps in the Eastern Sector in September 1969, a post which he held till May 1972. He was then appointed as GOC 11 Corps at Jalandhar for two years and was later appointed as GOC-in-C Southern Command in Pune. He was awarded the Param Vishist Seva Medal (PVSM) for service of the most exceptional order in 1976. Prior to his appointment as the Chief of Army Staff, he served as the Vice Chief of Army Staff. He retired on 31 May 1981, after completing nearly 40 years of distinguished military service.

General Malhotra served as the Ambassador of India to Indonesia from 1981 to 1984. He was appointed as the Governor of Punjab in 1990, when militancy in the state was at its height. A resigned as Governor of Punjab in August 1991. A keen sportsman, he was the President of the Equestrian Federation of India for nine years and was the Founding President of the Asian Equestrian Federation. He has also been the President of the Delhi Golf Club in New Delhi. He is a Trustee of the Nehru Trust for the Indian Collections at the Victoria & Albert Museum and has served as the President of India's largest NGO (Non-Governmental Organisation)- The National Association for the Blind-in New Delhi. In 1994, the University of Jammu conferred upon him the Degree of Doctor of Letters (Honours Causa). He is an active member of Kiwanis International in India. He is presently the Chairman of two charitable organizations-Shiksha and Chikitsa.

GENERAL K.V. KRISHNA RAO, PVSM
COAS, 31 May 1981-31 July 1983
Infantry, Mahar Regiment

General Kotikalapudi Venkata Krishna Rao assumed charge of the Indian Army, as the 12th Chief of Army Staff, on 31 May 1981. Born on 16 July 1923, he was commissioned into the Indian Army on 09 August 1942. He took over command of the 3rd Mahar on 14 July 1956. He commanded a brigade in the Ladakh Sector during the 1965 Indo-Pak War. During 1969-70, he commanded a Mountain Division in the Jammu sector. He always displayed a gift for leadership under fire and the high point came during the 1971 Indo-Pak War, when in a series of brilliant manoeuvres, his division captured the Sylhet area and liberated the north-east sector of Bangladesh. He was awarded the Param Vishisht Seva Medal (PVSM) for his most laudable command of the Mountain Division. In 1974, he took over a Corps in Jammu and was later appointed as the Deputy Chief of Army Staff (DCAS) in 1978.

Subsequently he served as the General Officer Commanding-in-Chief, Western Command in 1979. He attained the highest rank in his military career when he became Chief of Army Staff in 1981. He was the Colonel of the Mahar Regiment from June 1968 to June 1983. He presently serves as the Honorary Colonel of the Mahar Regiment.

Post retirement, General Rao was appointed as the Governor of Nagaland, Manipur and Tripura from June 1984 to 1989. He helped restore order to what was fast becoming a chaotic situation, with rising insurgency and political disarray. He was then appointed as the Governor of Jammu & Kashmir and he served from 11 July 1989 till 19 January 1990 and then for a second time from 13 March 1993 till 02 May 1998.

GENERAL A.S. VAIDYA
Padma Vibhushan, PVSM, MVC (Bar), AVSM
COAS, 31 July 1983-31 Jan 1986
Armoured Corps, Deccan Horse

General Arunkumar Sridhar Vaidya assumed charge of the Indian Army, as the 13th Chief of Army Staff, on 31 July 1983. Born on 27 January 1926, he was commissioned into the Indian Armoured Corps in 1945 and saw battle during the Second World War. He was the seventh post-independence commander of the 9th Deccan Horse, one of the oldest armoured regiments in the Indian Army. He commanded this regiment in the Battle of Asal Uttar during the 1965 Indo-Pak War and led the 2nd (Independent) Armoured Brigade in the Battle of Shakargarh during the 1971 Indo-Pak conflict.

During the 1965 Indo-Pak War, then Lieutenant Colonel Vaidya was in command of the Deccan Horse. From September 6th to 11th, his unit fought a series of actions in Asal Uttar and Cheema, both in Punjab. He showed inspiring leadership and remarkable resourcefulness in organising his unit and fighting against heavy odds and inflicted severe casualties on the Pakistan Army's Patton tanks. With untiring effort he moved from sector to sector with complete disregard for his personal safety, thereby inspiring his troops by his personal example. He was instrumental to a large extent in stemming thrusts by Pakistani armour in the battle of Asal Uttar and later at Cheema. For his exceptional bravery he was awarded the Maha Vir Chakra (India's second highest medal for gallantry).

During the 1971 Indo-Pak conflict, then Brigadier Vaidya was commander of an armoured brigade in the Zafarwal sector on the western front. He moved his brigade swiftly to get to grips with the Pakistan Army and took the enemy tanks by surprise. He employed his tanks relentlessly & aggressively and helped the division to maintain constant pressure & momentum of advance against the Pakistan Army. In the battle of Chakra and Dahira, the going was difficult due to hostile terrain combined with minefields. In a cool and confident manner, he undertook the crossing through the minefield and moved forward, disregarding his own personal safety. Through his inspiring leadership, the entire squadron pushed through the lane and quickly deployed itself to meet the Pakistan Army's counter-attacks.

During the Battle of Basantar in the Shakargarh sector, also during the 1971 Indo-Pak conflict, Brigadier Vaidya again displayed his professional skill and superb leadership. He got his tanks through one of the deepest minefields, expanded the bridgehead and repulsed a strong enemy counter-attack. In this battle, 62 Pakistan Army tanks were destroyed. Throughout, he displayed outstanding courage, great professional skill, indomitable will, foresight and imagination in fighting against the enemy in keeping with the best traditions of the Indian Army. For this he was awarded a second Maha Vir Chakra (known as the Bar to MVC).

Elevated to the rank of Major General in 1973, he held the appointments of Director Military Operations, Chief of Staff at Headquarters Southern Command and as Commandant Armoured Corps Centre & School.

Promoted to the rank of Lieutenant General in January 1980, he held the appointment of Master General of Ordnance and later as the General Officer Commanding of a Corps before being elevated to the appointment of General Officer Commanding-in-Chief of Eastern Command in June 1981. His tackling of the insurgency problems in his command has been particularly praiseworthy. He was awarded the Param Vishisht Seva Medal (PVSM) in 1983 for distinguished service of the most exceptional order.

General Vaidya took over as the Chief of the Army Staff from 01 August 1983 to 31 January 1985. During his tenure as Army Chief, he planned Operation Bluestar in 1984-a controversial military action against militant Khalistan separatists who barricaded themselves in the Sikh's most holiest shrine-the Golden Temple in Punjab.

He described the operation as the *most difficult and painful* decision of his career. He retired on 31 January 1986 after completing more than 40 years of service and retired to a quiet life in Pune. He was assassinated by Khalistan separatists on 10 August 1986, in retaliation for the Indian Army's attack on the Golden Temple. He was posthumously awarded the Padma Vibhushan-India's second highest civilian honour-for his tireless service to the nation.

An outstanding military leader, General Vaidya gave the Indian Army a very sound leadership and brought with him an aura of gallantry, valour and remarkable reservoir of combat experience befitting the head of the army. He had the distinction of being among the most decorated soldiers in the defence services.

OPERATION BLUESTAR, 05 JUNE 1984

As a result of the uniqueness of this operation, and the circumstances under which it occurred, the BHARAT RAKSHAK Team would like to clarify the purpose of this article. This article is not against Sikhs or Sikhism. It is purely meant to report the Indian Army's action at the Golden Temple against heavy odds. We do not intend to discuss the causes, the misrules, the politics, the scheming that led to this mess in the first place. This sad event hurt both the Indian Army which went in with a heavy heart and the patriotic community of Sikhs who have given so much to India.

"We went inside with humility in our hearts and prayers on our lips." General K. Sundarji

For the last three years Punjab was gripped by terror. The Pakistan-backed terrorist movement had acquired monstrous proportions. Not a day went by without massacres of Hindus, Sikhs, migrant workers and those who opposed the terrorists diktats. From Golden Temple, the most sacred symbol of Sikhism and seat of its religious power, hit lists were drawn up and death squads were dispatched under the guidance of the malevolent figure Jarnail Singh Bhindranwale. The chanting of the gurbani was now drowned by the staccato bursts of gunfire. Prominent Sikh figures were assassinated in the Golden Temple when they went to pray there. Pushed to the wall, the Indian Government under Mrs. Indira Gandhi, gave the signal for the most complex and largest anti-terrorist action in the world.

May 30 to June 2

As the death toll from extremist actions climbed, the Government started holding frequent consultations with the Army. On May 30th, units of the 9th Infantry Division based at Meerut, started moving in on to Amritsar and other important towns. Para-Military forces were placed around the temple. The extremists responded with heavy exchanges of fire lasting for hours. Meanwhile newly fortified positions were coming up all around. On June 1st, curfew was clamped and troops and para-militaries fanned along the 12,168 villages of Punjab. The Akalis were threatening a food movement agitation, designed to stop the movement of food grains to other states.

Last minute attempts to get the moderate Akalis to reach an agreement came to a naught. The state was then put under siege. Lt. Gen. Ranjit Singh Dayal, Chief of Staff Western Command was brought in as security advisor to the Punjab Governor. Men of the 12th Bihar Regiment fanned to take positions across the roof tops. Soon they realised that they were vulnerable to grenade attacks from the top of the 18th century towers and water tank.

The Biharis were moved to sandbagged windows in vacated houses. Similarly, men from the Garhwal Regiment and The Brigade of The Guards were moved on the other side of the temple. Tanks fanned out to guard sensitive villages to prevent communal killings.

June 3

By now the whole state has been secured. The Biharis watched the area of the clock tower, the main entrance and Brahm Buta Market, the Garhwalis, the Guardsmen and Punjabis overlooked the Chowk Parag Dass, Chhati Khui, Atta Mandi, Baba Atal and Buddhi Lutt Bazaar. The aim was to apply psychological pressure to break the extremists resolve. Officers used loud-hailers to ask them to surrender peacefully. The reply was automatic gun fire. The jawans replied with bursts of automatic fire of their own. The extremists responded with grenade and heavy machine gun fire from the top of water towers.

June 4

It was now evident that this was no rabble army, but a determined insurgent army fired up with religious fervour. It was decided to deal with them effectively. 106mm jeep-mounted RCLs were brought in to fire at the pillboxes. But the concrete pillboxes proved hard to crack and it was decided that stronger firepower was needed. A 3.7" howitzer was brought in. This was a risky move, as the artillery had to be elevated almost vertically and a miss would mean it would land on the top of houses. Thus the two elevated 18th century Bungas on either side of the langar, and the elevated water tank to the rear of the Teja Singh Samunsari Hall were targeted. The firing lasted five minutes, at the end of which the pillboxes were blown to pieces with sandbags and the sniper's bodies flying apart.

Maj. Gen. Brar, Lt. Gen. Sundarji and Gen. Vaidya: Tough Act

By now the senior commanders, Maj. Gen. Brar and Lt. Gen. Sundarji, had realised there was no way to avoid bloodshed. Brar went in and spoke to all the troops. Spending 30 minutes ate each location he explained the difficult and terrible mission at hand. It was not against Sikhs but against terrorists. This was to be a volunteer mission. Not one of the many Sikh officers, JCOs and ORs, opted out.

The die was cast for Operation Bluestar. The operation was to be launched in the following phases:

I-Initial Operations:

(a) BSF to secure Hotel Temple View by 9 pm, June 5th.

(b) CRPF to secure Brahm Boota Akhara by 10 pm, June 5th.

II-Phase 1

(a) 10 Guards to secure Northern Wing of the Temple Complex by 1 am, June 6th.

(b) 1 Para-Commandos:

  (1) Secure a foothold in the Akhal Takht at the earliest and not later than 1 am, June 6th.

  (2) Secure a foothold in Harmandir Sahib with divers and neutralise demolitions, if any, by 11:30 pm, June 5th.

(c) Special Frontier Force (SFF) to isolate Akhal Takht and secure western flank by 1 am, June 5th.

(d) 26 Madras to secure southern and eastern wings by 1:00 a.m., June 5th.

(e) 9 Kumaon to secure Guru Ram Das Serai and SGPC building by 1:00 a.m., June 5th.

III-Phase 2

(a) Mopping up all areas secured in Phase 1

IV-Phase 3

(a) 9 Kumaon-extend operations to secure the rest of hostel complex.

(b) Units of 10 Guards, SFF and 1 Para Cdo to secure rest of Temple Complex and check prisoners.

Others: 12 Bihar was to continue to cordon of the Temple with CRPF units under its command and provide fire support to any target within its span of observation.

MECHANISED UNITS

Armour: 16 Cavalry

(a) Three tanks to enter through the main temple entrance, initially for close protection for 10th Guards but thereafter for support to infantry, paras and SFF with machine gun fire.

(b) Three tanks to enter the langar area and provide machine gun fire for the 26 Madras.

Mechanised Infantry: 8 Mech Btn

(a) Four BMPs to carry para-commando/divers.

(b) Four BMPs and three Skot APCs to support the 26 Madras and Paras.

Reserves: 15 Kumaon-2 companies as backup for 9th Kumaon and 2 companies for any contingency tasks.

Central Rendezvous and Logistics Control-City Kotwali.

Divisional Tactical HQ-Roof Top outside Temple complex.

H-Hour for operation launch 10 pm, June 5th

One last minute attempt was made to avoid bloodshed. A senior civil administration member and a senior army officer through a public address system asked militants and devotees to come outside. From 4:30 pm to 7:00 pm the attempts continued. Only some 129 devotees many of them very sick were let go. The other hapless ones were held hostage inside, one used as a deterrent to the army.

1. Akal Takht
2. Darshani Deori
3. Harmandir Sahib
4. Sarowar
5. Parikrama
6. Main Entrance (Clock Tower)
7. Hotel Temple View
8. Brahm Buta Akhara

9-10. Ramgaria Bungas (Towers)

11. Guru Ramdas Langar -
12. Guru Ramdas Serai / Akal Rest house
13. Water Tank
14. Seraiside Entrance
15. Teja Singh Samundari Hall
16. Manji Sahib Congregation Hall
17. Guru Nanak Niwas
18. Baba Atal Gurudwara
19. Rear Entrance
20. Sikh History Library

At 7:00 pm troops started moving up to take their appointed positions. From the surrounding balconies, people watched the rumble of trucks and tanks, as night fell and a darkness of gloom settled in the city. In order to prevent a violent backlash there was a total shutdown of he telecommunication and electric system.

Punjab was virtually cut off from the rest of India. Initial operations went through as planned with the both the Hotel Temple View and Brahm Boota Akara secured with little resistance. It was however not surprising as they were isolated and only existed to provide early warning of the army's approach. However the battlements on the top of the clock tower were proving harder to knock out and thus H-hour was postponed by half an hour. At 10:30 pm the first phase of Operation Bluestar commenced.

THE TEMPLE COMPLEX

Main Entrance-North Side

At H-hour, the men of 10 Guards, under Lt. Col. Mohammed Israr geared up to maintain their reputation as one of the world's finest troops. At 10:30 pm, the leading elements of the 10 Guards moved through the main gate. Immediately they came under heavy and accurate machine gun fire, cleverly sited through wired enclosures on either side of steps. While some troops broke through the trap and reached the ground floor, others cleared the machine gun nests. For those who made it across the steps, another nightmare awaited.

For the couple of minutes they were caught in the open, before taking the cover of the Parikrama but then they were fired upon from the Parikrama itself. 20 soldiers were mowed down in the initial assault. Captain Jasbir Singh Raina, who had three days before done a recce of the temple was severely wounded in the leg by a burst of machine gun fire. This young Sikh officer in tremendous pain refused to evacuate but was eventually ordered to do so. Unfortunately he lost the use of the leg. The troops started inching their way towards the Akal Takht but were fired upon from the southern side.

Meanwhile each room had to be cleared along the Parikrama, many by hand-to-hand combat. Militants would come out and lob a few grenades and rush back in. As troops cleared a room and moved forward they found militants again appearing from the rooms. Unknown to the Army, was an elaborate structure of concealed manhole and underground passages. Meanwhile a machine gun site was fitted about 12 inches from the ground. This low sitting meant even crawling troops were hit. While this was going on, another group of men were preparing with cool and calm, that comes with being an elite unit. These men clad in black dungarees, with bullet proof vests made last minute checks on their specialised weapons. The Indian Army's youngest units-the Para Commandos-was about to be blooded. Their objective was to get a foothold in the Akal Takht and a foothold in Harmandir Sahib with the help of divers.

As they slipped in and made a dash across the Parikrama they met a similar fate to the Guardsmen. The Parikrama was exposed to fire from all four sides. Realising their predicament, the commandos dashed from pillar to pillar trying to cut off the suppressing fire. As they reached the Akhak Takht their misery was compounded by the devastating machine gun fire from the fortified Akal Takht, as well as the Harmandir Sahib and the area of Darshani Deori-Toshakana. Caught between the Sarovar on one side and the fortified concrete building on the other, the commandos had no option but to inch their way by fire and movement.

The Guards were asked to bring fire down on the northern side from whatever portions of the northern side they had secured. Meanwhile the senior officers were barking orders to ensure that under no condition was any fire to be returned on Harimandir Sahib. It is incredible that the orders were obeyed. The commanders were to note later that they never expected the troops to obey such orders. The mission of the divers to slip across the Sarovar was aborted as they would have not survived the murderous fire.

By midnight the Guards had secured the eastern half of the North Wing but the Western side was only 75% secured. Due to the severe casualties suffered by the first two companies, the third company was pressed in. Rather than wait for the complete clearance of the ground floor they were asked to secure a foothold on the first and second floor. This was deemed necessary to provide some sort of fire to the bogged para commandos and the SFF. One platoon climbed to the first floor using aluminium ladders. They then moved methodically clearing the rooms one by one by lobbing grenades and spraying it with fire. Another platoon likewise moved from the first to the second floor and started clearing the rooms. Troops moving up from the ground floor were suddenly fired upon by militants through an opening in the wall next to the staircase. Some casualties resulted, but the troops quickly wiped them out. By now 145 militants lay dead along with 19 Guardsmen. By 1 am, the Guards had secured their objective and could now bring covering fire for the beleaguered commandos.

The Para Commandos were still inching their way to the Akal Takht. This five-storied building was heavily fortified with all windows, balconies and other openings closed with brick masonry and sandbags, with small loop holes through which machine guns were being fired and grenades being lobbed. Together with a double storied building, the Nishan Sahib building and the Darshani Deori, they transformed the quadrangle into an ideal killing field. The leading team of para commandos made a desperate dash for the Darshani Deori. The foothold was needed to launch the CS canisters. Of the 35 men, only 12 made it. The remainder, including team leader Major Prakash Chand Katoch, were cut down. The SFF started with 50 men, had already 17 casualties (three dead). With midnight approaching, casualties mounting and the objectives far from being achieved, the situation was desperate.

Serai Entrance-Eastern Side

On the eastern side, the 26 Madras was expected to enter and then sweep the southern side of any resistance. The entry from the southern side was ruled out because of the narrow passage not allowing for entry of any vehicle. But two companies of 9 Garhwal were stealthily brought in, as backup near the Southern entrance. But they had been delayed by a steel gate which was much more formidable then expected. It needed a tank to ram it down. At H-hour, 26 Madras started to move in but came under a withering fire from atop the Langar, Guru Ram Das Serai, SGPC building, Manji Sahib and Gurdwara Baba Atal Rai. In addition the steel gate was proving difficult to break. 30 metres from the gate they came under fire from medium machine guns from the Deori itself. A section went ahead to lob grenades and clear it, but could not succeed. At this moment a sniper's bullet hit Lt. R.P. Ropiera killing him.

As casualties mounted, the CO-Lt. Col. Panikker, changed his original plan quickly and moved some of his troops in an opening on the south west side. This gave some relief but progress was slow as they had to fight it room by room, like the Guardsmen on the other side. At 11 pm, with 26 Madras behind schedule, the Garhwalis were asked to move in from the south side and secure a foothold on either side of Atta Mandi. They could then assist 26 Madras by laying down suppressive fire and allow 15 Kumaon to launch an attack on the Akal Takht from the south west. The committing of the reserves was decided based on the fact that the Guards were now more or less in control of the northern side. Garhwalis moved with little difficulty and by 1:30 am had secured the ground and upper floors of the southern gate. The 15 Kumaon, under Lt. Col. N.C. Pant, was in the process of building to launch an attack on the Akal Takht.

At 2 am the overall picture was as follows:

1. The 10th Guards suffering heavy casualties, had more or less secured the northern wing. Sporadic militant activity from concealed chambers was still a problem.
2. 26 Madras had stalled, but was now gaining ground between the eastern and southern wings. However there was still heavy opposition.
3. 2 companies of 9 Garhwal had secured a foothold in the southern gate.
4. 1 Para Cdo and SFF had bogged down within reach of the Akal Takht.

Reorganising

At this point Brigadier A.K. Dewan, an armoured corps veteran and Dy GOC of 15 Division had come to see if his troops (9

Garhwal) had reached their location. Brar placed Dewan in charge of 26 Madras, 15 Kumaon and the two companies of 9 Garhwal, and created an ad hoc task force. By 2:30 am, Brigadier Dewan took charge of the Garhwalis and Kumaonis while 26 Madras had still to join up. Meanwhile Maj. Gen. (retd.) Shahbeg Singh realising that the only way to win was to hold of the Indian Army till dawn, poured in an even higher volume of fire. Brar now sought Sundarji's permission to use tank fire to neutralise the Akal Takht's concrete defenses. Lt. General Sundarji watching the proceeding from the Divisional Tactical HQ, agreed and relayed the request to New Delhi.

Meanwhile reports started trickling of volatile Sikh masses gathering on the outskirts of Amritsar. In the meantime, in order to help the SFF and Paras, a tank was brought in and asked to switched on its search light. It was hoped that this would temporarily blind the defenders as well as allow the SFF and Paras locate some of the defences.

But unfortunately this move failed as the Xenon lamps filament burned out in a couple of minutes. When this happened, another tank was moved in followed by a third. Thus all 3 tanks were in the Parikrama. Meanwhile at 4 am, a Skot APC was brought in. Since it is a wheeled vehicle, the tank had to roll back and forth on the steps and crush the marble slabs. Only then could the APC be safely brought in. The APC was then supposed to take a squad right up to the Akal Takht.

The Guards were asked to fire a few 84mm Carl Gustaf rocket rounds at the Akhal Takht to precede the arrival of the APC. As the APC was approaching the Akal Takht, it was hit by an RPG-7 anti-tank launcher from the Akal Takht. This came as a complete shock as none had been expected. As the APC squad dismounted and retreated, the driver was shot by a sniper. By now dawn was approaching and soon the troops in the Parikrama would become sitting ducks. At 5:10 am the clearance to use tanks came from Delhi. The 3 tanks in the Parikrama, were asked to line up their machine guns on the Akhal Takht. Dewan had meanwhile readied for an assault, and the first Madrassis were trickling having cleared the southern wing.

The first assault was led by 'A' Company of 15 Kumaon. Led by Major B.K. Mishra, a group of men reached the footsteps of Akal Takht, the first group to make contact. As they climbed the stairs, a machine gun opened up from the inside and all seven men were mowed down. More machine gun fire rained from the base and the buildings on both side and the Kumaonis were thrown back with heavy casualties. It was clear that the tank machine gun fire was not enough. The Kumaonis fell back to reorganise, having suffered 7 killed and 23 wounded. 2 companies of 26 Madras were now asked to pick up where the Kumaonis left. In the darkness there was confusion as Kumaonis and Madrassis got mixed up. It was realised that the 2 machine guns at the entrance had to be eliminated for any chance to move in on the Akal Takht. A section of troops were asked to volunteer for this dangerous task. The group was led by Lt. Jyoti Kumar Dang and was formed into two sub groups.

One group led by Subedar K.P. Raman Ravi and 4 ORs was to destroy the bunker covering the staircase by hurling pole charges. Another led by the Lt and4 ORs was to rush the first floor and silence the MG there. As the groups reached the Akal Takht, 8-9 fortified machine guns opened up. Valiantly the two groups moved forward. Subedar Ravi and his men reached the bunker and were about to launch their charges when they were cut down by machine gun fire. Lt. Dang and his men also managed to reach the first floor only to be cut down by machine gun fire. Two of the wounded men managed to crawl back. Lt. Dang, although wounded, tried to pull the wounded Subedar Ravi with him but had to give up due to the heavy fire. The barbarism of the terrorists now came through. Subedar Ravi was dragged back, attached with sticks of dynamite and blown up in full view of the other troops. In spite of this, discipline still held. 26 Madras had suffered 14 dead and 49 wounded.

Progress of Operations in the Golden Temple

It was 7:30 am and daylight was well upon us. The temple complex marble was a sea of olive green and red as dead army personnel and terrorists lay sprawled all over. The Temple of God, was a full fledged fortress. With no other option the Generals authorised the tanks to use their 105mm main guns. The high explosive squash rounds smashed into the Akal Takht throwing up flames and masonry. This subdued the machine guns. Except for a few machine gun bursts it was now calm. All troops were asked to stay in the building they had secured and wait till dusk before launching an attack to clear the Akal Takht of any remaining militants.

In response to reports of angry mobs approaching Amritsar, 15 Infantry Division moved in and sealed of the routes leading to Amritsar. At 11 am a large number of militants rushed out of the Akal Takht on to the Parikrama and fled towards the gates. Most were cut down. Seeing that the troops were not firing on the Harmandir Sahib some of them jumped in the Sarovar and tried to swim towards it. They too were killed. This led to a group of militants emerging from the Akal Takht, waving white flags. Now the Akal Takht suddenly went silent. To the army commanders it indicated that either the top leadership of Bhindranwale, Maj. Gen. (retd.) Shabegh and Amrik Singh had either escaped or been killed.

The Hostel Complex

The main buildings of the Hostel Complex were the Guru Ram Das Langar, Guru Ram Das Serai, Teja Singh Samundari Hall, Guru Nanak Niwas, Manji Sahib and Baba Atal Gurdwara.

(1) Guru Ram Das Langar: double storied heavily fortified building commanding a view of the side entrances and open area leading to Parikrama.

(2) Guru Ram Das Serai (Akal Takht Rest House): 3 storied building, 228 rooms and seven halls.

(3) Teja Singh Samundari: houses the offices of SGPC and occupied by Longowal, Tohra, Ramoowalia and others.

(4) Guru Nanak Niwas: 4 storied building with fortified roof tops, 85 rooms and one hall.

As mentioned earlier the operations was in the hands of 9 Kumaon. The operation was to commence at 10 pm, with the simultaneous launch of the Paras and SFF. It had three Vijayantas, six BMPs and three Skot APCs to provide machine gun support. In addition they were to break open the gates to help 26 Madras to enter the eastern gate. On schedule, 9 Kumaon moved into the Guru Ram Das Serai. A company was deployed on each of the floors with the fourth held in reserve. The troops encountered opposition from each of the floors although it was lighter than the temple complex. Many a place hand to hand combat resulted. The troops secured all corners and stairwells, as the rooms were to be cleared later in mopping operations.

By 1:30 a.m. the building was isolated from the rest of the complex. Two companies were left behind to secure it while the rest led by Lt. Col. K. Bhaumik moved to clear the Teja Singh Samundari Hall. Now initial briefings had indicated a large number of devotees and Akali leaders in the building. In the dark Bhaumik realised that it would be impossible to separate the militants. He decided to block the exits and ask them to surrender. The building was isolated by 2:30 am and an emissary sent to establish contact with Tohra and Longowal. Both men had initially vowed to defend the Temple to their death but now agreed to surrender.

Major H.K. Palta with a few men went into meet the leaders which also included Ramoowalia, Akali Dal secretary Gurcharan Singh, SGPC member Bagga Singh and head of the Akhand Kirtani Jatha, Bibi Amarjit Kaur. The leaders were fearful that they might be targeted and needed protection. As the troops started leading them out a group of 350 devotees rushed out to join them. At this, the terrorists threw hand grenades in the crowd and sniped at them. Total chaos reigned as the Kumaonis tried to control the situations. While Major Palta managed to get Tohra, Longowal and Kaur in an APC, snipers got Gurcharan Singh and Bagga. It was 5 am, when things were under control. About 70 innocent devotees were killed or injured in the indiscriminate fire.

With 1 company left behind, the Kumaonis tackled the Guru Nanak Niwas. The clearing operations continued. Every now and then devotees would try to escape only to have the militants throw grenades at them and open fire. By morning, the Kumaonis had 600 hundred prisoners and controlling them absorbed manpower. By 10 am, the Hostel Complex was fairly secured by 9 Kumaon. There were terrorists holed up in manholes, tunnels and concealed basements. The only are of resistance continued to be the langar. The militants continued to pour machine gun fire and hurl grenades. The Kumaonis fired back with everything at their disposal. At one point the wheat and kerosene caught fire sending huge columns of smoke. Gas cylinder caught fire and exploded intermittently. This fighting however was a rearguard action allowing some 40 Babbar Khalsa activists to escape. By the early hours of the morning on June 7th, the fighting suddenly died down. Perhaps they had learnt the fate of their leaders in the Akal Takht.

Mopping Operations, 7th-9th June

Now the job of clearing the many rooms, concealed tunnels and basements began. A number of them were captured and handed over to the Punjab Police and intelligence agencies. Meanwhile other units began cleaning the remains of the battle. The snipers continued to take pot shots. When President Zail Singh was visiting the complex a sniper's round hit his bodyguard Lt. Col. M.P. Choudhary of the SFF in the arm. The sniper was spotted on the terrace and was gunned down. After his departure two companies of 10 Dogra joined 9 Kumaon, in the flushing operations. At this point a burst of gunfire from the area around the bunga wounded four soldiers. While the rest fanned out to search for the militants, Captain Ramphal of the Medical Corps and his nursing assistants were attending to the casualties.

Suddenly a group of militants emerged from a concealed tunnel and grabbed Captain Ramphal and 2 soldiers of 10 Dogra.

As the alarm was raised, the SFF and 10 Dogra got into position to clear the tunnel. The militants were asked to surrender. Their responses was to ask for the Head Priest Gianin Sahib Singh. When he was brought in the militants demanded that he come in. The scared Head Priest refused to go in and troops got ready to blast in. A demolition party crawled up and fixed explosives to the grill at the entrance. When it was blown up the SFF charged in and in the firefight, killed 7 militants inside only to find that the three soldiers had been executed in a inhumane manner. Their limbs had been chopped of. Search revealed cash, weapons and survival rations stashed away.

Behind the Akhal Takht, a lone militant jumped down and tried to make a getaway. He was caught and his turban fell away to reveal a wad of currency notes. Further interrogation revealed him to be one of many criminal elements which had taken refuge in the temple. He further indicated that many others were dumping valuables in the well behind during the course of the fighting. 12th Bihar and the Engineers lowered an anchor in the well. The first attempt pulled up 19 weapons and cash. As naval divers joined the search it revealed Rs.20 lakhs in cash sealed in trunks, gold and silver biscuits, transmitters and weapons and ammunition. A weapons manufacturing unit was discovered in a room at the top of the Deori with grenades, country pistols and rifles in various positions of manufacture. All this added to the ability to convert the holy Golden Temple into an armed fortress.

The army suffered 83 dead and 248 wounded. A total of 492 terrorists and others were killed and 86 wounded. About 1500 people were captured, including a number of Pakistanis. Thus ended the Indian Army's toughest operation. However a number of terrorists had fled to the countryside and the army had to launch Operation Metal to move around Punjab. These operations were relatively minor. The operations indicated the need for a specialised unit for such operations and led to the formation of the National Security Guards. Thus the next time around it was the NSG which was involved in Operation Black Thunder I and II at the Golden

Temple along with the Punjab Police. It would take a few more years before a reinvigorated Punjab Police led by K.P.S. Gill and backed by the army, would break the back of the terrorist movement.

GENERAL K. SUNDARJI, PVSM, ADC
COAS, 01 Feb 1986-30 April 1988
Infantry, Mahar Regiment

General Krishnaswamy Sundarji (formal name was Krishnaswamy Sundararajan) assumed charge of the Indian Army, as the 14th Chief of Army Staff, on 01 February 1986. Born on 28 April 1930 at Chenglepet in Tamil Nadu, he joined the Madras Christian College only to leave it before receiving a degree. Dr A.J. Boyd, who was then the highly distinguished principal of the college, was sorry to see him leave. He was commissioned into the Mahar Regiment in April 1946 and saw action in the North-West Frontier of Undivided India and later on in Jammu & Kashmir. In 1963, he served in the UN Mission in the Congo, where he was Chief of Staff of the Katanga Command and was mentioned in dispatches for his bravery. Later, he commanded the 1st Mahar from November 1963 to November 1965 and his battalion saw action in the plains during the 1965 Indo-Pak War.

During the 1971 Indo-Pak War, General Sundarji was the Brigadier General Staff of a corps in the eastern theatre and made valuable contribution in operations culminating in the liberation of erstwhile East Pakistan into Bangladesh. In March 1974, he was promoted to the rank of Major General and took over command of an infantry division in the plains. He was chosen by General KV Krishna Rao to be part of a small team for reorganizing the Indian Army, especially with regard to technology. He came to head the Mechanised Infantry regiment, which he had himself shaped, by inducting various battalions from the Indian Army's premier regiments. He was then appointed as the Deputy Chief of Army Staff in August 1981, where he threw himself into the Indian Army's modernisation activities.

General Sundarji was a graduate of the Defence Services Staff College (DSSC) at Wellington, the Command and General Staff College at Fort Leavenworth in the US in 1967-68, the Senior Officers Preventive Maintenance Course at Fort Knox, Kentucky and the National Defence College in New Delhi. He held an Master of Arts in International Studies from Allahabad University and a Master of Science in Defence Studies from Madras University. After graduating from Wellington, he held various command and staff appointments, including that of Chief of Staff, Katanga Command and took part in combat as part of the UN forces in the troubled African state of Congo. He was Mentioned-in-Despatches for his distinguished UN tenure. He was also awarded the PVSM in 1978 in recognition of his distinguished service of the most exception order. He took over as the GOC Western Command in 1984 and was involved in the politically-sensitive Operation Bluestar, to flush out Sikh militants holed up in the Golden Temple at Amritsar.

General Sundarji was amongst the most farsighted armoured corps commanders in the Indian Army. Despite being commissioned in the infantry, he was a keen student and admirer of tank warfare. He pioneered various operational guidelines, challenged his commanders to push the men & machines to the limits. In various exercises, he is known to have ordered tanks full speed up sand dunes in the Thar desert at 70° degrees Celsius. Amongst other things, he designed the flamboyant all-black uniform of the Indian Armoured Corps. Post his transformation of the Armoured Corps, he went on to create the Mechanised Infantry. With emphasis on speed, technology and mobile weaponry it is now an integral part of the Indian Army's Strike Corps. He is also credited for shaping modern Indian Army thinking. In his stint as the Commandant of the College of Combat in Mhow, he practically rewrote the Indian Army war manual with emphasis on speed, decisive action, technology and his abiding love-armour.

As Army Chief, his operations at Sumdorong Chu in 1986-known as Operation Falcon-has been widely praised. The Chinese had occupied Sumdorong Chu and General Sundarji used the Indian

Air Force's new air-lift capability to land a brigade in Zimithang, north of Tawang. The Indian Army took up positions on the Hathung La ridge, across the Namka Chu river, where India had faced a s humiliating defeat in 1962. The Chinse responded with a counter build-up and adopted a belligerent tone. Western diplomats predicted war and some of Prime Minister Rajiv Gandhi's advisers blamed General Sundarji's recklessness. But General Sundarji stood by his steps, at one point telling a senior aide, "Please make alternate arrangements if you think you are not getting adequate professional advice." The confrontation petered out.

Among the Indian Army's most articulate Generals, he guided and conducted the Indian Army's largest military exercise for its time, codenamed Operation Brasstacks, near the Indo-Pakistan border in Rajasthan. Conducted between December 1986 and January 1987, the exercise involved two armoured divisions, one mechanised division and six infantry divisions. The stated objective of Operation Brasstacks was to test new concepts of mechanization, mobility, and air support devised by General Sundarji. A man of immense wit, charm and style, he was also known as the 'scholar warrior' and a visionary with a brilliant mind.

Handsome with high cheekbones and a pugnacious jaw, and with his cap worn at a rakish angle, he fitted the glamorous image of the soldier and was married to Vani Sundararajan. He was afflicted by an ailment of the central nervous system and was hospitalised during March 1998. He passed away on 08 February 1999, at the age of 69.

OPERATION BRASSTACKS

Operation Brasstacks was a military exercise undertaken by Indian Army in Rajasthan during November 1986 and March 1987. It was one of largest mobilization of armed forces in the Indian subcontinent. Many regard this as one of the most critical point in relationship between India & Pakistan with regard to nuclear war.

The exercise's closeness to the border and the magnitude of it caused a situation where a war between India Pakistan looked imminent. There is still a considerable debate about the entire exercise as many believe that India in fact was preparing for a war against Pakistan.

Indian Army Rationale and Moves

The Indian army chief at that time was Krishnaswamy Sundarrajan populary known as Sundarji. Sundarji advocated modern methods of warfare and professionalism in the Indian army. According to Sundarji, Operation Brasstacks was carried out to test new concepts of mechanization, mobility, and air support.

The scale of the operation was bigger than any NATO exercise and the biggest land exercises since World War II. According to retired Lt General PN Hoon of the Indian Army, Operation Brasstacks was a mobilization of the entire army of India.

The entire exercise took place in the deserts of Rajasthan instead of the sensitive regions of Kashmir and the then restive Punjab. At one point of time nearly 400,000 Indian troops were deployed directly across the Pakistani state of Sindh leading to Pakistani fears that India was displaying an overwhelming display of conventional superiority and was in fact planning to invade Pakistan and dismember it by surgical strikes.

Pakistani Response

Pakistan's response was to mobilize its own forces near the Indian state of Punjab. The then president and army chief of Pakistan, General Zia ul Haq viewed the exercise as a direct challenge and threat to Pakistan and issued commands to his armoured units to move to the front lines.

By mid January, both the Indian army and the Pakistan army were facing eye ball to eye ball on the frontiers. The situation could have potentially lead to a war between the two *de facto* nuclear weapon states (India had already conducted a nuclear test in 1974 and Pakistan was also believed to possess nuclear weapons at that time).

Nuclear Saber-rattling

The nuclear threat was brought into the picture by the Pakistani nuclear scientist A Q Khan. Khan stated in an interview to Indian journalist Kuldip Nayyar that Pakistan would retaliate with the nuclear bomb towards any offensive move by India against Pakistan.

This threat by Pakistan was considered to have prevented an all out aggression by Indian army. India responded that it was re evaluating its options after this disclosure by Khan. Khan in fact retracted his comments after a few days.

End of Operation Brass Tacks

According to events that played out and stance taken by the Indian army, Operation Brasstacks was only an exercise and not supposed to be a provocative one. The media was involved after this and intense diplomatic maneuvres followed preventing any further escalation in hostilities.

Indian Prime minister Rajiv Gandhi and Pakistani President Zia ul Haq involved in Cricket diplomacy to resolve this issue towards a peaceful end.

GENERAL V.N. SHARMA, PVSM, AVSM
COAS, 30 April 1988-30 June 1990
Armoured Corps, 16 Light Cavalry

General Vishwanath Sharma assumed charge of the Indian Army, as the 15th Chief of Army Staff, on 30 April 1988. General Sharma belongs to a distinguished military family whose members have served in the Armed Forces for two generations and produced three Generals. He is the son of Major General Amarnath Sharma who retired as the Deputy Director General of Medical Services.

His oldest brother is none other than the late Major Somnath Sharma, who was awarded Independent India's first posthumous Param Vir Chakra-the highest medal for gallantry-on 03 November 1947 for the Battle of Bagdam in Kashmir in October 1947. His older brother, Lieutenant General Surindranath Sharma, retired from the Army as Engineer-in-Chief and his younger sister, Kamla Tewary, is a doctor retired from the Army as a Major. Lieutenant General Surindranath Sharma's youngest son, Major Gautam Shavnik, continues the long time family tradition of serving in the Indian Army.

General Vishwanath Sharma was educated at Sherwood College, Nanital and later at the Prince of Wales' Royal Indian Military College at Dehradun. He joined the 5th Regular Course at the Indian Military Academy (IMA), Dehra Dun and was the first recipient of the Rajputana Rifles Gold Medal for tactics and leadership. He was commissioned into the 16 Light Cavalry on 04 June 1950 and was on the rolls of this Armoured Regiment for 16 years. He has held important commands, staff appointments and instructional assignments. As a young Major, he saw action during the 1965 Indo-Pak War in the Lahore sector.

As a Lieutenant Colonel, he commanded the 66 Armoured Regiment and was later appointed as an instructor at the Defence Services Staff College, Wellington. During the 1971 Indo-Pak War, he served as the Colonel General Staff Operations of an Armoured Division. On promotion to Brigadier, he commanded a mountain brigade in an insurgency affected area and was awarded the Ati Vishisht Seva Medal (AVSM) for distinguished service. Later he commanded an armoured brigade in the Rajasthan desert was appointed Brigadier General Staff of a Strike Corps in the Western sector. In 1980, he was promoted to Major General and commanded a mountain division in the eastern sector. He then served as Deputy Director, General Military Operations at the Army HQ. He was promoted to Lieutenant General and took over command of a reserve Corps in the western sector in 1984.

General Sharma was awarded the Param Vishisht Seva Medal (PVSM) for rendering distinguished services of the most exceptional order in March 1986. He was later appointed Commandant of the prestigious College of Combat at Mhow. He is a graduate of the Defence Services Staff College (DSSC), Wellington and the National Defence College (NDC), New Delhi. He has had vast experience in serving in all border regions with their varied terrain and types of operations. He is considered an authority in both mobile operations and mountain warfare. He took over as General Officer Commanding-in-Chief, Eastern Command on 01 June 1987. He is the Colonel of the 66th Armoured Regiment and was appointed as the Honorary Army ADC to the President on 25 July 1987. He retired on 30 June 1990, after completing 40 years of distinguished service to the nation.

GENERAL S.F. RODRIGUES, PVSM, VSM
COAS, 30 June 1990-30 June 1993
Regiment of Artillery

General Sunith Francis Rodrigues assumed charge of the Indian Army, as the 16th Chief of Army Staff, on 30 June 1990. Born in Mumbai on 19 September 1933, he was educated at St Xaviers High School in Mumbai. He joined the Joint Services Wing of the Indian Military Academy in 1949 and was commissioned into the Regiment of Artillery in December 1952. An alumnus of the Defence Services Staff College, he commanded a Mountain Artillery Regiment from 1970 to 1971 and during the 1971 Indo-Pak War served as a General Staff Officer at a Corps HQ. In 1972, he was awarded the Vishisht Seva Medal (VSM) for distinguished service during the 1971 Indo-Pak War. He commanded a mountain brigade in high altitude from June 1975 to December 1977. In 1978, he attended a course at the Royal College of Defence Studies in the UK.

After serving as the Chief Instructor (Army) at DSSC for about three years, he took command of a division deployed in high altitude on becoming a Major General. In 1981, he earned his Master's Degree in Defence Studies. After a stint as the Chief of Staff of a Corps from 1983 to September 1985, he took over as the Director General Military Training (DGMT), on promotion to the rank of Lieutenant General in 1985. The next year, he took over the command of a corps in the northern sector, a post which he served for about three years. He was appointed as the Honorary

ADC to the President in 1987 and in 1988, was decorated with the Param Vishisht Seva Medal (PVSM).

He served as the Vice Chief of Army Staff (VCOAS) from 01 November 1987 to 20 April 1989, when the Indian Peace Keeping Force (IPKF) was deployed in Jaffna, Sri Lanka during Operation Pawan. He served as the GOC-in-C Central Command from 21 April 1989 to 31 October 1989 and later as the GOC-in-C Western Command from 01 November 1989 to 29 June 1990. He took over as the Chief of Army Staff (COAS) on 30 June 1990 and retired from service on 30 June 1993.

He is known among his compatriots as a visionary and a strategist. It was during his tenure that the Army started inducting women officers. His tenure, however, was not totally without controversy. A remark made by him that good governance of the country was also the Army's business, led to a debate in Parliament.

Post retirement, he served as the Director of the International Centre, Goa for nearly six years. He also served two terms on the National Security Advisory Board. He has also been engaged in social and literary pursuits and has also been delivering talks on strategic issues. He takes a keen interest in education and empowering children to achieve their potential. He was on the Executive Council of Goa University for seven years and on the Managing Committee of the Goa Chamber of Commerce & Industry. He was appointed as the 32nd Governor of Punjab on 09 November 2004 and is the second former Army Chief, after General Om Prakash Malhotra (Retd.) to hold that appointment. He is also a long standing member of the Goa Planning Board and is on the Board of Governors of the Goa Institute of Management. He is married to Jean Rodrigues and they have two sons and a daughter.

THE INDIAN ARMY IN SRI LANKA, 1987-90

Introduction-The Origins of the Sri Lankan Civil War

After Sri Lankan independence there was a steady rise in Sinhala chauvinism. Like in many other countries, where a majority ethnic group is upset by the advancement of a educated and hard working minority the result was a "Sinhala only" policy. This drove the Tamils out of traditional job and opportunities. As the educated class had no land to fall back, frustration began building up. A methodical Sinhala wedge was driven between Vanni and Trincomalee district. With all major industries being handed to Sinhalas, the only economy to fall back on was smuggling.

The Tamils were initially influenced by the Indian Freedom movements leadership like Gandhi, Nehru and Bose. But as the Indian method of peaceful mass resistance, satyagrahas, etc did not work the militancy of Netaji Bose provided the new approach.

To this day Netaji Bose is talked about in glowing terms. The high education state, accentuated political awareness, strong traditional pride and a growing sense of loss created an explosive mix. It led to the formation of various militant groups like the LTTE, ERPLF, EROS, etc. As the state responded heavy handedly the militants started hit and run tactics on the Sri Lankan Army and para-militaries. One such ambush caused the deaths of 13 soldiers. This triggered of major anti-Tamil riots in Colombo and elsewhere resulting in the massacre of hundreds of Tamils. This completed the separation of the two sides and a bitter civil war started.

Operation Poomalai-India Intervenes

The civil war in Sri Lanka between the Sinhalese majority and the Tamil minority had escalated. The situation had deteriorated to such an extent that in Jaffna, there was large scale casualties amongst civilians. The Indian Government tried to coerce the Sri Lankan government into halting the offensive against the LTTE (Liberation Tigers of Tamil Eelam). An initial attempt to send food and medical supplies, by boat, was prevented by the Sri Lankan government. This led to Operation Poomalai (Garland). On 4 June 1987, five AN-32s escorted by four Mirage 2000Hs air-dropped 24 tonnes of relief supplies.

This led to the Indo-Sri Lanka accord, to establish peace and normalcy in Sri Lanka on 29 July 1987. This was to be upheld by an Indian Peace Keeping Force (IPKF). The first phase envisioned the supervision of the surrender of arms by the various militant groups. Soon some 24 AN-12s and AN-32s flew into Palaly carrying two Indian Army battalions constituting the IPKF. On July 30th, Lieutenant General Depinder Singh, the Indian Army's GOC-in-C Southern Command flew into Jaffna to discuss arrangements with the Sri Lankan forces. The next few days saw the bulk of an infantry brigade comprising the Sikh Light Infantry, the Maratha Light Infantry, the Mahar Regiment plus supporting elements had landed in northern Sri Lanka. By August, the 54th Infantry Division under the command of Maj Gen Harkirat Singh and the 340th Indian Inf Bde had landed in Sri Lanka.

The composition was;

- 54th Infantry Division (Maj. Gen. Harkirat Singh GOC, Brigadier Kulwant Singh, Dy GOC):-
  - o Divisional Reserves
    - * 10 Para Commando (Jaffna)
    - * 65 Armoured Regiment
  - o 91 Infantry Brigade (Jaffna)
    - * 5 Madras Bn
    - * 8 Mahar Bn
    - * 1 Maratha LI Bn
- o 76 Infantry Brigade (Brigadier I.M. Dhar) (Munnar, Vavuniya, Mulliativu)
- o 47 Infantry Brigade (Trincomalee-Batticoloa-Amparai)
- o 340 Ind. Inf. Bde. (Trincomalee)

THE PROBLEM

The initial phase of the agreement called for the disarmament of the various militant groups followed by the formation of the Interim Administrative Council. This was to have proportionate representation from various groups but the LTTE wanted to dominate it. Part of this fascist outlook was the massacre of political rivals and Sinhalese groups. A group of captured LTTE militants committed suicide in the custody of the Sri Lankan Army. These gave the LTTE the excuse it wanted. The turning point was;

1. Automatic and mortar fire on IPKF post at Tellipallai
2. Ambush of CRPF convoy near Tellipallai (4 Jawans killed)
3. The kidnapping of five unarmed para commandos on their way to collect provisions. These men were brutally killed by 'neck lacing'. i.e. they had burning tires placed on their necks.

A political decision was taken to disarm the LTTE if necessary by force. Meanwhile on October 8th, the LTTE carried out mortar and machine gun attacks on IPKF patrols. Following a high level Defence Ministry meeting on October 10th, the IPKF commenced its operations, code-named 'Pawan' on the night of 11/12 October 1987.

Operation Pawan-The Battle for Jaffna

The rules of engagement for this operation were strict and once again tied the Indian Army's hands. Use of artillery, heavy weaponry and offensive air support was forbidden to minimise civilian casualty and damage to property. The Indian Army's plan was to cripple the LTTE guerrilla network by capturing its headquarters in Jaffna City, a task the Sri Lankan Army had tried this for many years but had not succeeded. Pushed by the political/bureaucratic establishment the Army made a hasty plan. However it had only 91st Brigade under Brigadier J. Ralli consisting of only three battalions. One was at the front, one at point Pedro and one west of Palaly.

Furthermore each battalion was staffed to only 50% and had none of its heavy weapons as they had not been expecting a fight. The IPKF push into the city was contested by the LTTE at every nook and corner. It had to fight against heavily armed guerrilla, in a heavily built up and densely populated urban area already fortified and extensively mined during the three years of war with the Sri Lankan Army. Both sides took heavy casualties. Furthermore all the approach roads were pitted with Claymore mines or huge drums filled with explosives, buried in the ground. The whole area was flooded with IEDs (Improvised Explosive Devices) which could be detonated by remote or radio control from over a kilometre away.

One such explosion killed 29 IPKF personnel. The attack took place along five axis to the city. A bold plan to make a heli borne assault on Jaffna University to capture the LTTE leadership was made. The plan involved a company of 10 Para Cdos. to act as path finders. They were to be followed by a company of Sikh LI. If all went to plan the heli borne troops would be linked with troops coming by land. On the night of 11/12th October 1987, the plan was put to effect. But unknown to the Indian troops, was the fact that the LTTE had sophisticated Japanese radio sets which were monitoring IPKF communications.

Heavy and sustained machine gun fire pinned down the commandos killing six of them instantly. The Mi-8s were damaged but made it back to base. A further flight of helicopters brought in a platoon from the Sikh LI. These came under even more intense fire. As the men from the Sikh LI ran out of ammo, they made a valiant bayonet charge. All but one perished. The commandos had conserved their ammo but were close to running out. Still they managed to hold out the entire night. Next morning their battalion commander, Lt. Col. Dalbir Singh personally led a column of T 72 tanks to relieve them.

At this point the major operational base for the IPKF was Palaly airbase. This was a hub of LTTE activity and therefore a constant battle to secure it from guerrilla attacks. The IPKF was badly overstretched. On October 15/16 it halted its advance to stabilize its front. A massive airlift was undertaken to reinforce it with 3 brigades and heavy equipment. These included T-72s and BMP-1s. The improvised controllers worked round the clock to fly in troops and equipment. While the IL-76s and An-12s moved the heavy equipment the AN-32s, Hs.748s and Indian Airlines B737s brought in the troops. So heavy was the traffic that the runway in

Tamabaram (Madras) cracked with the repeated take offs and landings. The Mi-8s and Mi-25s, as well as Cheetahs, were flown in. By end of October the IAF flew 2200 tactical transport and 800 helicopter sorties.

36 Infantry Division:

* 115 Infantry Brigade (Jaffna)
* 72 Infantry Brigade (Jaffna)
* 4 Bn of 5 Gorkha Rifles
* 13 Sikh LI Bn
* 41 Infantry Brigade (Jaffna)
* 5 Rajputana Rifles
* 18 Infantry Brigade
* 5 Para Bn

Independent:

* Elements of the 65 Armoured Regiment (Jaffna)

Now reinforced the fighting resumed. In some areas the anti-personnel mines were countered by rolling BMP-1s and T-72s over them. But there was another weapon in the LTTE arsenal which the IPKF found hard to combat-snipers. Located in buildings, treetops and even coconut palms, equipped with powerful telescopic infra-red sights they took a heavy toll. Helicopters flying below 2000 feet were shot at damaging five, although all were recovered. By selectively killing officers and radiomen the LTTE would bring advances to a grinding halt. Take the case of 4/5 Gorkhas. As part of 72 Brigade the battalion was supposed to move up to Jaffna and link up with the heli borne troops at the Jaffna University campus. There, it followed the T-72 tanks and rescued the Para Commandos. But while the tanks moved out, the Gorkhas bringing up the rear came under fire from four temples dominating the main road crossing in Uramparai.

Under orders not to fire back at temples, the Gorkhas tried to close in. The battalion adjutant, Major N.J.D. Singh-a tough Manipuri-was hit on the head and died instantly. Another company commander, Major Anil Gardner had the entire flesh of his leg blown off by a Claymore mine. Major A.A. Verghese the other company commander and the only Tamil speaker in the whole unit, went into a house full of crying women and children to comfort them.

As he turned to leave an old woman shot him in the back. It became disastrous, when Lt. Col. I.B.S. Bawa was shot just under his heart. Along with the other wounded he was moved to a dried up well, the only cover available. With the helicopters unable to come in because of withering fire the wounded had to wait for tanks to fight their way through. By the time they made it at 4:30 p.m., Lt. Col. Bawa died. Only two Officers in the battalion survived trough the fighting, One was the second-in-command Major Randhir Singh.

The other was a young subaltern, Lt. Raj Sinha, who had joined the Army in 1984 and experienced this battle after three years of service. Lt. Sinha was running from post to post seeing that the wounded were taken care of and fighting with the LTTE with whatever was left of the battalion along, with bullets whizzing past him, He could never imagine why the bullets went past him without hitting him. With just these two officers at the helm, the battalion became unfit for further operations till officer reinforcements were flown in. Elsewhere a BMP-1 of the 72 Brigade with Colonel D.S. Saraon was blown by a mine killing him and the entire complement of nine men. The IPKF was forced to improvise by having its officers avoid pips of ranks, wearing slouch hats and carry oversize back packs. As advances got bogged down, the battalions should have taken the time to manoeuvre around the defenders. Instead, due to pressure from New Delhi more troops were thrown, into the furnace. But the mines continued to harass the IPKF. Frustrated, the IPKF cut off power to Jaffna to counter it.

To compound the IPKF's problems, it was impossible to distinguish between the Tigers and civilians. Many a times they would open fire on a IPKF unit, hide their weapons and merge with the civilians. Sepoy Govindan, Madras Regiment, says, "It was impossible to say who was a Tiger and who was not. Everyone male or female above the age of 10, could be armed and dangerous. We saw little girls producing guns from under their frocks and shooting at us. How do you fight them?" The turning point came when IMSF commandos broke out of the besieged Jaffna port and cleared the heavily mined Navanturai Coastal Road. This allowed the crucial link up between 1 Maratha Light Infantry in the fort under Colonel T. Brar and the advancing troops of 41st Brigade. This sealed off the Nallur area.

It took two weeks of bitter and hard fighting for the IPKF to wrest Jaffna and other major cities from the LTTE. Unfortunately many of the LTTE had ex-filtrated out of Jaffna. All this time the Mi-25s were not authorised to be used. Finally as patience ran out, the order to use these powerful gunships was given.

In its debut at attacking LTTE entrenchments in Chavakacheri it was used to devastating effect. For only a handful of IPKF casualties; Chavakacheri was wrested from the LTTE. Contrast to the 600+ casualties in Jaffna, this speaks monuments of the political leadership of India. Battered in Jaffna, the LTTE fled southwards. Its hard core fighters moved to the safety of the jungles by skirting the coast of Jaffna from Point Pedro to Elephant Pass, sheltered by the impenetrable jungles and criss-crossed waterways of the Nittkaikulam jungles.

Shifting to the Jungles

With the LTTE slipping into the jungles the overstretched IPKF began to build up for the long haul ahead. The 36th Infantry Division along with 2 additional brigades was brought in. It took over responsibility for the Trincomalee-Batticaloa and Vavuniya sectors while the 54th Division consolidated in Jaffna. Then in Feb 88 the 4th Mountain Division and 57 Infantry Division came in and took over Vanni and Batticaloa sectors from the 36th. The Jaffna sector was the smallest, about 60 km by 30 km) with a population of 200,000. About 16 to 20 battalions were employed in this sector. Then began the daily rituals of mine and IED explosions, unearthing of arms and shootouts with groups of LTTE men. The town of Jaffna was under the charge of Brigadier Manjit Singh. A tough and temperamental individual, he would lead some of his operations from a BMP.

His impatience with his command led him to sack two of his COs, his Brigade Major and his Signal Officer. But his personal bravery and dynamism was beyond reproach and was later decorated with the MVC. He held Jaffna well although there was always tension in the town. When his Brigade was pulled off the task was passed on to Brigadier JS Dhillon. A man of few words Dhillon moved in quickly. He used his forces intelligently constantly thinking of changes. Small units scurried around the town in vans, cycles, mopeds and autos. They would scurry across backyards and over walls constantly changing their directions. Sometimes 3 to 4 columns would move in parallel in opposite directions, lashing out LTTE hideouts and also being able to provide covering fire. He made good use of the BMPs to keep the Eastern Coastal route clear.

The Vadarmachi town was held by Brigadier Samay Ram. He was a very calm man totally unperturbed. He was a hard thinker and was able to simulate the same in his subordinates. When his men were attacked from the Nallur Kandsawamy temple he refused to attack it back because of 30000 civilian refugees in the temple premises. The standoff was resolved when the LTTE keeping in mind civilian casualties choose to withdraw. A huge cache of arms and ammunition was found in the temple courtesy the son of the head priest an LTTE member. His excellent rapport with the locals, led to a lot of cooperation from the local heads. North of Jaffna extending into Kankesanthurai and Kayts island was the domain of Brig JK Ralli. Shrugging of the criticism of his units in the early battles he used innovative tactics and constantly evolving battle drills to keep the LTTE on its toes. He was the first to build an intelligence network from the ground up. A couple of units rehabilitated themselves into efficient outfits.

In the jungles of the South, around the Killinochi farmlands, rimmed by the thick jungles of Vanni were the forces of Brigadier

Jaspal Singh. The IPKF devised tactics to suit the terrain. In order to sustain operations for a longer time, without having to rely on air supplies, he established road axes for essential vehicles to penetrate the jungles for as far as possible. He planned artillery & mortar cover for all his vehicles ensuring immediate fire support. The Chetaks and Cheetahs were employed to guide artillery and Mi 25s towards the targets. Instead of indiscriminate jungle bashing, attacks were made on well identified targets. Wherever the opportunity arose for operations in flat farmlands BMPs were used aggressively. The area left of Pachchilaippali, the south eastern strip of land between Jaffna & Elephant Pass on the lagoon in the south were LTTE strongholds.

As all the routes to Jaffna and Vadamarachi passed through this the IPKF tried to make inroads here. But the LTTE wisely preferred to keep low and bypass the IPKF rather than confront them. But soon under the charge of Brigadier Panag, a veteran of the Naga campaign things began to change. LTTE trails were picked up and ambushes set constantly. While the coasts were being hit, Panag kept the pressure on land with a series of deceptive mobile posts. In the lagoons a number of frail assault boats manned by Colonel Dahiya's engineers kept engaging the superior LTTE water borne forces. South across the Killinochi belt in Mulaivithu was the largest concentration of LTTE camps and cadres. In charge of this area was Brigadier Palsokar. His men were involved in the maximum number of battles. Major action was observed in Alampil (May 88), Nittukaikulam (Sept 88) and Nayuru April May 89. These places were interconnected and heavily defended indicating the presence of the LTTE leadership.

Jungle Bashing: Operation Trishul and Viraat

About this time, the IPKF's doctrine of counter-insurgency against the LTTE was evolved. The answer was not to maintain strongholds in the Jaffna peninsula, but to actively conduct search and destroy missions against LTTE camps and bases in the dense tropical forests of the North. This 'Jungle Bashing' would involve aggressive patrolling by the individual infantry units. This also resulted in the casualties mounting steadily. but the professional pride and esteem of the Indian Army served to steel its morale.

The first phase of IPKF operations in the area was codenamed Trishul and Viraat. It spread out over the Northern provinces from Mannar to Mullaitivu and Elephant Pass to Vavuniya. As the heat turned up the LTTE started operating more from the Nittaikulam areas close to the lagoons and rivulets it new so well. This was where its supplies continued to be delivered. The LTTE was hit hard losing area commanders and leaders every day. In one instance an IPKF assault in Mullaitivu in Feb 88 almost trapped the IPKF's top leadership. A gallant rearguard action by Prabhakaran's guards ensured his escape.12 LTTE men were found dead after the fight.

Operation Trishul was launched in April 1988. Its result were modest, hundreds of weapons seized and few killed but it kept the pressure up. Operation Viraat was launched in May/June 1988. A force of 15,000 armoured personnel, infantrymen and paratroopers were used. During the operation the IPKF stumbled across well prepared defenses. It consisted of concrete bunkers with electric generators. A few guerillas were captured or killed but most melted away. But sometimes, the LTTE struck back. When they did do so, it was at the time and place of their own choosing. So vulnerable convoys and lone vehicles became the targets for ambushes. The LTTE were masters at the use of landmines and improvised explosive devices. For a while, these IED attacks were neutralised by the cutting off power to the Jaffna Peninsula. but it was not a permanent solution. Thus the Army suffered a number of causalities to these ambushes. Ambushes by gunfire were rare, and when carried out by the LTTE, they found that the army bounced back with great fervour. The army rose to the occasion in these small actions. Young officers and soldiers displayed extraordinary courage and bravery in the face of death.

Of particular mention would be two soldiers of 1/11 Gorkha Rifles. 1/11GR was one of the original battalions that was inducted for the fighting in Operation Pawan. After the Capture of Jaffna, its mission was primarily sending patrols on 'Search & Destroy' missions. One Patrol on such a mission on 16 March 1988 in the Vallankulam Pannai area ran into an ambush when enfilade gunfire rained down on them from the dense jungle growths. The Gorkhas hit the ground and returned fire. Slowly they organised themselves and extricated themselves out of the site. In the Melee, two Jawans got separated from the main column, Havildar Devinder Singh Gurung and Rifleman Rajender Bahadur Thapa were both pinned down by heavy fire. By the time they could extricate themselves, the main column has disappeared, as both were presumed to be missing in action. As both the jawans were making their way through the undergrowth, they came under fire from LTTE Snipers. In the exchange of fire, Havildar Gurung was hit in the thigh and was not able to move. Rifleman Thapa then picked up Havildar Gurung and carried him on his shoulders to a hut nearby, returning the odd burst that came his way with fire from his Ishapore rifle.

Once in the hut, Rifleman Thapa administered first aid to Havildar Gurung and surveyed the situation around him. The LTTE had identified the two soldiers hideout and slowly have started encircling the Hut from a distance. Even as the LTTE Militants slowly made their way to the hut, Rifleman Thapa picked them off with single shots from his Ishapore. His main concern was to save ammunition, and use it efficiently. Resisting the temptation to waste the ammunition in general direction of the militants, Rifleman Thapa used it only when he could clearly identify his target. The exchange of fire went on and on well into the next day. Early morning on March 17th, a patrol sent by 1/11GR in search of the two missing soldiers was drawn to the hut by the sound of gunfire. The LTTE Militants decided to call it a day on the sight of the approaching patrol and fled. Rifleman Thapa and Havildar Gurung were thus recovered safely. Rifleman Thapa kept a cool mind and as a result he was able to keep the LTTE Militants at bay for more than 17 Hours.

During the time, he fired only 22 rounds, and was well a target for hundreds of rounds fired by the AK-47 Rifles of the LTTE.

Two dead militants were recovered as well as another wounded LTTE man. It wasn't always the Jawan or the NCO that displayed such bravery and courage, young officers barely out of the Indian Military Academy (IMA) thrust into the sweltering Jungles of Jaffna too showed that they could give a fitting reply to the LTTE.

On 19 July 1988, a convoy of a two vehicles of the 7th Battalion of the Assam Regiment was making its way from Madurengkenikulam to Mangani to collect dry rations. In charge of the detail was a young subaltern, 2nd Lt. Rajeev Sandhu, who was barely six months out of the IMA. 2nd Lt. Sandhu was traveling in the Mahindra Jeep, leading the way to the 1 Ton Nissan truck which was trailing 50 meters behind the jeep. Driving the jeep was Sepoy NKKS Rajkumar, 2nd Lt. Sandhu was in the next seat. Sitting in the rear was L/Nk Nandeshwar Das and Sepoy Lalbuanga. As the vehicles reached a track junction, a rocket fired from the undergrowth hit the jeep, lifting it into the air and overturning it to the side. Immediately a fusillade of fire from the AK-47s straddled the overturned Jeep. When the volley of fire ended, and silence descended on the ambush site, the LTTE militants knew that this was one convoy that never made it to the Army base. They came out of their ambush positions to pick up the weapons and equipment of the fallen soldiers.

But one Indian Soldier still had his wits around with him. Out of the view of the militants, 2nd Lt. Sandhu, was dragging himself with his 9mm SMC Carbine out of the wreck. Both his legs were smashed when the rocket hit the jeep, the subsequent volley of fire had wounded him and he was bleeding profusely. He checked the other occupants of the jeep. None of them were conscious. In fact the initial blast of the rocket was borne by 2nd Lt. Sandhu. The machine gun fire that followed killed both Lance Naik Das and Sep Lalbuanga in the rear. Driver Rajkumar was wounded and unconscious. Sandhu tumbled out of the Jeep and crawled to a fire position. As one of the LTTE militants by the name of Kumaran approached the Jeep. Despite his legs being totally smashed and his body ridden with bullets, 2nd Lt. Sandhu lifted his carbine with blood soaked hands and sprayed Kumaran with bullets, killing him instantly.

However, the bleeding had already taken its toll. 2nd Lt. Sandhu succumbed to his wounds and injuries. A grateful nation recognised his bravery with the award of a Maha Vir Chakra in 1990. 2nd Lt. Sandhu was just 22 years old when he died in Sri Lanka. Incidents like these were what kept the LTTE from underestimating the fighting prowess of the Army. They knew that they could not compare the fighting calibre of the Indian Soldier to that of the Sri Lankan Army. The Indian Soldier was coming from a background of operational exposure in areas like the Jungles of North east and the Mountains of the North. Death and Hardship were not a stranger to him, thus He was more ready and more experienced in fighting back to the hit and run tactics of the LTTE.

As a prelude to the elections to the newly created North Eastern provincial council the IPKF launched Operation Checkmate. Operation Checkmate did bring some results, inflicting causalities on the LTTE. On one occasion, the IPKF almost caught the top LTTE Leadership consisting of Prabhakaran, Mahataya and others. But in the fluid situation, the LTTE leaders managed to slip out. Many camps and carefully sited positions of the LTTE were rooted out and destroyed. These measures ensured that the LTTE was in no position to disrupt the coming elections. The Jungle Bashing soon came to a halt, as the IPKF concentrated on the upcoming Provincial Council elections. Operation Checkmate ended by the middle of October 1988.

Consolidation, Elections, Victory and Withdrawal

With the LTTE in the jungles the ding dong battles continued. The LTTE underestimated the strength required to tie down the IPKF in Jaffna. So in August-September 88 an influx of LTTE cadres and junior leaders into the peninsula again started. Encounters and shootouts increased and many of these cadres and area leaders were wiped out. All this was achieved through aggressive patrolling rather than specific intel. The mounting pressure on the LTTE caused concerns among the religious leaders, erudite professionals and Senior Citizen groups. Upto now these groups had been mouthing LTTE drafted propaganda on IPKF massacres, destructions of civilian properties, infrastructure etc. The aim was to coerce the IPKF to restore the infrastructure so that the LTTE could use it to fight more vigorously.

The IPKF authorities continued to reason with various citizen groups about the need for a political understanding. The LTTE's stubbornness was highlighted at every opportunity. Little by little the IPKF made inroads into the civilians. The first talk of trying to reason with the LTTE emerged under the cover of a cautious ceasefire. Meanwhile the decimation of the LTTE's local leaders in the towns continued. Citizens of Kankesanthurai, Point Pedro, Killinochi and others indicated their willingness to reason with the LTTE. The turning point was the agreement of Chavakacheri to agree that too in writing. As a sign of easing tension the IPKF withdrew hundreds of checkpoints, road blocks and bunkers from the towns. But the LTTE did not budge and shooed away many of the citizenry, scolding them for their lack of understanding about the implications. The disappointed citizenry returned and subsequently could not question the IPKF on why it was destroying the LTTE.

Meanwhile Colombo issued the 13th Amendment to its constitution binging to life the North Eastern Provincial Council. Most normal life had been restored including posts, banking, trade etc. But the LTTE imposed mental barrier remained. The armed fight was not the answer as for every LTTE militant killed another would take his place as long as the idea of 'Eelam' remained. The answer was to hold take a chance and hold the political elections for the NEPC with hopeful LTTE participation. Once the IPKF suggested this idea the Indian Administrative service and Foreign Service under J. N Dixit took .charge. The various Tamil groups were asked to register as political parties. The EROS and LTTE refused. Even the moderate TULF, PLOTE and TELO opted out. Only the ERPLF agreed followed by the ENDLF. Jaffnaites were upset as they expected only the LTTE to represent them. A town meeting was arranged and an open invitation issued to the LTTE. Nut all this was to no avail and the ERPLF and ENDLF candidates were elected unopposed.

Although not accepted by the Jaffnaites and other Tamils the exercise allowed the holding of the Presidential elections as well as the Parliamentary elections. This time the EROS was persuaded to stand for the elections. This however did not please RAW. There was the threat of LTTE violence and electoral officers had the protected as well as pick up other employees for duty before they could become "absent". Barring a few cases of firing on IPKF patrols the elections went peacefully although he voter turnout was low. The whole thing was monitored by Commonwealth observers. The IPKF had done its duty sacrificing a few lives to bring democracy to this embittered land.

Now that some sort of political structure was restored the next step was to set up a body to monitor law and order. It would take some of the pressure of the IPKF but also enhance the feeling of self rule amongst the Tamils as well as create job opportunities. Mooted by General V.N. Sharma, Chief of Army Staff, its idea originated from British and French examples. Also with the Sri Lankan Police virtually moribund there was no other option. Colombo baulked at this while New Delhi backed the plan.

Unfortunately due to LTTE threats against traitors, Colombo's apathy the quality of the people attracted to the force was poor. This meant that the majority were recruited from the NEPC's ruling party. And once in the CVF they tried to enforce the interests of their party. It was a long ordeal to get the CVF going.

There were now three schools of thought in the IPKF:

1. Let the NEPC and CVF handle and reduce the IPKF progressively
2. Maintain the IPKF as long as it requires to implement the ISLA (internal estimates put it at 10 years)
3. Leave the problem to the NEPC and Sri Lankan Govt.

Meanwhile the pressure on the LTTE was to be continued.

Operation Baaz-Extension of Operations: With the success of the Provincial Council Elections and Sri Lankan Parliamentary elections the IPKF resumed operations. It now faced some hard choices. There needed to be a purpose to avoid drop in troop morale due to sense of aimlessness and lack of clarity in purpose. But while it figured out the best course of actions normal Operation Checkmate was resumed.

The aim was to continue to hound the LTTE forcing it to come to the peace talks. While parleys were going on in India the IPKF focused on the strongholds in the Nittikulam district north east of Vavuniya. This led to some fierce fighting including hand to hand. One such action took place on the shores of the Nayuru lagoon, south of Alampil. The shores of the lagoon are densely forested. One of the Battalions freshly inducted after the Operation Viraat was the 6th Battalion of the 8th Gorkha rifles regiment. 6/8GR was vested with the task of being the scout unit in the Jungle Bashing mission of Operation Baaz, and they started their operations in the last week of February. On 02 March 1989, two Companies of 6/ 8 GR set out on a 'reconnaissance mission'. This was a mission to search and weed out any LTTE elements, the details had 48 hours worth of rations with them while on the move. The Unit was not expecting much action. Till then, their activities in Sri Lanka involved only manning of road blocks and conducting searches at these road blocks. Their only hour of excitement was when they nabbed a hidden Dinghy and an outboard motor being carried in a Tractor-Trailer.

As the Lead platoons made their way through the thick and dense jungle, One of the sections in the front ran into an ambush. The LTTE men opened fire with their LMGs and AK Rifles, killing or wounded five of the Gorkhas. Though the Gorkhas returned fire, the LTTE casualties could not be ascertained. Even as the fighting was going on, the Gorkhas realised that they had stumbled upon the outer defences of a major base.

In such a case there would be a couple of tiers of defensive positions before the main camp a good 10-12 km behind. This was the reason the LTTE outer defences were holding their ground. This spurred on the Gorkhas to renew their assault with more fervour. By nightfall the fighting became confused. The Commanding Officer of the Gorkha's Colonel V.K. Bakshi sent back calls for more reinforcements.

As the Gorkhas ran out of ammo they drew their kukhris and waded into the LTTE. Somewhere along the line Colonel Bakshi was fatally wounded. By morning the fighting was all over a 4 km front. Helicopters flew in reinforcements. An infantry company dropped from the other side of the lagoon to help the Gorkhas ran into heavily booby trapped trails. By afternoon 5 battalions of the Army were in the area moving towards the lagoon. By March 7 when the operations were over 70 LTTE personnel were killed. The main group including the leadership melted away. Colonel Bakshi was awarded the MVC posthumously.

The Mi 8s continued to fly in reinforcements. After 2 days of build up the IPKF again resumed operations. By March 15 almost a full Division of IPKF troops were involved. The IAF intensified its operations. No 109 HU ferried in troops, ammo, equipment and food. MI 25 gunships operating out of China Bay flew large number of attack sorties guided in by Chetak helicopters. CASEVAC duties were shared by Chetaks and Mi-8s.

These operations had a telling effect on the LTTE. The IPKF meant business. It will not sit by in camps. It had the will and the ability to seek the Tigers in their lair even if it meant booby traps, mines and casualties. It was this mounting pressure, while no means a defeat but a steady decimation of its units which caused the LTTE to seek peace talks with the Sri Lankan Govt on April 25 1989. The IPKF had finally brought the parties to the table for a political solution which was the only long term solution in this type of ethnic conflict.

The LTTE Agrees for Peace Talks

The LTTE while not defeated was slowly being decimated. It had to confront the inexhaustible resources of the IPKF which was prepared to stay on for years. Its cadres and junior leaders were being wiped out regularly in the urban areas. It was primarily a jungle force albeit one with the support of the majority of Tamils. Still it was worried at the increasing influence of the moderate parties, the NEPC and the CVF. Little by little people were accepting the way of life. On the other side Colombo continued to hem and haw over the NEPC. Opposition to the accord led by the new President Premadasa.

Consumed by his hatred for the Indians he even opened up secret channels to the LTTE to arm them against the Indians. Premadasa demanded that the IPKF leave the Island and asked the Sri Lankan Armed forces to throw them out. Any movement of the Sri Lankan forces outside their barracks would kill the still alive ISLA. Lt Gen AS Kalkat warned that the IPKF would retaliate if fired upon by the Sri Lankans. IAF squadrons moved to the South while naval units moved of the Sri Lankan coast. Thanks to the professionalism of the Indian and Sri Lankan armed forces a conflict was avoided. Sri Lankan commanders must get major credit for a cool and tactful behaviour.

The NEPC was further losing support by forcefully trying to increase the size of the CVF. A new Govt also took power in India. The UF Govt of V.P. Singh was committed to the withdrawal of Indian troops. Events took a rapid turn when Colombo and LTTE under pressure from the Indians agreed to peace talks in June 1989. The LTTE finally had to come to the peace table. The Tamils were now paradoxically unhappy at the IPKFs departure but had to bear the start of a new ordeal. The IPKF started reducing its units progressively. On 23 March 1990 the last of the ships left Sri Lanka with men of the paras.

EPILOGUE

The last units of the IPKF came back in March 1990. They were received by representatives of the Union Govt although the local Govt of Tamil Nadu Chief Minister Karunanidhi stayed way. To their credit the IPKF did not scramble to get out like the

Americans in Vietnam. Still it was a sense of dejection, tiredness and disappointment. The IPKF had sacrificed so many of its officers and jawans to set a professional and secular example to the Sri Lankan Armed Forces and a sense of democracy to the Tamils. All this to no avail. The palm fringed towns, farms, placid lakes, beaches and lagoons soon descended into chaos. Within months the NEPC and CVF were in disarray.

The LTTE marched back in. And soon the peace between Colombo and the LTTE collapsed and bitter fighting resumed. The Tamils in Sri Lanka are being put through the meat grinder again. Many prominent Tamils who had so vociferously protested against the IPKF on the LTTE's behalf were gunned down at the first hint straying from the path. The supreme irony is that man who led the LTTE's brilliant fight against the IPKF Mahathayya was branded a RAW spy and tortured to a state of near death. He has not been seen since. It is believed that Mahathayya was done to death on Prabharkaran's orders. Voices now ask for the return of the IPKF but there is no one to listen to them.

The Sri Lankan Armed Forces were in retreat for the first half of the 90s. But since then they have regrouped and driven the war into the LTTE's camp. Jaffna is now back again in Colombo's hands and the LTTE back to the jungles. As this is being written at the end of this century the war is in a stalemate, for a brief period in early 2000, the LTTE hit back with spectacular gains in the Island. Erstwhile strong bastions like Elephant Pass and Chavakacheri in the Sri Lankan army's hands fell in quick succession to the LTTE. For a period, the fate of 22,000 soldiers of the Sri Lankan army seemed to hand in balance. This situation renewed the calls for India to intervene. Wisely, the Indian government stayed out of the conflict.

The Sri Lankan forces have since then, consolidated their positions. The stalemate continues. For the families of the 1,157 Indian Soldiers who died in Sri Lanka, it has been a life of bitter memories. Though the government has done its best to rehabilitate those affected by the conflict, It is pretty clear that unlike the Kargil conflict, where the entire country's population rallied behind the armed forces and the families of those who died defending Indian territory, there has been little or no awareness among the Indian public about the sacrifices made by these families. In short as one correspondent wrote "They died fighting someone else's war, remembered only by their families."

Unlike the Kargil war where the bodies of the dead soldiers were shipped back to their homes and the funeral rites were carried out with full military honours, the families of the martyrs in Sri Lanka received only the ashes. The practice then was to ship the bodies of the officers home, but the bodies of the other soldiers were cremated on the Sri Lankan soil itself. Amongst the Indian Army their is a marked reluctance to talk of the Sri Lanka episode. Only a couple of books have been written by officers who served there. The College of Combat did study the conflict and accordingly rewrite many of the tactics. But what is needed is an effort understand and highlight the political, military and intelligence bungling to the general public so that the sacrifice of the many men would not go in vain. This website is hopefully a small part of that process.

THE IPKF PERFORMANCE

The Indian Army had been accustomed to wars of 2 to 3 weeks. The COIN operations in the North East were not even close in comparison to what it had to handle in Sri Lanka. The 2½ year operations against the LTTE proved tough and many were found wanting. It was brutal toughening process for the Army as an institution.

Infantry

The war in Sri Lanka was primarily an infantryman's war and sadly the infantryman was found wanting in the initial stages of the war. There are a number of valid reasons for this, from organisational neglect to operational mistakes to inadequate equipment.

Organisationally, the Army and its senior leadership had been caught up in the process of fighting the next war with Pakistan in a NATO/Warsaw Pact type clash. The emphasis in the preceding years was big exercises with mechanised forces and division and Corps level manoeuvres. The basic principles of infantry combat were neglected due to lack of time & resources committed to the above mentioned exercises. Furthermore periodic tinkering with the rank structure at the unit level, caused units & sub units to stall at the death or wounding of its commander. No matter how many JCOs and NCOs are present, true responsibility & ability rest with the officers and it is unfair of JCOs and NCOs to be expected to fill the breach without any long term training.

Operationally almost all the units in the initial phases were not to full strength. Brigades were without 1 or 2 battalions and battalions without 1 to 3 companies. Many were away in course, at firing ranges and on leave. Self imposed restrictions meant hardly any supporting fire. A brigade had six 105mm guns for fire support. Maps were in short supply and antiquated. The Battle of Jaffna was fought by units with maps of 1937! Till Tamil language courses were set up, there was a shortage of translators. The LTTE had fought and built up this environment since 1983. In contrast the Indian Army had fought its last war in 1971.

The cumulative effect of all this was a tendency to crowd in numbers. The basic tactics of fire and movement was absent. Patrols would go out in large numbers making it easy for the LTTE to keep track of them. In fact it was possible to monitor the position of IPKF patrols from LTTE intercepts. The IPKF patrols failed to use this to lure enemy ambushes into traps. Add to this the impatience of the Generals caused more troops to be thrown into this furnace. Fire discipline was poor resulting in a tendency to fire off all the ammo at the enemy. patrols would advance in single file and would leave and return by the same way. More worrying was the tendency to allow weapons to be snatched from the dead and wounded. Add to this the IPKF equipment at the unit level was poorer than the LTTEs. The Indian soldiers' semi-automatic SLRs were no match in close quarter combat to the LTTE's AK-47s. The LTTE also had better webbing, lightweight machine guns and superior radios. The standard issue DMS boot, rotted in the jungle. The VM series of radio sets were too weak in built up areas. The non availability of nickel cadmium batteries meant the ANPRC-25 radio sets could not be used as standard sets.

The other problem was the aging officer corps. There were commanding officers and company commander who were in the 40 to 45 age bracket. While the younger Majors and Lt Cols performed well, these older men were found wanting. One such commander would go into operations riding the BMP open hatch. A veteran of the 1971 war, he brushed aside his men's warnings. One day a burst a heavy machine gun fire ripped him up.

The IPKF slowly learnt to cope the hard way, in the field. Training bases were provided to train the newly inducted men the techniques of urban combat and COIN operations. Camouflaged canvas was used to create an LTTE like webbing. While some men converted their 7.62mm SLRs into full auto, the army equipped a few men in every section with the 7.62 IC with burst fire. However there were two opinions about the success of this version. While some felt its barrel would drop after a burst of fire, others felt it was fine. The Army also imported 70,000 AK-47s from Eastern Europe and flew them straight to Sri Lanka. Using the principle of infrared beam shooting, torches with extremely focused light was strapped to the rifles and the circuit connected to the trigger guard, for point & shoot. Metal sheets and thick wooden planks, help deflect bullets from sift vehicles. Sandbags were used in the beds of trucks to soften the impact of mines.

In the end whatever the shortcomings there was an abundance of courage and heroism. Even in situations with more than half the men dead or wounded there was no panic and positions were held tenaciously.

Special Forces

This was an ideal war to utilize special forces. Initially however the special forces were part of the division HQ. Later a separate

Special Forces HQ, was created to better utilize them. Initially the Special forces were used like normal infantry and suffered from many of the same problems. The only difference was superior battle craft skills and better fire discipline saved the day. Later as they were used in small groups, using speed & deception, they performed exceptionally well. However there was a paramount need for better & lighter equipment, more long life rations for lengthier missions and their own helicopters and supporting fire.

The other special force in Sri Lanka was the Indian Special Marine Force (ISMF) now called the Marine Commando Force (MCF) or MARCOS. This unit made its debut in the IPKF operations and came through with flying colors. Being a small startup force it did not get caught in the infantry mode, the Paras got in to.

Mechanised Forces

The terrain is not suitable mechanised operations.. It had built up areas, lagoon, and water-logged fields. Tanks were used in direct fire mode to blast opposition in built up areas. They were used to get units surrounded by the enemy to safety. eg. Paras in Jaffna Univ raid. Initial deployment was poor with no supporting infantry on the flanks, but once the infantry battalions were to full strength they were well flanked with infantry. The T-72s managed to cope with the narrow lanes, an indication of its size and manouevrability. It was exposed to severe RPG-7 fire that helped determine its weak points. About three T-72s were lost due to drums packed with 200 kg of explosives. These had been inserted before the road was tarred.

A number of BMPs were also deployed. While some commanders complained about lack of terrain to use it effectively, others did adapt and make good use of it wherever possible. Mostly it had to be used in the dismounted role as fire support platform. In the initial stages, some BMPs were lost to LTTE drum mines. Both, T-72s and BMPs, were used to run over anti personnel mines and IEDs. Overall losses of both T-72s and BMPs were less than 10.

Artillery

Deployment of artillery was restricted, because of political orders to not use heavy weapons. Although as an area weapon it was not always the weapon of choice to flush a couple of houses full of LTTE militants, it was useful in speeding up advances when troops were held up especially outside of the built up area. The artillery observers operating with infantry units performed well. Observers lying in Cheetahs were not only useful to help being down fire, but also in forcing the LTTE to not fire its mortars lest they give away their positions.

However the paucity of guns resulted in their deployment in troops and many a times fire support to patrols were limited. The lack of night vision devices limited AOP flights.

Engineers

The Engineers were in action from the time they set foot in Sri Lanka. Even before the conflict started they were involved in defusing booby traps and mines. In fact the first casualty was an engineer and two sappers in August 1987. The engineers were involved in a number of tasks, many of them civil reconstruction projects. On the military side they provided;

1. Support to infantry troops by laying mines and booby traps and defusing those of the LTTE.
2. Building helipads and roads to maintain axes of supply as far as possible.
3. Their assault boats (BAUTs) were used for patrolling and raiding the various lagoons.
4. Improvise and extend the airfields at Palaly, make the jetty at KKS functional.

On the civil side: they were involved in repairing accommodations, electric and water supplies to the towns and hospitals as well as repairing roads. The sheer variety and ingenuity of the Tiger's use of explosives came as a rude shock in the beginning. The use of plastic jerry cans and coconut shells to negate mine sweeping devices was a novelty. Still most of the casualties were due to carelessness on the part of individual or groups.

Signals

This was one of the more secretive units of the IPKF. Led by Chief Signals Officer, Southern Command, Major General Yashwant Deva, the first task was to set up a communication hub. After scouting the locations, Mandapan in Tamil Nadu was selected. It would extend broad band microwave communication to the island, interface it with the mainland troposcatter and other field communications. The relevant info about the defunct Indo-Sri Lanka microwave system (1979) was dug up and with the help of the Sri Lankan Army reactivated. With a considerable amount of innovation all Sri Lankan cities and towns were linked into our own.

Once the IPKF was inducted C3I nodes were created in Plalay, Trincomalee, Vavuniya and Batticaloa. They provided;

1. HF radio with Burst Error Control System for Teleprinter
2. Troposcatter links and satellite channels
3. Hot lines from HQ OFC down to Divisional and Brigade HQ

But it was in SIGINT (Signals Intelligence) that the Signals were hard pressed. The Tiger's ran an extremely efficient communications network based on Japanese ICON sets utilizing (148-150 MHz). The receiver could lock on to one of 10 preset frequencies which posed problems for intercepting. These were overcome with the capture of a few sets. These captured sets were later used for jamming the LTTE network. The captured set would be utilised for generating the required frequency and then amplify it. LTTE messages were short and used a number of codes. Intercepts were quickly recorded before passed on for transalation and analysis.

In order to locate LTTE transmissions, Hungarian Direction Finding equipment was flown in. The success of this is mixed. LTTE transmitters in Tamil Nadu continued to be active for a long time. VHF sets were weak for built up areas. In the future the trend should be HF sets. Radio procedures were outdated and tended to be verbose. Many a time the communications were irrelevant. Better use should have been made of other Indian languages to delay deciphering. Ground-to-air communication was poor. Many a times, the solution was to have the army officer sit in the helicopter with an PRC 25 set, to provide communications between the pilot and ground troops.

Logistics-Army Service Corps

If there was one are where the IPKF performed magnificently it was in logistics. Originally an Army Maintenance Area was created in Madras. Even then supplies came through Supply Depot, Madras it meant to cater to 10,000 troops. But the number of troops increased rapidly forcing a rethink in strategy. Although the best process would be to obtain most of the requirements in the island itself, the resultant price increase would have caused a furor. So everything had to be brought in from India.

To store petrol and aviation fuel, more tankers were brought in. Till adequate storage facilities were developed, surplus fuel from transport aircraft were offloaded in Palaly. The aircraft then flew to Colombo for refueling before flying back to India. The logistics also required coordination between all three services. Everyday late at night men from the three wings would hash out plans to ensure an uninterrupted flow of materials the next day. The men of the ASC also organised their own security while transporting goods to various units. This was the first time such composite operations were carried out and everything had to be learnt.

RAID ON JAFFNA UNIVERSITY, 12 OCTOBER 1987

The Indo-Sri Lanka accord, to establish peace and normalcy in Sri Lanka was signed on 29 July 1987. The first phase involved the supervision of the surrender of arms by the various militant groups. This was to be followed by the formation of the Interim Administrative Council with proportionate representation from various groups. The LTTE however wanted to dominate it. This led to attacks by the LTTE on IPKF personnel. A political decision was taken to disarm the LTTE if necessary by force. Meanwhile on October 8th the LTTE carried out mortar and machine gun attacks on IPKF patrols. Following a high level Defence Ministry meeting on October 10th, the IPKF commenced its operation code-named Pawan on the night of 11/12 October.

THE BATTLE

Jaffna University (JU) was the tactical headquarters of the LTTE. The Indian military leadership planned a quick commando raid to round up the leadership and thus cut short the Battle for Jaffna. The JU area was extremely built up. From the air the city was packed with the red & green of tiled roofs and palm trees. There were just two open patches, a football field and a smaller playground.

The plan was to land a company of 70 men from 10 Para Cdo. to secure the football field. A second wave was to follow with a company of the 13th Sikh LI. If all went to plan the heliborne troops would be linked with troops coming by land. But unknown to the IPKF, the LTTE had intercepted IPKF radio communications and knew the plans. It had sighted the landing zone and was waiting. The first wave of Mi-8 flew in and began disgorging the Para Cdos. They immediately came under heavy fire especially from 0.50 machine guns. The LTTE had the range and position right.

Sepoy Lok Ram recounted, "We thought everything was fine but as we were sliding out of the helicopter we came under heavy fire from all sides. It was an impossible situation, as people would come out of the houses fire at us and disappear right back. There were gunmen on tree tops including coconut trees. Since we were ordered not to use heavy weapons it was impossible to advance. We were fighting an enemy we could not even see."

What followed is the most painful story of the Battle of Jaffna. In the dark with heavy machine gun fire the second wave of choppers brought in a platoon of Sikh LI and landed on the other smaller playground. This was a few yards from the Jaffna University but is separated by several lanes of booby trapped buildings. The Sikhs soon realized something was wrong as they landed smack on the LTTE's battlements. Bullets rained on them.

The three helicopters were hit and pilots barely managed to nurse them back to Palaly. Their grim assessment: The platoon was likely to be wiped out as would any reinforcements. The commanders made the devil's choice: leave the platoon to its fate.

Fate was hopelessly cruel to the young commander of the platoon, Major Birendra Singh. The first man to get hit on landing was the radioman. This severed contact from Palaly. They could reach the commandos on short range walkie talkies. The commandos asked him to join them. But like a good infantryman he waited for the rest of his company. Little did he know that it was not coming. And by the time he knew he was encircled.

The first assault came at dawn. The troops fought valiantly and repelled it. As more assaults were launched the situation became grim. Each assault left them with less men and ammunition. Finally at 11:30 a.m. on October 12th, with the last bullet fired the troops led a bayonet charge. They were cut down to the last man but one. That man, Sepoy Gora Singh, was taken POW and later released. Sepoy Singh helped to reconstruct one of the most poignant battles in the history of the Indian Army.

For the LTTE this was a morale booster. The Sikhs were stripped of their weapons, uniform and equipment. Their bare bodies were displayed at the nearby Nagaraja Vihar temple and then burnt with a barrel of oil. The battle field was littered with pieces of Sikh LI's uniforms and equipment along with thousands of.50 MG shells. Meanwhile the commandos were still holding out. Their commander, Lt. Col. Dalbir Singh, led a rescue mission with three T-72 tanks. The roads were hopelessly booby trapped. The commander of the tank group, Major Anil Kaul, improvised brilliantly. Knowing the rail tracks passed behind Jaffna University, he drove his tanks on the Palaly-Jaffna rail line. Passing through the narrow lanes, an RPG-7 fired on him, hitting the turret. The explosion severed his wedding ring finger. Splinters hit him in the eye and arm. His men put him on morphine and they fought their way to the Para Cdos. A little later the 4/5 Gorkhas and remainder of the 13 Sikh LI linked up.

The Para Cdos superior training saved the day. They conserved ammo and even picked up all their dead and weapons. For 18 hours they prayed and fought. The LTTE leadership came perilously close to getting wiped out. It's Chief, Prabhakaran, was injured in the foot. The 13 Sikh LI now holds a special Ardas & Akhand Panth on October 12th every year to honour their 30 lonely and gusty comrades on the brutal killing fields of Jaffna University.

Fallen members of the Jaffna Raid

13 Sikh Light Infantry	10 Para Cdo
Major Birendra Singh	Naik Babu Lal
Subedar Sampuran Singh, VrC	Naik Ganga Ram, VrC
Havildar Ajit Singh	Naik Lakhmi Singh
Havildar Swaran Singh, SM	Naik Umesh Pandey
Havildar Kashmir Singh, SM	Naik Manohar Singh Rathore
Lance Havildar Sher Singh, SM	Paratrooper Manuwa Kujur
Naik Surjit Singh	-
Naik Gurmail Singh	-
Naik Mukhtiar Singh	-
Naik Satwinder Singh	-
Lance Naik Hira Singh	-
Lance Naik Manjit Singh	-
Lance Naik Darshan Singh, SM	-
Sepoy Lal Singh	-
Sepoy Ranjit Singh	-
Sepoy Kuldip Singh, VrC	-
Sepoy Jarnail Singh	-
Sepoy Sohan Singh	-
Sepoy Gurdial Singh	

Sepoy Gurbax Singh -
Sepoy Gurnam Singh -
Sepoy Satnam Singh -
Sepoy Joginder Singh -
Sepoy Sakinder Singh -
Sepoy Bakshish Singh -
Sepoy Somnath Singh -
Sepoy Harjinder Singh -
Sepoy Sukhwant Singh, VrC -
Sepoy Sukhwinder Singh -

-SPECIAL FORCES IN SRI LANKA

At the signing of the Indo-Sri Lanka accord, an Indian Peace Keeping Force was sent to help in the disarming of the Tamil militants and oversee a ceasefire. Amongst the first troops to land as part of the IPKF, was the 10 Para Commando. This was the beginning of the long involvement of Special Forces in the Sri Lankan conflict. The Para Commandos were also the last unit to withdraw from the island.

10 Para Commando is attached to the Western Command, and was optimised for Desert Operations in Rajasthan. It has been also referred to as Desert Scorpions. However like all elite troops, they would soon adapt to the rigours of urban combat and jungle warfare thrust upon by the LTTE. The first incident for 10 Para Commando would be a sign of the problems ahead. As the accord was souring, a five-man, unarmed Para Commando unit, out to pick up rations was surrounded by the LTTE in the market place. The men were lynched publicly, by neck lacing (have burning tires placed around their necks).When the inevitable fighting started, 10 Para Commando spearheaded many of the thrusts. A company of Para Commandos were involved in a heli-borne assault to capture the LTTE leadership in Jaffna University. Unaware that their radio communications were monitored, the commandos flew in Mi-8s and landed on a soccer field. They were immediately pinned down

by a hail of gunfire. 6 commandos were killed instantly. The commandos knew that further helicopter sorties were impossible. They collected their dead and fanned out towards the objective. But in the booby trapped alleys of Jaffna University it proved to be a difficult task. As daylight approached, they came under observed fire and broke of contact. Observing excellent fire discipline and battle craft they kept the LTTE at bay till a column of tanks with their CO, Lt. Col. Dalbir Singh, broke through to rescue them.

As the Indian Army realised it was overstretched, it paused to build up. Among the units flown in were the 5th Para Btn. However its deployment was marked by confusion. It was initially assigned to the 18th Brigade, then shifted to 72nd Brigade before being reassigned a week later to 18th Brigade. Consequently both brigades could not use the resources properly. After the Jaffna operations, 5th Para shifted to the East while 10th Para Commando was in the Jaffna area.

Slowly the nature of operations shifted from elite infantry to true special forces operations. The advantage of using Special Forces in quick raids sunk in and subsequently a Special Forces HQ was formed to control all special forces in the theatre. 10 Para Commando made a heli-borne assault in the town of Moolai in November. 25 LTTE men were killed and a large quantity of arms seized.

The Para battalions continued to rotate to give the other units combat experience. A 12-man unit was also stationed in Colombo to provide security to the Indian mission. 9 Para Commando replaced 10 Para Commando in early 1988. It conducted a series of air assaults in the coastal swamps around Mullaittivu.

While the Paras did participate in the grand operations, involving multiple battalions, it was in small strike units when they provided spectacular successes. However various deficiencies were thrown up, some which could be addressed while others had to be addressed in the future.

Initially the Paras were used as infantry and tended to make the same mistake of seeking security in large numbers. Once the small unit value was realised, there was a dramatic improvement in operations. Small units would go out to set ambushes. In order to go native, they would be barefoot or wear slippers like the LTTE personnel. But in spite of all this their ability to operate for prolonged periods was limited. One of the main problems was water. The few fresh water resources in the deep forests was either booby trapped or poisoned by the LTTE. This meant carrying your own water.

Perhaps this necessitates the need for a elite jungle warfare unit, capable of sending five-man sections in the jungle to live of the land for prolonged period of times. Another need was for them to have their own helicopters. In addition the individual weapons and ancillary equipment were bulky and needed to lightened considerably. On the midnight of 21 October 1987, an Indian Navy destroyer moored 5 miles outside Jaffna Harbour. 18 men slipped over the sides into two Gemini motorised assault craft.

Clad in black wet suits with light sub machine guns, underwater explosives and daggers strapped to their sides they were a deadly lot. Each Gemini craft towed a wooden raft strapped with more explosives.

The target: the narrow & heavily mined channel leading to the Guru Nagar jetty, the hub of LTTE supplies to Jaffna city. In addition to the booby traps, LTTE snipers and machine guns overlooked the channel from high rise building around it.

The journey took three painstaking hours as they had to pause to unhook the mines, every few, now & then. Once in sight they switched to the wooden rafts and paddled so that noise of the Gemini craft would not give them away.

One team attached explosives to the jetty while the other sorted the LTTE's Yamaha motor equipped 35 knot speed boats. While placing explosives on the boats they were spotted and came under a hail of machine gun fire. They fired back at the tell tale flashes. Within five minutes the 2 Gemini craft roared back into the harbour and opened up covering fire.

By dawn, the 18 men were back on their mother ship with no casualties. This was the second mission of the newest special force of the Indian Armed Forces, the Navy's Indian Special Marine Force. Patterned & initially trained after the US Navy Seals, they soon proved capable of taking any mission on land, air or sea. Their debut occurred a few days before, when they were air dropped in the beleaguered Jaffna Fort. With the help of 10 Para Commando, they broke out and cleared the heavily-mined Navanturai Coastal Road, all the time under constant fire from roof tops and sniper positions. This allowed the crucial link up between 1 Maratha Light Infantry in the fort and the advancing elements of 41st Brigade.

Three days after the Jaffna lagoon raid they were back to destroy the remaining boats. This time they swam for more than a mile under water to reach their targets. Under fire they suffered a few wounds but managed to destroy the remaining boats. Lt. Arvind Singh in charge of all three raids was awarded the MVC (Maha Vir Chakra) for his outstanding performance. Throughout the IPKF operations, the IMSF was used to launch raids in the areas bordering the lagoons.

The IPKF operations gave the first opportunity to use special forces to their full potential. The war against the LTTE required a combination of stealth, surprise, speed and innovation which the special forces could offer. However a combination of factors from lack of good intelligence, paucity of equipment for independent operations, poor personal equipment and initially the fear of failure, prevented them from being very successful. The last is especially pertinent.

Initially there was a tendency not to operate in small units because of the possibility of getting wiped out by a rebel unit and the disgrace that it would bring to the regiment. But as the going got tough, small unit raids were launched on specific intelligence and paid rich dividends. More importantly the experience would come in handy in the future, when low intensity war in Kashmir, escalated to dramatic proportions in the mid-90s.

GENERAL B.C. JOSHI, PVSM, AVSM, ADC
COAS, 30 June 1993-19 November 1994
Armoured Corps, 64 CAV and 2 Lancers

General Bipin Chandra Joshi assumed charge of the Indian Army, as the 17th Chief of Army Staff, on 30 June 1993. Commissioned in the Indian Army in December 1954, into the Armoured Corps, he has held important command and staff appointments which include staff officer with the UN Force in Gaza, Brigadier General Staff at a Corps Headquarters and as a Military Advisor in Australia from May 1973 to October 1976. He is credited with raising the Rashtriya Rifles in 1990 to fight an insurgency in Kashmir. He commanded an Armoured Regiment in the Western Sector during the 1971 Indo-Pak War. He has also commanded an Independent Armoured Brigade and an Infantry Division. He commanded a Corps in the Eastern Sector and was also the General Officer Commanding-in-Chief, Southern Command. He has also held the appointment of Additional Director General of Perspective Planning (ADGPP) and Director General Military Operations (DGMO) at the Army HQ.

He had three tenures as an Instructor in the Armoured Corps Centre & School and was also a Directing Staff in the College of Combat, Mhow. General Joshi has been a recipient of the Param Vishisht Seva Medal (PVSM) and the Ati Vishisht Seva Medal (AVSM) for distinguished service of the most exceptional order. He passed away on 19 November 1994, at a military hospital in New Delhi at the age of 59 as a result of a heart attack. He had complained of chest pain after he played a round of golf that morning and died soon afterward in the hospital. He was due to retire in December 1995.

GENERAL SHANKAR ROYCHOWDHURY, PVSM, ADC
COAS, 22 Nov 1994-30 Sept 1997
Armoured Corps, 20 Lancers

General Shankar Roychowdhury assumed charge of the Indian Army, as the 18th Chief of Army Staff, on 22 November 1994.

Born in Calcutta on 06 September 1937, he was educated at St. Xavier's School, Calcutta, Allen Memorial School and St. George's College, Mussoorie. He entered the Joint Services Wing of the Armed Services in 1953 as a Cadet. He was commissioned into the 20th Lancers of the Armoured Corps from the Indian Military Academy (IMA), Dehra Dun on 09 June 1957.

He saw action at the Chamb-Jaurian sector in the 1965 Indo-Pak War and in the Jessore and Khulna during the 1971 Liberation War.

He commanded 20 Lancers from 1974-76, an Independent Armoured Brigade from December 1980 to July 1983 and an Armoured Division from May 1988 to May 1990. He subsequently commanded 16 Corps in Jammu and Kashmir from 1991-92. He is a graduate of the Defence Services Staff College (DSSC) and held several staff and instructional appointments, including that of Director General Combat Vehicles dealing with the Arjun MBT.

He was awarded the Param Vishisht Seva Medal for distinguished service and valuable contribution. He took over as General Officer Commanding–in-Chief, Army Training Command (ARTRAC) in August 1992. He became the Army Chief upon the untimely death of his predecessor, General B.C. Joshi, on 22 November 1994. He retired from the Indian Army on September 1997, after completing 40 years of distinguished service to the nation. Post retirement, he became a member of the Rajya Sabha and has highlighted defence related issues with great passion & vigour in Parliament.

Investing in the armed forces is like paying premium for insurance. It pinches while paying, but the insurance is what saves you when the disaster strikes-General Shankar Roychowdhury

GENERAL V.P. MALIK, PVSM, AVSM, ADC
COAS, 30 Sept 1997-30 Sept 2000
Infantry, Sikh Light Infantry

General Ved Prakash Malik assumed charge of the Indian Army, as the 19th Chief of Army Staff, on 30 September 1997.

Born on 01 November 1939 at Dera Ismail Khan (present-day Pakistan), he was commissioned into the Sikh Light Infantry on 07 June 1959. He saw action in the 1962 Indo-China border conflict in the Ladakh sector. He commanded the 10th Sikh LI on the Indo-China border and played an active role in counter-insurgency operations in Nagaland from 1974 to 1977.

His other assignments include Instructor in the Senior Command Wing at the College of Combat from 1977-78, Joint Planning Staff in the Military Wing of the Cabinet Secretariat from 1979-80, Deputy Brigade Commander of an Infantry Brigade from 1980-82, Colonel of an Infantry Division from 1982-83 and Commander of the 162nd Infantry Brigade in Jammu & Kashmir from April 1983 to December 1985, where he earned the Ati Vishist Seva Medal (AVSM).

In 1986 he attended the National Defence College (NDC) in New Delhi. He served as Deputy Director General of Military Operations from 1987 to 1990 during which he dealt with operational plans for the defence of northern borders as also two international operations-IPKF (Indian Peace Keeping Force) operations in Sri Lanka and Operation Cactus in Maldives. In mid-1989, he was appointed GOC-in-C of the 8th Mountain Division which was initially deployed in counter-insurgency operations in NEFA (North East Frontier Agency). He saw service in J&K again to conduct COIN operations in the Kashmir Valley from December 1989 till May 1991.

He also held the office of Additional Director General of Operational Logistics, at Army HQ from 1991 to mid-1992. Along with operational responsibility of the Indo-Pak border, he commanded XI Corps in Punjab from August 1992 till March 1994 during which he over saw anti-militant operations.

A graduate of DSSC, General Malik was posted to Military Ops. Directorate at Army HQ in the section dealing with COIN operations. He attended the Higher Command Course at the College of Combat, Mhow and was posted as an instructor in the Tactical Wing at the

Infantry School, also in Mhow. As Commandant of the Defence Services Staff College (DSSC) in Wellington, from April 1994 to July 1995, he was instrumental in updating the syllabus and computerisation of staff work. In July 1995, he was appointed GOC-in-C Southern Command before being shifted to Army HQ in New Delhi as the Vice-Chief of Army Staff (VCOAS) in August 1996. He was decorated with the Param Vishist Seva Medal (PVSM) by the President of India, in the 1996 Republic Day Parade.

General Malik assumed the charge of Indian Army on 30 September 1997 and concurrently with the appointment, he took over as Chairman of the Chiefs of Staff Committee with effect from 01 January 1999. He coordinated and oversaw the planning & execution of Operation Vijay to successfully defeat Pakistan's attempted intrusion in the Kargil sector during May to July 1999.

He was felicitated with the *Excellence in Leadership* award by the Atur Foundation of Pune and also the *Distinguished Fellowship* of the Institute of Directors, New Delhi in 1999. The Doon Citizens' Council gave him the *Pride of the Nation* award in July 2000. He was Colonel of the Sikh LI from 1990 to 1998 and continues to be Honorary Colonel of the regiment for life. He retired on 30 September 2000, after completing more than 41 years of distinguished military service. During his tenure he was the Colonel of the Sikh Light Infantry.

General has settled in Panchkula, near Chandigarh and since retirement, keeps himself engaged spreading awareness and sharing his views on India's national security challenges and international relations, in India and abroad. He was a member of the National Security Advisory Board (NSAB) for two years.

Currently, he is an independent director on the board of some well-known private sector companies and advisor to various foundations and trusts. He has authored and edited various defence related books and has written chapters and articles for several other security-related books.

GENERAL S. PADMANABHAN, PVSM, AVSM, ADC

COAS, 30 Sept 2000-31 Dec 2002

Regiment of Artillery

General Sundararajan Padmanabhan assumed charge of the Indian Army, as the 20th Chief of Army Staff, on 30 September 2000. Born in Trivandrum, Kerala on 05 December 1940, he is an alumnus of the prestigious Rashtriya Indian Military College (RIMC), Dehra Dun and the National Defence Academy (NDA), Khadakwasla in Pune. He was commissioned into the Regiment of Artillery after graduating from the Indian Military Academy (IMA) on 13 December 1959.

His illustrious career included several prestigious command, staff and instructional postings, besides having participated in numerous operations. He is a graduate of the Defence Services Staff College (DSSC) at Wellington in 1973 and the National Defence College (NDC) at New Delhi. He commanded an Independent Light Battery from August 1975 to July 1976 and later on commanded the Gazala Mountain Regiment from September 1977 to March 1980. This mountain regiment is one of the oldest artillery regiments of the Indian Army and has participated in several wars.

He served as Instructor Gunnery at the School of Artillery in Deolali, been a Brigade Major of an infantry brigade on its raising and served as Colonel General Staff of a Mountain Division from January 1983 to May 1985, where he was awarded the Vishisht Seva Medal (VSM). He has also spent two tenures as Instructor at the IMA. Within army circles, he is affectionately known as Paddy. He commanded an Independent Artillery Brigade and a Mountain Brigade before attending the prestigious NDC course at Delhi.

He commanded an Infantry Brigade from December 1988 to February 1991 at Ranchi, Bihar and Punjab and was then appointed as the General Officer Commanding of an Infantry Division in Punjab from March 1991 to August 1992. He served as Chief of Staff, 3 Corps from September 1992 to June 1993. After his promotion to Lieutenant General, he was commander of the 15

Corps in the Kashmir valley from July 1993 to February 1995. It was during his tenure as the 15 Corps Commander, that the Army made big gains over the militants in Kashmir and could even scale down its operations. He was awarded the Ati Vishisht Seva Medal (AVSM) for his services as the 15 Corps Commander.

General Padmanabhan held the appointment of Director General Military Intelligence (DGMI) after the successful culmination of which, he took over as the GOC of the Northern Command at Udhampur on 01 September 1996. Before being appointed as the Chief of Army Staff, he was the GOC of Southern Command. He retired on 31 December 2002, after completing more than 43 years of distinguished military service. He is a prolific writer and has even authored two books. He presently resides in Chennai.

4

Indian Air Force

The Indian Air Force is the air arm of the armed forces of India. Its primary responsibility is to secure and preserve peace within Indian airspace, and to conduct aerial warfare during a conflict. The Indian Air Force was officially established on October 8, 1932 as an auxiliary air force of the Indian Empire. In 1945, King George VI conferred the prefix *Royal* in recognition of its services during the World War II. After India achieved its independence from the United Kingdom in 1947, the Royal Indian Air Force served the Union of India and after India became a republic in 1950, the prefix was dropped.

Since independence the Air Force had been involved in several conflicts with neighbouring Pakistan and in 1962 with China. In 1961, the IAF played a crucial role during liberation of Goa and in 1971, during the Bangladesh liberation war. Apart from combat operations during war, the IAF is often called upon during natural disasters to provide relief to victims.

The President of India is Commander in Chief of the Air Force. Chief of the air staff, an Air Chief Marshal, is the commander of the Air Force. In 2002, for his service during the 1965 Indo-Pakistan war as Air Chief Marshal, Arjan Singh was given the honorary rank of Marshal of the Air Force. Officers holding this rank never retires and is the ceremonial chief of the Airforce. Approximately 170,000 men and women serve in the Air Force and with over 1,500 aircraft in active service, it is the world's fourth largest. Other than the officers and airmen, the IAF employs a large number of non-combat and civilian personnel for day to day affairs.

Large number of aircraft in the Air Force's inventory are aging Soviet era MiGs and due to their ongoing decomissioning, the IAF fleet is shrinking. Therefore, in recent years, the IAF has undertaken an ambitious expansion and modernization program. With lengthy delays in the development of an indigenous replacement fighter, Indian launched the Multi-Role Combat Aircraft (MRCA) program. Under this program the IAF plans to induct 126 fighter jets at a cost of US$12 billion. India is increasingly projecting its power beyond South Asia. To assist its foreign policy, Government of India has authorized to increase the force level from 39.5 squadrons in present to 42 squadrons in 2022.

MISSION

Mission of the air force is defined by the Armed Forces Act of 1947, Constitution of India and the Air Force Act of 1950, in the aerial battlespace, as: *Defence of India and every part thereof including preparation for defence and all such acts as may be conducive in times of war to its prosecution and after its termination to effective demobilisation.* Moreover, the air force, along with the other branches of the armed forces, can assist local and state governments; if assistance is sought by such government during natural disasters and for maintaining internal security.

History

The Indian Air Force was established, as an auxiliary air force, when the Indian Air Force act was passed on October 8, 1932. On April 1, 1933, The IAF commissioned its first squadron, No.1 Squadron, with four Westland Wapiti biplanes and five Indian pilots. The Indian pilots were led by Flt Lt (later Air Vice Marshal) Cecil Bouchier. Until 1938, No. 1 Squadron remained the only squadron of the IAF even though two more flights were added. During the Second World War, the Air Force had grown to 7 squadrons in 1943 and to nine squadrons in 1945. In recognition of the crucial role played by the IAF, King George VI conferred it the prefix *Royal* in 1945.

After Indian independence in 1947, Royal Indian Air Force (RIAF) was bifurcated. Three of the ten operational squadrons and facilities located within the borders of Pakistan were transferred to Royal Pakistan Air Force.

In 1947, when a conflict broke out over the control of erstwhile principality of Jammu & Kashmir, the Maharaja of the state decided to accede India in order to receive military help. The day after instrument of accession was signed, the RIAF was called upon to mobilize armed troops into the war-zone. This led to the eruption of full scale war between India and Pakistan without a formal declaration. During the war, the RIAF did not engage Pakistan Air Force in air-to-air combat; however, provided effective transport and close air support to the Indian troops. When India became a Republic in 1950, *Royal* title was dropped to become the Indian Air Force.

In 1960, when Belgium's 75-year colonial rule of the Congo ended abruptly, widespread violence and rebellion engulfed the nation. IAF aircraft arrived in Congo to support United Nations Operation in the Congo and started undertaking operational missions in November. The unit remained there until 1966, when the UN mission ended.

During the Sino-Indian War of 1962, India's military planners failed to deploy and effectively use the IAF against the invading Chinese forces. Three years after the Sino-Indian conflict, India went to war with Pakistan again over Kashmir. Learning from the experiences of the Sino-Indian war, India decided to use its air force extensively during the war. This was the first time the IAF actively engaged an enemy air force. However, instead of providing close air support to the Indian Army, the IAF carried out independent raid missions against Pakistani Air Force (PAF) bases. These bases were situated deep inside the Pakistani territory, making IAF fighters vulnerable to anti-aircraft fire. During the course of the conflict, the

PAF enjoyed qualitative superiority over the IAF because most of the jets in IAF's fleet were of World War II-vintage. Despite this, the IAF was able to prevent the PAF from gaining air superiority over conflict zones. By the time the conflict had ended, Pakistan claimed to have shot down 113 IAF aircraft while the Indians claimed that 73 PAF aircraft were downed. More than 60% of IAF's air combat losses took place during the disastrous battles over Kalaikunda and Pathankot.

After the 1965 war, the IAF underwent a series of changes. In 1966, the Para Commandos regiment was created. With an intention of increasing its logistics supply and rescue operations ability, the IAF inducted 72 Avro 748s which were built by Hindustan Aeronautics (HAL) under license from Avro. India started to lay more stress on indigenous manufacture of fighter aircraft. A total of 147 HAL HF-24 Marut, designed by the famed German aerospace engineer Kurt Tank, were inducted into the air force. HAL also started working on a new improved version of the Folland Gnat, known as HAL Ajeet. During 1960s, the IAF also started inducting MiG-21 and Sukhoi Su-7 fighters which had a top speed of Mach 2. The induction of these advanced fighter jets was the beginning of close collaboration between India and the Soviet Union.

By late 1971, the intensification of the independence movement in erstwhile East Pakistan, war was inevitable. On November 22, 1971, 10 days before the start of a full-scale war, four Pakistani Air Force (PAF) F-86 Sabre jets attacked Indian and Mukti Bahini positions near the international border. Three of the 4 PAF Sabres were shot down by IAF's Folland Gnats.On December 3, India formally declared war against Pakistan following massive preemptive strikes by the PAF against Indian Air Force installations in Srinagar, Ambala, Sirsa, Halwara and Jodhpur. But the plan failed as the IAF had anticipated such a move and no major losses were suffered. The Indian Air Force was quick to respond to Pakistani air-strikes, following which the PAF carried out mostly defensive sorties. Within the first two weeks, the IAF had carried out almost 2,000 sorties over East Pakistan and also provided close air support to the advancing Indian Army. IAF also assisted the Indian Navy in its operations against the Pakistani Navy and Maritime Security Agency in the Bay of Bengal and Arabian Sea. On the western front, the IAF destroyed 29 Pakistani tanks, 40 APCs and a railway train during the famed battle of Longewala. The IAF pursued strategic bombing of West Pakistan by carring out raids on oil installations in Karachi, the Mangla Dam and a gas plant in Sindh. Similar strategy was also deployed in East Pakistan and as the IAF achieved complete air superiority on the eastern front, the ordnance factories, runways, and other vital areas of East Pakistan were severely damaged. By the time Pakistani forces surrendered, the IAF claimed that 94 PAF aircraft, including 54 F-86 Sabres. The IAF had flown over 6,000 sorties on both East and West fronts; including sorties by transport aircraft and helicopters. Towards the end of the war, IAF's transport planes dropped leaflets over Dhaka urging the Pakistani forces to surrender, demoralizing Pakistani troops in East Pakistan. The Indian Army too acknowledged the immense role which the IAF played towards a speedy, decisive and favorable end to the conflict.

In 1984, India launched Operation Meghdoot to capture the Siachen Glacier, in the contested Kashmir region. IAF's special helicopters, capable of flying in extremely thin air, airlifted hundreds of Indian troops to Siachen. Launched on April 13, 1984, this military operation was unique because of Siachen's inhospitable terrain and climate. The military action was successful, given the fact that under a previous agreement, neither Pakistan nor India had stationed any personnel in the area. The Indian forces, facing no odds, took control over most of the heights on the glacier.

On May 20, 1999, during Kargil conflict, the Indian Air Force was called in to provide close air support to the Indian Army. Due to Kashmir's high altitude and rigid terrain, the IAF initially expressed its reservations to deploy the slow-moving Mil Mi-8/17 helicopters which had a service ceiling of 10,000 feet. These concerns materialized when the Pakistani forces shot down an IAF Mi-8 helicopter and two fighter jets, MiG-21 and MiG-27, that had reportedly strayed into Pakistan's airspace. After the initial setbacks, the IAF deployed the Mirage 2000 which not only had better defense equipment compared to the MiGs, but also gave IAF the ability to carry out aerial raids at night. The Mirages successfully targeted enemy camps and logistic bases in Kargil and within days, their supply lines were severely disrupted. The IAF also deployed its radars and the MiG-29 fighter jets in vast numbers to keep check on Pakistani military movements across the border. The MiG-29s were also used extensively to provide fighter escort to the Mirage 2000. At the height of the conflict, the IAF conducting over forty sorties daily over the Kargil region. The IAF's operations in Kargil not only boosted the morale of the Indian Army, but also paved the way for the early recapture of Muntho Dhalo and Tiger Hill. By July 26, the Indian forces had successfully liberated Kargil from Pakistani forces and Islamist militants. On August 10, 1999, IAF MiG-21s intercepted a Pakistan Navy Breguet Atlantic which was flying over the disputed region of Sir Creek. The aircraft was shot down killing all 16 Pakistani Navy personnel on board. Indian experts believe that the Atlantic was on a *probing mission* to gather information on IAF air defence.

Since late 1990s, the Air Force is modernizing its fleet to counter challenges in the new century. The fleet size of the IAF has decreesed during this period due to the retirement of old aircraft. As new aircraft enter service and numbers recover, the IAF plans to have a fleet of 42 squadrons.

STRUCTURE OF THE IAF

The President of India is the Supreme Commander of all Indian armed forces and by virtue of that fact is the notional Commander of the Air force. India's Ministry of Defence under the Defence Minister oversees the Air Force, by way of direct civilian leadership. The Prime Minister and the National Security Council provide indirect leadership by shaping government security policy. A Chief of the Air Staff in the rank of Air Chief Marshal commands Air Head Quarters and provides military leadership. He is assisted by six officers: a Vice Chief of the Air Staff, a Deputy Chief of the Air Staff, the Air Officer in Charge of Administration, the Air Officer in Charge of Personnel, the Air Officer in Charge of Maintenance, and the Inspector General of Flight Safety. In January 2002, the government conferred the rank of Marshal of the Air Force on Arjan Singh making him the first and only *Five Star* rank officer with the Indian Air Force and ceremonial chief of the air force.

Commands and Structure

The Indian Air Force is divided into five operational and two functional commands.

Operational Commands	Functional Commands
• Central Air Command (CAC), headquartered at Allahabad, Uttar Pradesh • Eastern Air Command (EAC), headquartered at Shillong, Meghalaya • Southern Air Command (SAC), headquartered at Thiruvananthapuram, Kerala • South Western Air Command (SWAC), headquartered at Gandhinagar, Gujarat • Western Air Command (WAC), headquartered at Subroto Park, New Delhi	• Training Command (TC), headquartered at Bangalore, Karnataka • Maintenance Command (MC), headquartered at Nagpur, Maharashtra

Each Command is headed by an Air Officer Commanding-in-Chief in the rank of Air Marshal. The purpose of an operational command is to conduct military operations using aircraft within its area of responsibility whereas the responsibility of functional commands is to maintain combat readiness. Aside from the Training Command at Bangalore, the center for primary flight training is located at the Air Force Academy in Hyderabad, Andhra Pradesh, followed by operational training at various other schools. Advanced officer training for command positions is also conducted at the Defence Services Staff College; specialized advanced flight training schools are located at Bidar, Karnataka, and Hakimpet, Andhra Pradesh (also the location for helicopter training). Technical schools are found at a number of other locations.

Bases

The IAF operates over 60 air bases, with more being built or planned. They are grouped under one of the five Regional Air Commands.

Western Air Command is the largest Air Command. It operates 16 Air bases from Punjab to Uttar Pradesh. Eastern Air Command operates 15 Air bases in Eastern and North-eastern India: Central Air Command operates 7 Air Bases in Madhya Pradesh and surrounding states of central India. Southern Air Command, a strategically important Air command, in line with India's latest doctrine of protecting the vital shipping routes. It operates 9 Air bases in Southern India and 2 in the Andaman and Nicobar Islands. South Western Air Command is the front line of defence against Pakistan, this important Command operates 12 air bases in Gujarat, Maharashtra and Rajasthan.

Wings

Wing is a formation intermediate between Command and Squadron. A Wing generally consists of two or three IAF Squadrons and Helicopter Units and along with the Forward Base Support Units (FBSU). FBSUs do not have or host any Squadrons or Helicopter units but act as transit airbases for routine operations. In times of war, they can become full fledged air bases playing host to various Squadrons. In all, about 47 Wings and 19 FBSUs make up the IAF.

Squadrons

Squadrons are the field units and formations attached to static locations. In other words, a Flying Squadron is a sub-unit of an air force station which carries out the primary task of the IAF. All fighter squadrons are headed by the Commanding Officer with the rank of Wing Commander. Some Transport squadrons and Helicopter Units are headed by the Commanding Officer with the rank of Group Captain.

Within this formation structure, IAF has several service branches for day to day operations. They are:

Flying Branch	Technical Branch	Ground Branch
• Flying	• Engineering • Logistics	• Administration • Accounts • Education • Medical & Dental • Meteorological

The rank structure of IAF is based on the rank structure of the Royal Air Force. The Air Force has a strength of 170,000 personnel. The highest rank attainable in the IAF is Marshal of the Indian Air Force conferred by the President of India after exceptional service during wartime. MIAF Arjan Singh is the only officer to have achieved this rank. The head of the Indian Air Force is the Chief of the Air Staff. The Air Chief Marshal is Fali Homi Major. The members of the IAF are commissioned or enlisted in one of the service branches.

Officer

Anyone holding the citizenship of India can apply to be a an officer in the Air Force as long as they satisfy the eligibility eligibility criteria. There are four entry points to become an officer. Male applicants, who are between the ages of 16½ and 19 and have passed high school graduation, can apply at the *Intermediate* level. Men and women applicants, who have graduated from college (3 year course) and are between the ages of 18 and 28 years, can apply at the *Graduate* level. Graduates of engineering colleges can apply at the *Engineer* level if they are between the ages of 18 and 28 years. The age limit for the flying and ground duty branch is 23 years of age and for technical branch is 28 years of age.

After completing master's degree, men and women between the ages of 18 and 28 years can apply at the *Post Graduate* level. Post graduate applicants do not qualify for the flying branch. For technical branch the age limit is 28 years and for the ground duty branch is 25. At the time of application all applicant must be single. From the applicants the IAF selects candidates for officer training. After complition of training, the applicant becomes an officer.

Airmen

The duty of an airman in the Indian Air Force is to make sure that all the air and ground operations run smoothly. From operating Air Defence systems to fitting missiles, they are involved in all activities of an air base and give support to various technical and non technical jobs.

The recruitment of personnel below officer rank as an Airman in the IAF is conducted through All India Selection Tests and Recruitment Rallies. All India Selection Tests are conducted at the Airmen Selection Centres (ASCs) located all over India. There are 14 Airmen Selection Centers, spread all over India. These centres are under the direct functional control of Central Airmen Selection Board (CASB) with administrative control and support by respective commands. The role of CASB is to carry out selection and enrolment of airmen from the Airmen Selection Centers for their respective commands.

Candidates initially take a written test at the time of application. Candidates passing the written test undergo physical fitness test, an interview, conducted in English, and medical examination. Candidates for training are selected from individuals passing the battery of tests based on their performance. Upon completion of training, an induvidual becomes an Airman.

Some MWOs and WOs are granted honorary commission in the last year of their service as an honorary Flying Officer or Flight Lieutenant before retiring from the service.

NON COMBATANTS ENROLLED AND CIVILIANS

Non Combatants Enrolled (NCs(E)) were established in British India as personal assistants to the officer class, and are equivalent to the *orderly* or *sahayak* of the Indian Army.

Almost all the commands have some percentage of civilian strength which are Central Govt. Employees. These are regular ranks which are prevalent in ministries. They are usually not posted outside their stations and are helpful in administration and usual office and technical work. More than 250 different designations exists.

IAF Aircraft

The Indian Air Force has a strength of over 1,500 aircraft. Most of the IAF's aircraft are of Soviet/Russian origin. The Air Force also operates some aircraft from Britain and France. Hindustan Aeronautics Limited under licence produce some of the Russian and British aircraft in India. The exact number of aircraft in service with the Indian Air Force cannot be determined with precision from open sources. Apparently reliable sources provide notably divergent estimates for a variety of high-visibility aircraft.

Air superiority and multi-role combat aircraft:

- IAF Su-30 MKI
- IAF Jaguar
- Il-78 landing at Lajes, Portugal

These aircraft are primarily for air defence and superiority purposes. However, most of them have significant strike, offensive support capabilities. The IAF possesses several multi-role fighter jets that perform these functions. The Sukhoi Su-30MKI is the IAF's prime air superiority fighter. The Su-30K variant was first acquired in 1996. In 1996, the IAF signed a US$1.6 billion contract with Russia for the supply of 50 Su-30MKIs and the technology transfer and license to manufacture 140 Su-30MKIs by Hindustan Aeronautics Limited. The twin seater, multi-role fighter has a maximum speed of 2500 km/h (Mach 2.35) and has a service ceiling of 20,000 meters. The aircraft, with one mid-air refueling, can travel as far as 8000 km, making it an effective platform to deliver strategic weapons. In 2007, US$700 million were spent to upgrade IAF's remaining 10 Su-30Ks & 8 SU -30MKs to MKI Std variant and signed a contract for the supply of 40 additional MKIs with Russia.

MiG-29s are dedicated air superiority fighters of the IAF. The MiG-29 (NATO: *Fulcrum*) has a top speed of 2,445 km/h (Mach 2.3) and is armed with a 30 mm cannon along with R-60 & R-27 R missiles. The IAF was began deploying MiG-29 in 1984 and was the second air force to do so. Since their induction, the IAF's MiG-29s have undergone a series of upgrades including more efficient and powerful radar (Zhuk-ME), weapons system and upgraded engine.

Mirage 2000s, capable of flying at 2,500 km/h (Mach 2.35), are the IAF's premier multirole fighter jet. These aircraft can carry a wide range of weaponry including two 30 mm integral cannons, two *Matra Super 530D* medium-range missiles, two *R550 Magic* close combat missiles and various ground attack munitions.

Since 1963, over 450 MiG-21 combat aircraft have been serving the IAF. Most of these MiGs have been upgraded since induction. In 1996, India signed a US$300 million deal with Russia to upgrade 125 MiG-21 *Bis* and a multi-million dollar deal was awarded to Israel's Elta for upgrading the avionics of the MiGs. Due to their frequent crashes, the MiG-21s have been dubbed *flying coffins* by the media. As of 2007, about 250 MiG-21s remain in service with the Indian Air Force and are planned to be replaced by the indigenously-built HAL Tejas starting 2010.

STRIKE, ATTACK AND OFFENSIVE SUPPORT AIRCRAFT

Squadrons of Jaguar and MiG-27 aircraft serve as the IAF's primary ground strike force. The twin-engine Jaguar IB, with a top speed of Mach 1.6, is capable of carrying nuclear weapons. The IAF has 100 Jaguar IS and 8 maritime strike Jaguar IM aircraft. The single-seater MiG-27 carries one GSh-6-30 six-barreled 30 mm cannon, 4000 kg of general-purpose ordnance, SPPU-22 and SPPU-6 gun pods, and various guided air-to-surface missiles. In January 2009,India has successfully completed the upgrade programs on the Air Force's MiG-27 ground attack fighter aircraft. DRDO carried out the avionics upgrades on the fighter aircraft. In the upgraded MiG-27s, the avionics system is built around a modular mission computer termed Core Avionics Computer (CAC). The upgraded ground attack fighters are equipped with Inertial Navigation and Global Positioning System (INGPS) providing accurate navigation during aircraft sorties. To provide more accuracy to the aircraft's weapon systems, accurate ranging sensors such as Laser Designator Pod (LDP) and Laser Ranger and Marked Target Seeker (LRMTS) have been integrated in it also. To improve situational awareness of the pilot during air combat, a digital map generator has been integrated along with a digital video recording system, which helps in mission analysis and debrief support.

RECONNAISSANCE AND AIRBORNE EARLY WARNING AIRCRAFT

In 2004, the IAF ordered 3 IAI Phalcon Airborne Early Warning radar system from Israel Aerospace Industries, which is considered to be the most advanced AEW&C system in the world. The air force will use 3 newly-acquired Ilyushin Il-76 Phalcon as a platform for these radar. In May 2008, India appears to have ordered an additional three Phalcon radar equipped IL-76 from Israel, pushing up the value of the deal from US$1.1 to 1.5 billion. An Indian defense delegation headed by Defense Secretary Vijay Singh, visited Israel in November 2008 to discuss the purchase of the planes and missiles from Israel Aerospace Industries (IAI). It has been reported that India has placed a follow up order for 3 more Phalcon radar equipped IL-76 from Israel at a cost of $1.5 billion, pushing the total number to be acquired up to 6. The first Phalcon arriveed in

India on January 13, 2009 and are expected to be commissioned into service by 2010.

Transport Aircraft

The IAF operates 25 Ilyushin Il-76 for military transport duties such as heavylift, at all operational levels. The Il-76 MD is a strategic air-lifter with a payload of 95,000 lb and a range of over 5,000 km (2,700 nm; 3,100 statute miles). In 2003, the IAF orderd 6 IL-78MKI aircraft from Uzbekistan and are fitted with aerial refueling pods from Israel. India took delivery of the tankers in 2004.

IAF has a fleet of 64 Avro 748 which has a payload of 5,136 kg (11,323 lb) and has a range of 1,715 km (926 nm; 1,066 mi). The air force also operates a fleet of 94 twin-engined turboprop Antonov An-32 and 73 Dornier Do 228 utility aircraft. In an effort to infuse fresh life into its transport fleet, the Indian Air Force will begin an upgrade programme for its Antonov An-32s and Dornier Do 228s in 2009.

Unmanned Aerial Vehicles

The primary role of unmanned aerial vehicles (UAVs) is to provide aerial surveillance and reconnaissance. The IAF operates IAI Malat built Searcher II and Heron UAVs. Israel Aircraft Industries and Aeronautical Development Establishment (ADE). India's leading unmanned aerial vehicle research agency are also jointly developing three new UAVs.

UAVs can also be used as a *pilot-less target aircraft.* HAL *Lakshya,* indigenously-developed pilotless target aircraft, was inducted into the IAF in July 2005. Another UAV, the HAL *Nishant* Remote Piloted Vehicle (RPV) has also been developed, with an endurance of over 3 hours.[92] The UAV can be used for carrying out ground attacks and aerial surveillance.

Helicopters

An important objective of the IAF is to support ground troops by providing air-cover and by transporting men and essential commodities across the battlefield. For this purpose the Air Force maintains a fleet of helicopters. Helicopters in service with the IAF are:

Light Utility	Medium Utility	Heavylift	Attack
• HAL Dhruv • HAL Chetak • HAL Cheetah	• Mi-8 (*Hip*) • Mi-17 (*Hip-H*)	• Mi-26 (*Halo*)	• Mi-25/35 (*Hind*)

On October 15, 2006 India agreed to acquire 80 Mi-17 helicopters from the Russian Federation in a deal worth approximately US$662 million.

Training Aircraft

HPT-32 Deepak is IAF's basic flight training aircraft for cadets. Developed during the late 1970s, it has been in service with the IAF since 1984.

The IAF uses HAL HJT-16 Kiran mk.I for intermediate flight training of cadets and HJT-16 Kiran mk.II provides Stage II flight training. In 2004, the IAF placed an order for 66 BAE Hawk Mk 132 Advanced Jet Trainers in a deal worth over 1 billion GBP. Deliveries began in November, 2007 and induction in February, 2008. Pilot instructors and engineers have already been trained in the UK, and the aircraft is scheduled to replace mk.II. HAL is developing HJT-36 *Sitara* to replace Kiran mk.I.

WEAPONS

Surface to Air Missiles

- Isayev SA-3 Goa: The Indian Air Force is considering upgrading its Pechora SA-3 missiles with Polish help whilst it waits for the Akash. According to Janes Missiles and Rockets (December 2005), the IAF would like to conduct the Newa-SCM upgrade package upgrade to 20 S-125M Pechora-CC systems, using primarily the Tatra 8x8 chassis, which is licence-built in India. Installation on specially adapted heavy equipment trailers or Tatra 8x8 vehicles was studied at the request of the Indian Air Force. It incorporates a new

ZNO-X digital transmitter/receiver block developed by the Przemyslowy Instytut Telekomunikacji (PIT) to replace the original magnetron-based hardware. The unit uses digital technology, including digital frequency synthesis, and has automatic built-in test facilities. While the ZNO-X is an expensive upgrade, it significantly improves system performance. Most of the upgrade work would be done in India, although the core elements of the upgrade would be delivered from Poland.Pechora SAM will be phased out by 2012.

- SA-5 Gammon
- SA-8 Gecko
- SA-10 Grumble
- SA-16 Gimlet - MANPAD

Air to Air Missiles

- Vympel AA-8 Aphid
- Matra Magic 2
- AA-7 Apex
- Matra Super 530
- Vympel AA-10 Alamo
- Vympel AA-11 Archer
- Vympel AA-12 Adder

Air to Surface Missiles

- Zvezda AS-10 Karen
- Aerospatiale AS-30L
- Hawker-Matra Martel Missile
- Kolomna AT-6 Spiral
- Molniya AS-14 Kedge
- Zvezda AS-17 Krypton
- BAe Sea Eagle
- Raduga AS-18 Kazoo

Future Aircraft

- Medium Multi-role Combat Aircraft

The IAF plans to rise the strength of its combat fleet to 42 squadrons by 2022. The Air Force will reach the peak of strength with the induction of the planned Su-30 MKIs, Jaguars, Medium Multi-role Combat Aircraft (M-MRCA), Fifth Generation Fighter Aircraft (FGFA), the Light Combat Aircraft (LCA) and medium combat aircraft (MCA).

The Indian Air Force operates around 250 MiG-21 aircraft. Due to metal fatigue and outdated equipment, many MiG-21s used in training have crashed over the past six years, killing over 50 IAF pilots. Also, they are nearing the end of their service life having been in the IAF for many decades and are being decommissioned at an increasing pace. The IAF initially planned to replace the MiG-21 fleet with indigenously-built HAL Tejas aircraft by 2006. However, the target could not be met due to developmental delays and a US sanction, following the Pokhran-II nuclear tests, which blocked the delivery of GE F404 engines - a crucial component of the LCA.

The Indian Air Force has a requirement for combat aircraft to replace the MiG-21 in service. The Mirage-2000 were considered as a replacement. However, Dassault announced that it has shut down the assembly line of the Mirage-2000. Hence the IAF included the Mig-35, Gripen and F-16 in its itinerary of consideration. This was the first time in the IAF's history that an American aircraft was being considered. Later the number of manufacturers was widened to include heavy-weight aircraft like the F/A-18 Super Hornet, the Eurofighter Typhoon, and Dassault Rafale. In an interview, the then Air Chief of the IAF M. Shahindra Pal Tyagi admitted to allowing heavy-weight aircraft to compete, "to allow more competition".

The limited series production of the indigenous LCA Tejas aircraft is ongoing at Hindustan Aeronautics Limited. The aircraft is supposed to get full operational clearance by December 2010, as the Tejas' development has been accelerated. It is believed that the MRCA's procurement may take a much longer time than Tejas' induction in the IAF, and its subsequent mass production. The air force has issued an Intent (RoI) for procurement of MRCA (Multi Role Combat Aircraft). The following aircraft are participating: Russian MiG-35, French Rafale, European Eurofighter Typhoon, Swedish Gripen and the US F-16IN. Besides the F-16s, the US has also offered the sale of F/A-18E/F Super Hornet combat aircraft. IAF pilots and technicians are familiar with earlier aircraft from MiG and Dassault and would need minimal retraining. Infrastructural and logistical support for maintenance and spares would also be easier for these aircraft compared to the unfamiliar Gripens, F-16s and F/A-18s.

Apart from the 126 multi-role combat aircraft (with an option for another 74 aircraft), 110 Su-30MKI air superiority fighters (out of the 230 Su-30MKI fighters ordered at cost of 8.4 billion US$, 120 are already in service with the IAF), 220 Light Combat Aircraft, 47 Jaguar combat aircraft, 4 Tu-22M3 bombers, the Indian Air Force has signed contracts for 66 BAE Hawk Mk.132 trainers (deliveries in the pipeline), 80+ combat helicopters, 3 new Long Range UAVs, 8 mid-air refueling planes, 225+ HJT-36 Sitara Intermediate Jet Trainer aircraft and some additional medium-range transport aircraft. The Indian Air Force planned to upgrade its fleet of MiG-29 aircraft in 2007. India awarded Russia a $965 mn contract to upgrade its multi-role MiG-29 warplanes, on Monday March 10, 2008. The two post-Cold War allies signed the deal on Saturday March 8, 2008 to extend the life of India's fleet of 70 MiG-29 jets another 15 years from their current 25 years. Russia will re-arm the twin-engined MiG-29s with air-to-air missiles, modern bombs, increased fuel capacity and the latest avionics, the contract said.

- Hawk AJT: Deliveries of the first order of 66 Hawk 132 Advanced Jet Trainers began in November, 2007 with induction in February, 2008. An order for 57 (40 for IAF and 17 for Indian Navy) more was placed in 2008. The Hawk, along with the HJT-36, will serve the IAF's future fighter training needs.

- C-130J Hercules: Indian Air force signed a deal to acquire 6 C-130J Super Hercules in early 2008 for US$1.06 billion. Lockheed Martin will deliver the planes on 2011.
- Light Helicopters: A tender for supply of 317 light helicopters will be floated by Ministry of Defence combining the requirements of Indian Air force (125) and Indian Army (197). The Navy is too likely to join this tender. The requirements of Indian Navy being 50–60 Helicopters and this is likely to increase the tender to 367. Unnamed Defense Ministry official stated that Letters of interest have been sent to Kamov, Bell, Augusta Westland and Eurocopter. Last week, Bell withdrew from the race, citing differences in offset clause with the Government of India. HAL has also recently joined the race with its Light Observation Helicopter (LOH). Although it is still on the drawing board, HAL officials seem to be confident to deliver in time.
- Medium Lift Helicopters: During Russian President Dmitry Medvedev's visit to India in December 2008, the two countries inked a deal for the supply of 80 Mi-17V-5 (also known as Mi-171) medium lift helicopters at a cost of US$1.2 billion. The two countries had earlier negotiated a price of $650 million, but early in 2008 Russia asked for a revision of the contract price. Russia is expected to deliver the Mi-171 to the IAF in 2010. The deal also envisages a US$405 million "offset" obligation by Russia. The new choppers, which have an 18,000 ft operational ceiling, will replace 50 Mi-8s currently in service with the IAF, some of which are over 35 years old, and boost IAF's capability to support high-altitude posts in Siachen and Ladakh sectors. The helicopter will come with the circuitry and hard points to carry weapons.
- Heavy Lift Helicopters: Indian Air Force has circulated the Request for Information for Heavy Lift Helicopters to the vendors. For this contract, the bidders could include Boeing's CH-47 Chinook, Sikorsky and Russian MI's. Indian Air

Force has the requirement of 6 such helicopters. This information was provided by Chief of Air Staff Air Chief Marshal F H Major on February 6, 2008.

- VIP Helicopters: Indian Air force had floated a tender in 2006 for supply of 12 VIP Helicopters and 4 Medium Lift Helicopters to replace Mi-8 Helicopters of VIP Squadron. IAF concluded the trials of competing helicopters, Augusta Westland EH-101 and Sikorsky S-92 in the period of January 14—19, 2008.The government is on the verge of clearing a US$300 million deal to purchase 12 advanced VIP helicopters from Italian armament major Augusta Westland EH-101. Owned by Finmeccanica, the Italian firm had fielded the EH101 — whose variant, US101, serves the US President — to compete for the Indian tender floated some two years ago. Based on the contract schedule, the first helicopter is likely to join the air force fleet around 2011.
- Attack Helicopters: Indian Air Force has plans to induct two more squadrons (22) of Attack Helicopters, capable of operating in high altitudes. The new purchase would give the force capability to operate helicopter gunships in both day and night as also in high altitude areas like Siachen, Jammu and Kashmir and North-East. It would give an option to armed forces as it can be deployed in fighting militants in insurgency-prone areas. The US aviation giant Boeing's world best seller AH-64A Apache helicopters, Russian Kamov and MI series and European consortium EADS would be bidding for the IAF's order, which could run up to more than a billion US dollars. A request for proposals has been issued to seven companies for the supply of 22 attack helicopters for the Indian Air Force. The new helicopters will replace IAF's aging fleet of Mi-35 helicopters. The contract is estimated to be worth US$500 million. The deal is expected to be finalized within two years and supply completed over the next three years. The qualitative requirements are as follows: twin engine, high maneuverability,

anti-armor capability, all weather capability and all terrain capability. The helicopters are likely to be equipped with an electronic warfare and self protection suite developed by EADS and India's Defense Avionics Research Establishment. Competing for the order will be: Boeing AH-64D Apache Longbow, Eurocopter Tiger, AgustaWestland AW129, Bell AH-1Z SuperCobra, Kamov Ka-50, Mil Mi-28, and HAL's Light Combat Helicopter. Boeing said in October, 2008 that it won't bid for a contract to supply 22 helicopters due to time constraints. HAL's Light Combat Aircraft, which is still underdevelopment, is expected to take to the air sometime this year. However the government had canceled the tender, as only 3 of the top 5 companies participated in the entire process & none could match the qualitative requirements of the IAF. The Indian Defence Ministry has said that soon a new tender will be floated for the same.

Under Development

- HAL Tejas: The IAF will also buy 220 indigenously-built HAL Tejas Light Combat Aircraft. It has already ordered a total of 28 Tejas aircraft. Weaponization is underway as an LCA Tejas successfully test-fired a Russian R-73 close-combat air-to-air missile off the coast of Goa in October, 2007. These aircraft are expected to enter service in 2010.As on February 3, 2009, LCA has completed 1011 Test Flights successfully using these prototypes: TD1-233, TD2-298, PV1-182, PV2-107, PV3-120, LSP1-33, and LSP2-38.
- Medium Combat Aircraft: India is also planning to develop a fifth generation aircraft called Medium Combat Aircraft or MCA. Development(HAL & ADA) work on the MCA is awaiting government approval and design phase is in its early stages. The Medium Combat Aircraft (MCA) is a twin-engined 5th generation stealth mutlirole fighter being developed by India. It will complement the HAL Tejas and the Sukhoi Su-30MKI in the Indian Air Force. The main

purpose of this aircraft is to replace the aging SEPECAT Jaguar & MiG-27. Design work on the MCA has been started.

- Fifth Generation Fighter Aircraft : In 2001, the Ministry of Defence signed a deal with Russia to jointly develop and fund the FGFA/PAK FA , Perspektivnyi Aviatsionnyi Kompleks Frontovoi Aviatsyi (*Future Air Complex for Tactical Air Forces*) program. The program was initiated to develop a fifth generation fighter aircraft to fill a role similar to that of Lockheed Martin's F-22 Raptor in all aspects. Initially, Mikoyan-Gurevich's Project 1.44 was expected to get the contract. However, Sukhoi Aviation Corporation came up with a more cost-effective aircraft and won. Design work has commenced on Sukhoi's experimental Su-47 Berkut aircraft. PAK FA proves to be a very ambitious program and the estimated costs for developing the aircraft vary between US$15–20 billion. However, it was announced in August, 2007 by Russian Air Force Commander Alexander Zelin that the development stage of the PAK FA project is complete without any Indian involvement and an Indo-Russian pact on building a fifth-generation fighter has only recently been agreed. The new project may effectively result in the development of an export version of the Russian PAK FA or very closely based on the PAK FA's final article. An official project name had not been assigned to this possible Indo-Russian fifth-generation fighter aircraft development programme as of November, 2007. Sukhoi has already started construction of a prototype which is expected to feature super maneuverability, super cruise, stealth and precision in destroying ground and sea targets. Flight tests of the fighter are due to begin as early as 2009, and the aircraft may go into production by 2015. The Sukhoi and HAL will sign a formal contract to jointly develop the fighter at the beginning of 2009, the head of the United Aircraft Corporation said on Friday, December 5, 2008.

"We are planning to conclude the contract at the beginning of next year," Alexei Fedorov said. According to the latest reports FGFA will have its first flight by 2015 or before 2015.

- HAL HJT-36 Sitara: The HAL HJT-36 Intermediate Jet Trainer carried out its maiden test flight in 2003 and is all set to enter service within the next 5 years. HAL recently signed a deal with Russian company Saturn DDB for supply of a specially designed engine for the trainer.
- Multirole Transport Aircraft: India's Hindustan Aeronautics (HAL) and Russia's United Aircraft Corporation (UAC) will form a joint-venture in mid-2009 for the development of a Multirole Transport Aircraft, which will replace the IAF's ageing fleet of Antonov An-32s. Both HAL and UAC will invest US$300 million each on the program.
- HAL Light Combat Helicopter: Hindustan Aeronautics Ltd is developing an Attack Helicopter for the IAF based on HAL Dhruv. It is being designed to fit into an anti-infantry and anti-armour role and will be capable to operate from altitudes an 6,500 metre. HAL selected the M621 cannon incorporated in a Nexter THL 20 turret for the gun armament of the helicopter. The helicopter will have a glass cockpit with multifunction displays, a target acquisition and designation system with FLIR, Laser rangefinder and laser designator. Weapons will be aimed with a helmet mounted sight and there will be an electronic warfare suite with radar warning receiver, laser warning receiver and a missile approach warning system. First flight of HAL LCH (Light Combat Helicopter) is expected in 2009.
- Airawat (AEW&C): India has also revived the Airavat Project, which was India's first attempt in developing an indigenous AEW aircraft. According to various sources, Centre for Airborne Systems (CABS), is coordinating the Rs.1,800-crore effort to develop an indigenous airborne early warning and control system (AEW&CS), scheduled to be completed

by 2012.The AEW&CS will comprise of an indigenous radar and control system mounted on a Brazilian Embraer EMB-145 regional jet. Under a $210 million deal signed with Brazilian aviation company Embraer in summer 2008, Embraer will supply India 3 EMB-145s with the system mounted on them. The CABS is looking for an experienced partner who will be responsible for integrating the Active Array Antenna Unit (AAAU), other antennas, trans receiver modules and various sub systems being developed by Indian defense laboratories onto the three Brazil manufactured EMB-145. It has sent a request for proposal to six vendors - Israel's Elta, the European consortium EADS, France's Thales, Sweden's SAAB Erikson and the United State's Raytheon and Northrop Grumman. The vendors have time till the third week of January 2009 to submit their proposals. The first EMB-145 is scheduled to be delivered in 2011 and the complete system will be flight tested by the DRDO along with the Indian air force from 2012.

Aerospace Command

The IAF is setting up an aerospace command. This command will have space technology including satellites available to them. This command is said to be utilised by all the three services of the Indian armed forces and also for civilian purposes by ISRO.

A specialized surveillance satellite for the IAF will be operational by the end of 2010. The satellite will enable the IAF to carry out precise strikes against targets like terrorist training camps.The Satellite has been named RISAT 2 and will use an Israeli Synthetic Aperture Radar mounted on a ISRO developed satellite bus and will be launched on a fast track basis in the aftermath of the 2008 Mumbai attacks in place of the civilian RISAT 1.

Surface to Air Missile Systems

- Trishul(Trident): Development of Trishul is complete. It has met the IAF requirements during its various developmental flight trials. DRDO is presently in dialogue with IAF for possible induction. Frontier India reports that Indian Air force is considering to induct small quantity to meet partial requirement of LLQRM (Low Level Quick Reaction Missile) System. However it is not known if IAF has placed a formal order of Trishul SAM System.

- SPYDER (*S*urface-to-air *PY*thon and *DER*by): Indian Air force plans to acquire 18 Spyder SAM Systems at a cost of Rs. 1800 crore (approx. $395.4 million). A typical squadron consists of 1 Mobile Command and Control Unit and 4 Mobile Firing Units with missiles, each with their own built-in power supplies. SPYDER will reportedly replace India's Russian-made OSA-AKM (SA-8 Gecko) and ZRK-BD Strela-10M (SA-13 Gopher) SAM systems. If the deal is approved RAFAEL would be the prime contractor, and Israel Aircraft Industries the major subcontractor. But recently Defence Ministry has ordered a probe into the deal following allegations of illegal influencing of the purchase process. Central Vigilance Commission is reviewing the deal. It was reported in February, 2008 that Rafael is to sign Production Transfer Program (PTP) agreement with Tata Power for maintenance and production of the SAM System. Cabinet Committee on Security (CCS) cleared the deal in January 2008. It was reported on August 18, 2008 that the Defence Acquisitions Council had approved the deal for 18 SpyDer systems at a cost of Rs. 1800 crore. On December 14, the Government of India informed the upper house that India has signed a deal with Rafeal for the supply of 18 SPYDER missile system.
- Maitri LLQRM (Low Level Quick Reaction Missile): DRDO is in talks with MBDA to develop Maitri LLQRM for Army, Air force and Navy. Sources said that DRDL is preparing feasibility report and is awaiting formal clearance from defence ministry.

- Akash: Indian Air force has approved the induction of Akash Missile System and had initiated the process of inducting the system. Akash has successfully demonstrated its performance through number of flight tests. DRDO and IAF jointly began a ten day intensive trial of Akash on December 13, 2007 aimed at making IAF familiar with the system. Defence News reports that IAF has already ordered two units (squadrons) of Akash which are likely to be inducted by 2009.

Surface to Surface Missiles

- Prithvi II: 250 km Prithvi-II Ballistic Missile is under IAF service which could be used to target airfields, command and control centers etc.

Air to Surface Missiles

- DRDO- NPO Mashinostroeyenia Brahmos- Air launched version under Development

5

INDIAN NAVY

India is a maritime nation strategically straddling the Indian Ocean with or substantive seaborne trade. The country's economic well being is thus very closely linked to our ability to keep our sea-lanes free and open at all times. Besides, India has other maritime interests as well. Our island territories situated on our Western and Eastern seaboards are at considerable distances away from the mainland. To ensure their sustained development, umbilical linkages with the mainland and maritime security protection are essential pre-requisites of our maritime security. Our offshore assets within the Exclusive Economic Zone (EEZ) of 2.02 million sq. kms, fisheries and deep sea interests, major and minor harbours and the overall seaward security of long coastline and island territories are other vital aspects of our maritime dimension and Navy's responsibilities.

Indian Navy has consciously taken the difficult route of indigenisation in consonance with the national endeavour towards self-reliance.

The Navy embarked upon a programme for indigenous construction of ships and development of major sub systems, sensors and weapon systems with the help of Defence Research and Development Organisation (DRDO) and Defence Public Sector Understandings (PSUs). Commissioning of the indigenously built destroyer, INS Delhi on November 15, 1997, & commissioning INS Mysore on June 2, 1999 have enabled the Navy to become a builder's Navy and not just be a buyer's Navy. Self-reliance through indigenisation has been the Navy's guiding philosophy over the last half century.

The Indian Navy is organised into three regional commands:

- HQ Eastern Naval Command, Visakhapatnam;
- HQ Western Naval Command, Mumbai; and
- HQ Southern Naval Command, Kochi.

The Indian Navy is divided into the following broad categories

- Administration;
- Logistics and Material;
- Training;
- The Fleets;
- The Naval Aviation; and
- The Submarine Arm.

The origins of the modern Indian navy are traced to a maritime force established by the East India Company in the seventeenth century. This force had a variety of names—the Bombay Marine, the Indian Navy, and the Indian Marine. In 1934 the Royal Indian Navy was established, with Indians serving primarily in lower-level positions. After independence the navy was the most neglected of the three services because the national leadership perceived that the bulk of the threats to India were land-based.

The first efforts at naval rearmament emerged in the 1964-69 Defence Plan, which called for the replacement of India's aging fleet and the development of a submarine service. Between 1947 and 1964, fiscal constraints had prevented the implementation of ambitious plans for naval expansion. Consequently, many of the vessels were obsolete and of little operational value. As part of this expansion program, the British helped develop the Mazagon Dock shipyard for the local production of British Leander-class frigates. The Soviets, however, were willing to support all phases of the planned naval expansion. Accordingly, they supplied naval vessels, support systems, and training on extremely favorable terms. By the mid-1960s, they had replaced Britain as India's principal naval supplier.

During the 1980s, Indian naval power grew significantly. During this period, the naval facilities at Port Blair in the Andaman Islands, in the Nicobar Islands, and in Lakshadweep were significantly upgraded and modernized. A new line of Leander-class frigates was manufactured at Mazagon Dock in collaboration with Vickers and Yarrow of Britain. These frigates, redesignated as the Godavari class, have antisubmarine warfare capabilities and can carry two helicopters. During the 1980s, plans were also finalized for the licensed manufacture of a line of West German Type 1500 submarines (known as the Shishumar class in India). In addition to these developments at Mazagon Dock, the naval air arm also was upgraded. India purchased nearly two squadrons of the vertical and short takeoff and landing (VSTOL) Sea Harriers to replace an earlier generation of Sea Hawks.

In the mid-1990s, India was preparing for a major modernization program that was to include completion of three 5,000-ton Delhi-class destroyers, the building of three 3,700-ton frigates based on Italian Indian Naval Ship (INS)-10 design, and the acquisition of four hydrographic survey ships. Also to be built were an Indian-designed warship called Frigate 2001; six British Upholder-class submarines; an Indian-designed and Indian-built missile-firing nuclear submarine—the Advanced Technology Vessel—based on the Soviet Charlie II class; and an Indian-designed and Indian-built 17,000-ton air defense ship capable of carrying between twelve and fifteen aircraft. The air-defense ship will be, in effect, a replacement for India's two aging British aircraft carriers, the INS Vikrant , the keel of which was laid in 1943 but construction of which was not completed until 1961 and which was slated for decommissioning by 2000, and the INS Viraat , which entered service in 1987 and is likely to be decommissioned by 2005. The problems encountered with modernizing these and other foreign-source ships led India to decide against acquiring an ex-Soviet Kiev-class aircraft carrier in 1994.

In the spirit of international military cooperation, India has made moves in the early and mid-1990s to enhance joint-nation interoperability. Indian naval exercises have taken place with ships from the Russian navy and those of Indian Ocean littoral states and other nations, including the United States.

Naval headquarters is located in New Delhi. It is under the command of the chief of naval staff—a full admiral. The chief of naval staff has four principal staff officers: the vice chief of naval staff, the vice chief of personnel, the chief of material, and the deputy chief of naval staff. The total strength of the navy in 1994 was 54,000, including 5,000 naval aviation personnel and 1,000 marines (one regiment, with a second reportedly forming).

Women were inducted into the Indian navy for the first time in 1992, when twenty-two were trained as education, logistics, and law cadres. In 1993 additional women were recruited for air traffic control duties. By 1994 there were thirty-five women naval officers.

The Indian navy is deployed under three area commands, each headed by a flag officer. The Western Naval Command is headquartered in Bombay on the Arabian Sea; the Southern Naval Command in Kochi (Cochin), in Kerala, also on the Arabian Sea; and the Eastern Naval Command in Vishakhapatnam, Andhra Pradesh, on the Bay of Bengal. Additionally, the navy has important bases in Calcutta and Goa.

The Southern Naval Command is responsible for naval officer training, which occurs at the Indian Naval Academy in Goa. Officer candidates are largely drawn from the National Defence Academy. After commissioning, officers are offered specialized training in antisubmarine warfare, aviation, communications, electronic warfare, engineering, hydrography, maritime warfare, missile warfare, navigation, and other naval specialties at various naval training institutions, many of which are collocated with the Training Command headquarters on Willingdon Island, near Kochi.

The Indian Navy is the naval branch of the armed forces of India. It currently has approximately 55,000 personnel on active duty, including 5,000 members of the naval aviation branch and 2,000 marine commandos, making it the world's fifth largest navy. The

Indian Navy currently operates more than 155 vessels, including the INS *Viraat*, the only full-deck aircraft carrier operated by a country in Asia or the Western Pacific, along with operational jet fighters.

Though the primary objective of the navy is to secure national maritime borders, India also uses its navy to enhance its international relations through joint exercises, port visits and humanitarian missions, including disaster relief. In recent years, the Indian Navy has undergone extensive modernization and expansion with an intention to increase its capabilities as a recognized blue-water navy. By 2020, the Navy is expected to operate three aircraft carriers and three nuclear submarines.

Role

The Indian Navy sees several principal roles for itself:

- In conjunction with other armed forces of the union, act to deter or defeat any threats or aggression against the territory, people or maritime interests of India, both in war and peace;
- Project influence in India's maritime area of interest, to further the nation's political, economic and security objectives;
- In cooperation with the Indian Coast Guard, ensure good order and stability in India's maritime zones of responsibility.
- Provide maritime assistance (including disaster relief) in India's maritime neighbourhood.
- To play a key role as part of 'a pluralistic security order' for a better world.

History

India has a maritime history dating back to 5,000 years. The first tidal dock is believed to have been built at Lothal around 2300 BCE during the Indus Valley Civilization, near the present day Mangrol harbour on the Gujarat coast. The Rig Veda written around 1500 BCE, credits Varuna with knowledge of the ocean routes and describes naval expeditions. There is reference to the side wings of a vessel called Plava, which give stability to the ship under storm conditions. A compass, Matsya yantra was used for navigation in the fourth and fifth century AD.

The earliest known reference to an organization devoted to ships in ancient India is to the Mauryan Empire from the 4th century BCE. Emperor Chandragupta Maurya's Prime Minister Kautilya's Arthashastra devotes a full chapter on the state department of waterways under *navadhyaksha* (Sanskrit for Superintendent of ships) . The term, *nava dvipantaragamanam* (Sanskrit for sailing to other lands by ships, i.e. Exploration) appears in this book in addition to appearing in the Buddhist text, *Baudhayana Dharmasastra* as the interpretation of the term, *Samudrasamyanam.*

Sea lanes between India and neighboring lands were the usual form of trade for many centuries, and are responsible for the widespread influence of Indian Culture on other societies. Powerful navies included those of the Maurya, Satavahana, Chola, Vijayanagara, Kalinga, Maratha and Moghul empires . The Cholas excelled in foreign trade and maritime activity, extending their influence overseas to China and Southeast Asia.

During the 17th and 18th centuries, the Maratha and Kerala fleets were expanded, and became the most powerful Naval Forces in the subcontinent, even defeating European Navies at various times. The fleet review of the Maratha navy took place at the Ratnagiri fort in which the ships Pal and Qalbat participated. The 'Pal' was a three masted fighter with guns peeping on the broadsides. The Maratha Kanhoji Angre and Kunjali Marakkar, the Naval chief of Saamoothiri were two notable naval chiefs of the period.

Colonial Era

The British Indian Navy was established by the British while India was a colony. The first Indian to be granted a commission was Sub Lieutenant D.N Mukherji who joined the Royal Indian Marine as an engineer officer in 1928. Indian sailors started a rebellion also known as the The Royal Indian Navy mutiny, in 1946 on board ships and shore estabilshments which spread all over India. A total of 78 ships, 20 shore establishments and 20,000 sailors were involved in the rebellion. When India became a republic on 26 January 1950, it became known as the Indian Navy, and its vessels as Indian Naval Ships (INS). On 22 April 1958 Vice Admiral R. D. Katari assumed office as the first Indian Chief of the Naval Staff.

Operation Vijay

The first involvement of the Navy in any conflict came with the success of *Operation Vijay* in the 1961 liberation of Goa. After Portuguese troops fired at commercial vessels and fishing boats passing near Anjadip Island, the decision was taken to militarily intervene to liberate Goa from Portuguese colonial holding. The Indian ships provided fire support to navy and army landing troops. During the operation, the *INS Delhi* sank one Portuguese patrol boat. The Portuguese frigate *Alfonso de Albuquerque* was also sunk after a brief fight.

Indo-Pakistan Wars

The Navy has been involved in two wars with Pakistan. While its activity in the Indo-Pakistani War of 1965 largely involved patrolling of the coast, it played a significant role in the bombing of Karachi harbour in the 1971 war. The name given to the attack was *Operation Trident*, which was launched on December 4. Owing to its success, it has been celebrated as Navy Day ever since. The attack was followed by *Operation Python* before the center of conflict shifted to the eastern India-Pakistan border and the Bay of Bengal. To show solidarity with its ally Pakistan, the United States sent a nuclear carrier task force led by the *USS Enterprise* into the Bay of Bengal. A task force led by *INS Vikrant* was stationed to counter the *Enterprise* task force; Soviet Navy submarines also trailed the U.S. task force. A confrontation was averted when the U.S. task force moved towards South East Asia, away from the Indian Ocean.

The sinking of the Pakistani Navy's lone long-range submarine *PNS Ghazi* under unexplained circumstances, enabled an easy Indian blockade of East Pakistan.. The missile boats *INS Nirghat* and *INS Nipat* each sank a destroyer; the *INS Veer* destroyed a minesweeper. The naval aircraft, Sea Hawks and Alizés, operating from the *Vikrant* were also instrumental in sinking many gunboats and merchant navy vessels. There was one major casualty, the frigate *Khukri* (sunk by the *PNS Hangor*), while the *Kirpan* was damaged in the western sector of conflict. Ultimately, the naval blockade of Karachi Port and the complete blockade of East Pakistan's ports were successful in cutting Pakistani troops off from reinforcements, supplies, and evacuation routes. These actions proved decisive in India's victory in the war.

Type of Vessel	Indian Navy losses	Pakistan Navy losses
Destroyers	Nil	2, PNS Khaibar and Shahjahan*(damaged)
Frigates	1, INS Khukri**	Nil
Submarines	Nil	1, PNS Ghazi
Minesweeper	Nil	1, PNS Muhafiz
Navy Aircraft	1, (Alize)	Nil
Patrol boats and Gunboats	Nil	7 Gunboats and 3 patrol boats
Merchant Navy and others	Nil	11 (including one US ammunition ship)
Loss on land	Nil	Missile attack on Karachi harbour and oil installations.

*PNS Shahjahan was presumably damaged beyond repair.

**The second frigate *INS Kirpan* was damaged although it remained in service later on after salvaging it.

Operation Cactus

In 1988, the Indian Navy joined the Indian Air Force in successfully thwarting a coup attempt by PLOTE in the Maldives. A naval maritime reconnaissance aircraft detected a vessel hijacked by PLOTE rebels. One of the hostages on-board included a senior Maldivian minister and *Operation Cactus* was launched to secure the vessel. After military intervention by INS *Godavari* and Indian marine commandos, the rebels surrendered.

In October 1999, a coordinated effort by the Indian Navy and the Indian Coast Guard led to the rescue of a hijacked Japanese cargo ship, MV *Alondra Rainbow*, from pirates.

Operation Talwar and Parakaram

During the Kargil conflict between India and Pakistan in 1999, the Western and Eastern fleet of the Indian Navy were deployed in northern Arabian Sea. Known as *Operation Talwar*, this was primarily done to not only safeguard India's maritime assets from a Pakistani naval attack, but also to deter Pakistan from initiating a full-scale war with India by blocking its naval sea-trade routes. Indian Navy's aviators and commandos also fought along side Indian Army personnel during the Kargil war.

The Indian Navy took part in military exercises during the 2001–2002 India–Pakistan standoff. More than a dozen ships from the navy were deployed during the exercise, codenamed *Operation Parakaram*. Later in 2001, the Indian Navy provided escort to American warships traveling through the Strait of Malacca to take part in *Operation Enduring Freedom*.

Disaster Relief

During the 2004 Indian Ocean earthquake crisis, the Indian Navy deployed 27 ships, 19 helicopters, 6 naval aircraft and over 5000 Naval personnel in disaster relief operations. These deployments were a part of various area-specific relief operations including *Operation Madath* in the Indian states of Andhra Pradesh and Tamil Nadu, *Operation Sea Waves* in the Andaman and Nicobar Islands, *Operation Castor* in Maldives, *Operation Rainbow* in Sri Lanka and *Operation Gambhir* in Indonesia. This was one of the largest relief mobilizations that the Indian Navy had undertaken. Indian Naval groups were able to start large scale rescue operations in neighboring countries within 12 hours from the time of the tsunami, and was the first foreign navy to reach the affected areas.

The quick deployment of forces during relief operations was a testing ground for the Navy's amphibious, as well as force projection capabilities. Deficiencies in the response led to modernization of the naval forces after the tsunami, including the acquisition of Landing Platform Docks (LPD) like the INS *Jalashwa* (formerly the USS *Trenton*), as well smaller amphibious vessels.

Operation Sukoon

During the 2006 Israel-Lebanon conflict, the Indian Navy evacuated 2,280 Indian nationals and people of various other nationalities, including four 436 Sri Lankan and 69 Nepali citizens, from war-torn Lebanon. This operation was named *Operation Sukoon*, meaning "Peace and tranquility". In the year 2006, ten naval doctors from India served for 102 days on USNS *Mercy* and conducted about 10 medical camps in Philippines, Bangladesh, Indonesia and East Timor. Indian Navy has also provided relief materials to survivors of cyclones in Bangladesh and Myanmar. Two ships from the Indian Navy carried the first international aid material for the victims of Cyclone Nargis in Myanmar.

ANTI-PIRACY OPERATIONS IN SOMALIA AND SEYCHELLES

Piracy off the coast of Somalia has caused significant concerns in India as most of its sea-trade routes pass through the region. The Indian Navy responded to these concerns by deploying the frigate INS *Tabar* in the Gulf of Aden in October 2008. Within a month of its deployment, the *Tabar* had prevented attempts by pirates to board two cargo ships and also destroyed a pirate "mother ship". As of November 11, 2008, the frigate had escorted 35 ships safely through the pirate-infested region.

The pirates have hijacked a fishing trawler from Thailand and made it their mothership. There were also reports of India deploying destroyer INS *Mysore* to augment the frigate INS *Tabar* in anti-piracy operations. On November 21, 2008 India was granted permission to enter Somalian territorial waters to intercept suspected pirate vessels. 23 pirates were arrested by Indian Navy while attempting to hijack a merchant ship near the Gulf of Aden. Anti-piracy patrols were carried out after a request was made by the Seychelles government, resulting in the arrest of nine pirates. Further ships has been send to give a boost to anti-piracy operations.

Personnel

Each of the three Naval Commands has an active Flag Officer Commanding in Chief. The commander of the Navy is the Chief of Naval staff (CNS). As of 31 October 2006, the CNS is Admiral Sureesh Mehta. The CNS is assisted by several other high ranking officers.

While the provision for the rank of Admiral of the Fleet exists, no officer of the Indian Navy has yet been conferred an equivalent rank. Both the Army and Air Force have had Field Marshals (Sam Manekshaw and Cariappa) and Marshal of the Indian Air Force (MIAF) (Arjan Singh) appointed.

Organization

The Indian Navy is divided into the following broad categories:

- Administration
- Logistics and Material
- Training
- The Fleets
- The Naval Aviation
- The Submarine Arm

Commands

The Indian Navy operates four Commands. Each Command is headed by a Flag Officer Commanding-in-Chief in the rank of Vice Admiral.

Commands	HQ Location	Current FOC-in-C
Western Naval Command	Mumbai	Vice Admiral Jagjit Singh Bedi
Eastern Naval Command	Vishakhapatnam	Vice Admiral Nirmal Kumar Verma
Southern Naval Command	Kochi	Vice Admiral Sunil Krishnaji Damle
Far Eastern Naval Command	Port Blair	Vice Admiral Vijay Shankar

The Far Eastern command, a joint Navy, Army and Air force command was set up in the Andaman and Nicobar Islands in 2001 as a strategic area of defence. The joint command is entrusted with security of the Malacca straits and the Indian Navy plays a major role in it by patrolling the area with the Indonesian Navy, Royal Malaysian Navy and Royal Thai Navy. India and Australia signed an agreement to provide maritime security in the Asia Pacific region.

In 2005 the Navy received a huge boost when *INS Kadamba* was commissioned at Karwar, 100 km from Goa. This is the third operational naval base after Mumbai and Vishakapatnam and the first to be controlled exclusively by the Navy.

The other bases share port facilities with civilian shipping, but this one is for purely military purposes. Built under Phase I of the multi-billion dollar 'Project Seabird', it has been described by naval pundits as the largest such base in the region, and will add strategic depth to the Navy.

Asia's largest Naval academy INS Saamoothiri, will be inaugurated at Ezhimala, on January 2009 by the Prime Minister of India. Another naval base is being planned for the eastern shores, near Vishakapatnam at a cost of US$ 350 million. The base, which will be located fifty km south of Vishakapatnam in Rambilli Mandal, will have comprehensive anti-aircraft, anti-submarine and amphibious capability.

The Indian Navy is setting up a monitoring station in Madagascar, to patrol the coast of Mozambique to monitor and prevent terrorist activities and piracy.

Marine Commando Force

The Marine Commando Force (MCF), also known as *MARCOS*, is a special forces unit that was raised by the Indian Navy in 1987 for direct action, special reconnaissance, amphibious warfare and counter-terrorism. In 1988, the MARCOS successfully rescued several hostages, including Maldives' then-Minister of Education, aboard a ship hijacked by PLOTE mercenaries during Operation Cactus.

The MARCOS are also deployed to prevent infiltration through the Jhelum and Wular Lake and are involved in covert counter-terrorism operations in and around lakes and rivers in Jammu and Kashmir. The MARCOS were also involved in the rescue mission of hostages captured by the terrorists in Taj Mahal Palace & Tower luxury hotel in Mumbai as part of a large terrorist attack in Mumbai metropolis in November 2008.

Ships and Weapon Systems

The names of all the commissioned ships (and Naval Bases) of the Indian Navy start with INS, meaning 'Indian Naval Ship'. The fleet of the Indian Navy is a mix of domestic built and foreign vessels and is expanding with new inductions. India often builds destroyers, frigates and corvettes. The Navy currently operates the *Delhi* and *Rajput* class destroyers. The frigates in the service include the latest *Shivalik* class, *Talwar* class, *Godavari* class, *Nilgiri* class and *Brahmaputra* class. The Indian Navy is acquiring from abroad the Kiev class aircraft carrier *Admiral Gorshkov* (INS *Vikramaditya*), improved *Talwar* class frigates, and the *Scorpène* class submarines. The carrier INS *Viraat* will be retired by the end of 2012 after the induction of the first domestically built *Vikrant* class aircraft carrier.

In 2006, India purchased the 16,900 tonne USS *Trenton*, an Austin-class amphibious transport dock, for 48.44 Million USD. The ship was renamed INS *Jalashwa* and commissioned on June 22, 2007 at Norfolk, Virginia. Six H-3 Sea King maritime utility transport helicopters were also purchased and will operate from the ship which arrived at the Eastern Command's Vishakhapatnam Naval base in September, 2007 and was promptly inducted into the Indian Navy. One corvette, INS *Prahar*, sank after colliding with a merchant vessel.

Submarines and AUVs

The Indian Navy currently maintains a fleet of 16 diesel powered submarines. These are primarily of Russian and German origin. India signed a deal for six *Scorpène* submarines with MESMA air-independent propulsion, and construction has begun. These submarines will join the Indian Navy from 2010-11 onwards. The Indian Navy may arm its *Kilo* class submarine fleet with the BrahMos cruise missiles after successfully completing test launches from the submarine. India will issue request for proposals for another six submarines in financial year 2008-09.

The National Institute of Oceanography has developed the Autonomous Underwater Vehicle (AUV) that has applications in the field of Oceanographic research. Also an Autonomous Surface Vehicle (ASV) has been developed.

Nuclear Powered Submarines

In January 1988 India leased for three years an ex-Soviet Charlie class nuclear powered guided missile submarine with eight Ametist (SS-N-7 Starbright) anti-shipping missile launchers. In the Indian Navy, the ship was christened INS *Chakra*, and the submarine was manned by an Indian crew. Upon expiration of the ship leasing term in 1991, the submarine was returned to Russia and joined the Pacific Fleet of the Russian Navy.

India has been working since 1985 to domestically construct a nuclear-powered submarine, one that is based on the Soviet Charlie II-class design, detailed drawings of which are said to have been obtained from the Soviet Union in 1989. The secretive project is known as the Advanced Technology Vessel (ATV) project. The nuclear reactor is reported to have been fitted into the submarine's hull. The Prototype Testing Centre (PTC) at the (Indira Gandhi Centre For Atomic Research, Kalpakkam, will be used to test the submarine's turbines and propellers. A similar facility is operational at Vishakapatnam to test the main turbines and gear box.

Once the vessel is completed, it may be equipped with Sagarika/ Agni-III ballistic missiles and advanced Indian made sonar systems. According to defense sources, the ATV is expected to be launched in 2009 and commissioned in 2010. Each unit will cost one billion U.S. dollars.

India is reportedly paying two billion dollars for the completion of two Akula-II class submarines which were 40-60% completed. Three hundred Indian Navy personnel are being trained in Russia for the operation of these submarines. India has finalized a deal with Russia, in which at the end of the lease of these submarines, it has an option to buy them. According to report, the first submarine will be commissioned into the Indian Navy in September, 2009. The first submarine will be named INS Chakra, it is currently undergoing trials in the Pacific ocean.

Aircraft

The naval air-arm is an important component of the Indian Navy. The Indian Navy air arm consists of Sea Harrier jets that operate from the aircraft carrier INS *Viraat* and also from INS *Jalashwa*. Recently, the Harriers were modernized for Beyond Visual Range missile capability. The Kamov-31 provide the Airborne Early Warning cover for the fleet. In the anti-submarine role the Sea King, Ka-28 and the domestic built HAL Dhruv are used. The MARCOS use Sea King and HAL Dhruv helicopters while conducting operations. Reconnaissance operations are carried out by Tupolev 142, Ilyushin 38, Dornier Do 228 aircraft, as well as HAL Chetak helicopters. The UAV arm consists of around 30 UAVs like Heron and Searcher-IIs that are operated from ships and shore for better surveillance. The Indian Navy also maintains a four aircraft aerobatic display team, the *Sagar Pawan*. The Sagar Pawan team will be replacing their present Kiran HJT-16 aircraft with the newly developed HJT-36 aircraft. The Indian Navy has also placed an order for 8 P-8I Poseidon long-range maritime reconnaissance (LRMR) aircraft.

The Indian Air Force also has a maritime strike role, providing support to the Indian Navy. It operates SEPECAT Jaguar and Sukhoi Su-30MKI Aircraft in this role. The Jaguars are armed with the Sea Eagle missile, which will be replaced with the Harpoon missile. Su-30MKI and the Il-38 will be armed with the air-launched version of the Brahmos cruise missile.

Weapon Systems

The Indian Navy uses modern technology and weapon systems, some of which are domestically developed. Others, like the BrahMos supersonic cruise missiles, are jointly developed with Russia. Some major strides in defense research. There are reports on the joint development by India and Israel of the Barak-II missile system, an improved, longer range version of the Barak-I air defence missile which is operational on Indian Navy ships. The Barak-I is used on most of the main ships of the Indian Navy. The Indian Navy's nuclear deterrence capability is based on *Sukanya* class ships armed with the *Dhanush* ballistic missiles that has a range of 350 km.

India has a number of foreign made cruise missile systems, including the Klub SS-N-27. It also has its own Nirbhay cruise missile systems under development. The Sagarika (Oceanic) submarine launched ballistic missile (SLBM), which has a range of at least 700 km (some sources claim 1000 km) forms part of India's nuclear triad. Another successful program has been the adaptation of the Yakhont anti-ship missile system into the BrahMos by the NPO and the DRDO. The BrahMos has been tailored to Indian needs and uses a large proportion of Indian-designed components and technology, including its fire control systems, transporter erector launchers, and its onboard navigational attack systems. The successful test of Brahmos from INS Rajput (D51) provides Indian Navy with precision land attack capability.

ELECTRONIC WARFARE AND SYSTEMS MANAGEMENT

Sangraha is a joint electronic warfare program of the Defence Research and Development Organisation (DRDO) and the Indian

Navy. The system comprises a family of electronic warfare suites, such as Ajanta and Ellora, for use on different naval platforms capable of intercepting, detecting, and classifying pulsed, carrier wave, pulse repetition frequency agile, frequency agile and chirp radars. The systems employ a modular approach facilitating deployment on various platforms like helicopters, vehicles, and small ships. Certain platforms, apart from ESM (electronic support measures), have ECM (electronic countermeasure) capabilities. Advanced technologies like multiple-beam phased array jammers are employed in the system for simultaneous handling of multiple threats.

The Indian Navy also relies on information technology to face the challenges of the 21st century. The Indian Navy is implementing a new strategy to move from a platform centric force to a network-centric force by linking all shore-based installations and ships via high-speed data networks and satellites. This will help in increased operational awareness. The network is referred to as the Navy Enterprise Wide Network (NEWN). The Indian Navy has also provided training to all its personnel in Information Technology (IT) at the Naval Institute of Computer Applications (NICA) located in Mumbai. Information technology is also used to provide better training, like the usage of simulators and for better management of the force.

Fleet Reviews

The President of India is entitled to inspect his fleet, as he is the supreme commander of the Indian Armed Forces. The first President's fleet review by India was hosted by Dr. Rajendra Prasad on October 10, 1953. President's reviews usually take place once in the President's term. In all, nine fleet reviews have taken place, the most recent being in February 2006, when President Dr. APJ Abdul Kalam took the review. The Indian Navy also conducted an International fleet review named *Bridges of Friendship* in February 2001 in Mumbai. Many ships of friendly Navies from all around the world participated, including two from the U.S. Navy.

Once in two years navies from the Indian Ocean region meet at the Andaman and Nicobar Islands and the event is named as *MILAN* (Sanskrit: Get together).

Naval Exercises and Cooperation

India often conducts naval exercises with other friendly countries designed to increase naval interoperability and also to strengthen cooperative security relationship. Some such exercises take place annually like the *Varuna* with the French Navy, *Konkan* with the Royal Navy (UK), *Indra* with Russian Navy, *Malabar* with the U.S. Navy and *Simbex* with the Republic of Singapore Navy. The Indian Navy also conducted exercise with the People's Liberation Army Navy in 2003 and will send ships to the South China Sea to participate in the fleet review. In 2007, the *TROPEX* (Theatre-level Readiness Operational Exercises) was held during which Indian Navy experimented the doctrine of influencing a land and air battle to support the Indian Army and the Indian Air Force. Apart from the Indian Ocean, India has steadily gained influence in the Pacific Ocean. In 2007, Indian Navy conducted naval exercise with Japan Maritime Self-Defense Force and U.S Navy in the Pacific and also signed an agreement with Japan in October 2008 for joint naval patrolling in the Asia-Pacific region.

India has also held naval exercise with Vietnam, Philippines and New Zealand. In 2007, India and South Korea decided to conduct annual naval exercise and India participated in the South Korean international fleet review. In addition, Indian Navy will also be increasing naval cooperation with other allies, particularly with Germany and Arab states of the Persian Gulf including Kuwait, Oman, Bahrain and Saudi Arabia. India held the first Indian Ocean Naval Symposium (IONS) with an objective to provide a forum for all the littoral nations of the Indian Ocean to cooperate on mutually agreed areas for better security in the region. The Indian Navy is increasingly used in international diplomacy. Since 2000, the Indian naval ships have made port calls in Israel, Turkey, Egypt, Libya, Greece, Oman, Thailand, Indonesia, Australia, New Zealand,

Tonga, South Africa, Kenya, Qatar, Oman, United Arab Emirates, Bahrain, Kuwait[112] and other countries in 2005-2007.

Exploration

The Indian Navy regularly conducts adventure expeditions. The sailing ship and training vessel INS *Tarangini* began circumnavigating the world on 23 January 2003, intending to foster good relations with various other nations; she returned to India in May of the following year after visiting 36 ports in 18 nations. INS Tarangini returned to port, after a ten month long overseas voyage named Lokayan 07. A solo circumnavigation voyage named 'Sagar Parikrama' is planned for 2008-09 by Cdr. Dilip Donde.

Lt. Cdr. M.S. Kohli led the Indian Navy's first successful expedition to Mount Everest in 1965; the Navy's ensign was again flown atop Everest on 19 May 2004 by a similar expedition. Another Navy team also successfully scaled Everest from the north face, the technically more challenging route. The expedition was led by Cdr Satyabrata Dam, belonging to the elite submarine arm. Cdr. Dam is a mountaineer of international repute and has climbed many mountains including the Patagonias, the Alps among others. This team's record is unmatched by any other navy. The Navy was also the first to send a submariner to summit Everest.

An Indian Navy team comprising 11 members successfully completed an expedition to the Arctic pole. To prepare, they first traveled to Iceland, where they attempted to summit a peak. The team next flew to eastern Greenland; in the Kulusuk and Angmassalik areas, they used Inuit boats to navigate the region's ice-choked fjords. They crossed northward across the Arctic Circle, reaching seventy degrees North on skis. The team scaled an unnamed peak of height 11,000 feet and named it "Indian Peak".

The Indian Naval ensign first flew in Antarctica in 1981. The Indian Navy succeeded in Mission Dakshin Dhruv 2006 by traversing to the South Pole on skis. With this historic expedition, they have set the record for being the first military team to have successfully completed a ski traverse to the Geographic South Pole. Also, three of the ten member team - the expedition leader - Cdr. Satyabrata Dam, leading medical assistants Rakesh Kumar and Vikas Kumar are now amongst the few people in the world to have visited the two poles and summited Mt. Everest. Indian Navy became the first organization to reach the poles and Mt.Everest.

Ongoing Expansion

In 2004, India bought the Russian aircraft carrier, *Admiral Gorshkov* for the equivalent of US$1.5 billion. It will cost an additional US$1.5 billion to refit, and is expected to join the Indian Navy in 2012 as INS *Vikramaditya.* A further US$700 million will be spent to purchase 12 single-seat MiG-29K and four dual-seat MiG-29KUB fighters, six Kamov-31 attack and reconnaissance anti-submarine helicopters; also included are training facilities for pilots and technical staff, delivery of simulators and spare parts, and establishment and maintenance of Indian Navy facilities. Upgrades include removing missiles from the carrier foredeck to make way for a 14.3-degree ski-jump. The Mig-29's will be delivered to the Indian Navy in 2008.

In April 2005, India began construction of a 40,000 tonne *Vikrant* class aircraft carrier at a cost of 4,000 crore and scheduled to operate 30 aircraft, including Naval LCA, MiG-29K, and Sea Harrier combat aircraft, as well as HAL Dhruv, Ka-31, and Sea King Mk.42 helicopters. Four turbine engines will power the ship. The carrier is being constructed by state-run Cochin Shipyard Limited and will be commissioned by 2012-13. The Indian Minister of State for Defence, Pallam Raju, went on record in September 2006 stating that the aircraft carrier is likely to be commissioned by 2011. There are plans to build more aircraft carriers domestically. The Indian Navy is currently undergoing rapid expansion and modernisation. Yantar, a plant in Kaliningrad, Russia, was awarded a US$1.56 billion contract to build three additional 1135.6 frigates. The increased price is due to more sophisticated armaments such as BrahMos cruise missiles. The Navy has government approval for an additional eight warships.

The Indian Navy is also planning to induct 8 P-8I maritime patrol aircraft for Rs. 8,500 crore. The first aircraft will be delivered 4 years after the signing of the contract.

Future Prospects

India is expected to spend about US$40 billion on military modernization from 2008 to 2013. A major chunk of those purchases were made for the Indian Navy. Work on the third aircraft carrier is to start in 2010 and will be inducted into the Navy by 2017. India is currently focusing on expanding its submarine fleet. Also newer technology like the Unmanned Underwater Vehicle (UUV) is being developed for the Indian Navy to protect the littoral domain.

After ordering six Scorpene submarines as part of Project 75, Indian Navy is now on the look out for six next-generation submarines in a project worth over Rs 30,000 crore. These six diesel-electric submarines built in India under Project-75I, will be equipped with air-independent propulsion boosting their operational capabilities and will have high degree of stealth, land-attack capability and ability to incorporate futuristic technologies. RFI has been issued to Rosoboronexport, French (Armaris), HDW and other firms, two rounds of discussions have already taken place. The RFP or global tender will be issued in late-2008 or early-2009.

The RFP (request for proposal) for six MRMR aircraft with anti-submarine warfare (ASW) capabilities was issued on July 11, 2008 to Italian Alenia Aeronautica's ATR-72-500MP aircraft, Brazilian Embraer P-99 , French Dassault's Falcon 900DX and Russian Antonov-72P. The contract is expected to be signed by June 2009 and deliveries to begin by 2012. The contract is estimated to cost Rs. 1,600 crore. The Navy is also planning to induct more UAVs. The India-Israel joint venture to convert the Chetak helicopters into unmanned UAV's that can operate from ships is progressing steadily. All these will be linked with space-based reconnaissance systems. On January 13, 2009, India has issued a request for proposals (RFPs) for six Medium Range Maritime Reconnaissance (MRMR) aircraft. The new aircraft, which will replace the aging fleet of 10 Islander aircraft in service, are to be equipped with an Airborne Early Warning system. The Indian Coast Guard has an additional requirement for six MRMRs without an Airborne Early Warning system. The MRMR is required to have a range of 500 nautical miles and an endurance of 6 hours. Aircraft competing for the order include a variant of Boeing's P-8I, and possibly the turboprop ATR-72MP, EADS C-295, Dassault's Falcon 900MPA and Embraer P-99A platforms. For the Coast Guard RFP, contenders could be the ATR-42MP, C-295 or CN-235MP.

Indian Navy has issued a tender for procurement of 16 advanced, multi-role naval helicopters to AgustaWestland, EADS and Sikorsky. The order is likely to be expanded to 60 helicopters. The helicopters will be equipped with anti-ship and anti-submarine warfare equipment including cruise missiles and torpedoes, and also be capable of being refuelled in flight. The type will operate from both naval vessels and land bases.

Global bids has been floated to acquire eight mine countermeasure vessels (MCMVs), to replace the twelve Pondicherry class ocean minesweepers in service. France's DCN International, Fincanteri of Italy, Izhar of Spain, Kangnam of South Korea and Northrop Grumman of the U.S have been invited to participate in the bidding process. Six of the craft will be produced at Goa shipyard under transfer of technology.

With the recent and ongoing upgrades and inductions, independent analysts expect that the Indian Navy may soon become a blue-water navy. India's navy is already among the most powerful in the region, and with further upgrades in the future, aims to control the Indian Ocean Region, from the coast of East Africa to Australia. India is also the only Asian navy to regularly operate aircraft carriers. The aim is to have a total of three Aircraft carrier's resulting in two fully operational Carrier battle group's and an additional Aircraft carrier eventually in refit making India an operating Blue-water navy.

6

PARA-MILITARY FORCES

INTRODUCTION

The Para-Military Forces assist the Police, as and when required, to maintain law & order in their respective States. They come under the control of the Central Government, namely the Ministry of Home Affairs (MHA). There are several Para-Military Forces in India. Some of the prominent ones are listed below:

HOME GUARD

The role of the Home Guard is to service as an auxiliary to the Police in maintenance of law, order and internal security, help the community in any kind of emergency such as an air-raid, an earthquake, etc., help in the maintenance of essential services, promote communal harmony, assist civil administration in protecting weaker sections, participate in socio-economic and welfare activities and perform civil defence duties. The Home Guard are trained to use .303 Rifles and Sten guns. They are also trained in fire fighting. Some also have access to light machine guns. Home Guards are of two types - rural and urban. In border states, Border Wing Home Guard battalions have also been raised, which serve as an auxiliary to the Border Security Force (BSF). The total unauthorised strength of the Home Guards in the country is at 472,000 however the actual strength is at 416,000 personnel. The organisation is spread over in all states and union territories except in Arunachal Pradesh and Kerala. The Home Guard was raised in 1946 under the Home Guard Acts & Rules of States/Union Territories. They are recruited from various cross sections of people such as doctors, engineers, lawyers, teachers, employees of public & private sector organisations, college & university students, agricultural & industrial workers, etc., who give their spare time to the organisation for betterment of the community. All citizens of India, who are in the age group of 18-50, are eligible to become members of the Home Guard. Normal tenure of membership in Home Guards is three to five years. A Home Guard, whenever called up for duty/training, is paid duty/training allowance at prescribed rates to meet out of pocket expenses. Members of Home Guard with three years services in the organisation are trained in the Police in maintenance of law and order, prevention of crime, anti-dacoit measures, border patrolling, flood relief, fire fighting, prohibition, elections and social welfare activities. In the event of a national emergency, some portion of civil defence work is also entrusted to the Home Guard. The Ministry of Home Affairs formulates the policy in respect of role, target, raising, training, equipping, establishment and other important matters of the Home Guard. Expenditure on Home Guard is generally shared between the Centre and State Governments as per the existing financial policy.

BORDER SECURITY FORCE

Till 1965 India's borders with Pakistan were manned by the State Armed Police Battallion. Pakistan attacked Sardar Post, Chhar Bet and Beria Bet on 9 April, 1965 in Kutch. This exposed the inadequacy of the State Armed Police to cope with armed aggression due to which the Government of India felt the need for a specialized centrally controlled Border Security Force, which would be armed and trained to man the International Border with Pakistan. As a result of the recommendations of the Committee of Secretaries, the Border Security Force came into existence on 01 Dec 1965, and Shri K F Rustamji was the first chief and founding father.

ROLE OF THE BSF:

"SECURITY OF BORDER OF India and matters connected therewith".

TASKS OF THE BSF: The tasks of the BSF are divided as follows:

(a) Peace time:

1. Promote a sense of security among the people living in the border areas.
2. Prevent trans border crimes, unauthorized entry into or exit from the territory of India.
3. Prevent smuggling and any other illegal activity.

In the last few years the BSF has, in addition to their duties, been deployed for counter insurgency and internal security duties

(b) War Time:

1. Holding ground in less threatened sectors.
2. Protection of vital installations.
3. Assistance in control of refugees.
4. Anti-infiltration duties in specified areas.

ETHOS: The BSF, in its 41 years of existence, has emerged as an elite force of the country having excelled with distinction in the 1971 war with Pakistan. Its ethos is "Any task, any time, any where" and the BSF has given blood and sweat to execute its motto "Duty Unto Death".

BORDER FENCING /FLOOD LIGHTING/ROADS: The concept of border fencing, flood lighting and construction of roads has been introduced with the aim to stop infiltration/exfiltration on the Western and Eastern borders.

DO YOU KNOW ?

a) The BSF contributes every year a number of personnel for services for UN Mission in Kosovo and Bosnia.
b) During the Kargil conflict in May-July 1999, the BSF remained on the heights of the mountains and defended the integrity of the country with all the might at its command in unison with the Army.
c) BSF personnel have been performing Internal Security Duty in Manipur for the last two years and have been successfully fighting insurgency in those areas.

d) During the earthquake in Gujarat on 26th January 2001, the BSF was the first to reach out to help the distressed people.

e) During the communal disturbances in Gujarat recently, BSF personnel went all out to restore amity and brotherhood among the people.

f) The BSF took over the erection of the border fencing in Jammu & Kashmir and it was successful in its task despite all attempts of Pakistan to scuttle our efforts.

g) The BSF has been defending the borders along with the army and checking infiltration on the borders during the current standoff with Pakistan.

ACHIEVEMENTS OF BORDER SECURITY FORCE

ACHIEVEMENTS OF BORDER SECURITY FORCE

Year	Militants/ Extremists Killed	Militants/ Extremists Appr	Surrender	Arms	Ammunition	Contrabands (In Crores)	Explosive (in Kgs.)
1990	433	905	33	1445	167259	136.758	1511.15
1991	647	1099	407	2250	183575	33.434	215.2
1992	524	2224	187	1728	96182	37.738	246.95
1993	442	1919	16	980	72517	57.327	398.15
1994	327	1315	24	1302	123341	163.310	1105.1
1995	194	1036	38	1300	138874	131.880	564.12
1996	127	932	114	1007	72564	50.980	3266.019
1997	128	499	40	666	51616	44.647	406.862
1998	162	223	20	585	61802	34.538	287.532
1999	247	262	12	591	49768	39.702	1073.94
2000	284	221	7	702	54192	46.326	436
2001	334	295	38	693	49496	65.928	463
2002	334	299	23	711	46992	85.486	452.52
2003	213	160	19	449	35118	105.893	1157.89
2004	129	148	61	360	75888	122.77	1006.8
2005	147	130	14	448	89939	125.05	363.58
2006	68	53	29	213	13917	199.81	417.5
2007	42	39	43	199	62136	198.18	54.55
2008	29	29	41	128	5560	257.79	228.1
2009 (Jan)	03	02	-	18	113	14.37	-
TOTAL	4814	11790	1166	15775	1450849	1951.917	13654.963

SUPREME SACRIFICES MADE BY BORDER MAN

BSF CASUALTIES

Year	KILLED	INJURED
1990	92	280
1991	91	416
1992	142	597
1993	124	629
1994	99	569
1995	69	401
1996	63	287
1997	47	129
1998	66	211
1999	80	273
2000	114	380
2001	110	329
2002	114	409
2003	56	231
2004	60	150
2005	24	150
2006	13	115
2007	2	49
2008	7	62
2009 (Jan)	2	2
TOTAL	1375	5669

THE RASHTRIYA RIFLES

Genesis

The last decade of the 20th century was particularly bloody for Kashmir. By May 1990 it was clear that Kashmir valley was in the grip of an insurgency of intensity not seen before. It started out in the urban areas and then spread to the countryside. The army which till then was the guardian of the international border (IB) and the line of control (LOC) was called in to assist in Counter Insurgency (CI) ops. Based on its experience with low intensity conflicts in Nagaland, Sri Lanka and Punjab, the Indian Army was quite wary of trying to replicate strategy and tactics successfully used elsewhere. By 1993 the army had got together a doctrine for the low intensity conflict in Kashmir. In Nagaland for example, the army had learnt that physical domination of each and every village was one way to combat insurgency. Long experience had taught the army the value of the grid system. In this system the whole terrain was divided into a grid. Each node at any given time would have a platoon worth of ready to move soldiers, the so called quick reaction team which would mutually reinforce other nodes. All would be covered with heavier fire support and have adequate logistics.

However the grid often looked better on paper than on the ground. The obvious reason for this was the terrain. In the Wanni jungles of Sri Lanka where the grid had been successfully applied, civilians and villages were few and far between, and so attack helicopters and artillery could be used. This enabled heavy firepower to be brought in to support troops in the grid in minutes. Now the Kashmir valley is very densely populated and there is fear of collateral damage from using heavy fire support. So troops fighting CI had to do without it. To makeup for that the grid had to be more densely packed. This is where the army saw the need for additional forces such as the Rashtriya Rifles (RR).

The army got the go-ahead to create the RR from the Vishwanath Pratap Singh government in 1990. The initial sanction was for two sectors Head Quarters (HQs) each of three battalions. When General B.C. Joshi became Army Chief, the promise his predecessor - General Sunith F. Rodrigues - made about making the Pathankot-based 39 Division and the Bareilly-based 6 Mountain Division available for Kashmir was pending. He pushed a long-held army view, that India was involved in an extended counter-insurgency akin to the Naga problem in the North-East. Hence a new force - like the Assam Rifles - was needed which could be permanently located in the area to counter the insurgents. And that using these divisions for CI would be playing into Pakistani hands. He instead pushed for setting up 10 more RR sector HQs - 30 battalions or the equivalent of three divisions. It was also felt that in the bargain the Army would have three additional battle-hardened divisions, ready for rear guard action during war. In 1994, the Narasimha Rao government gave a conditional go-ahead for a period of three years.

RR Organization

All units of the Army have an organizational structure called the War Establishment (WE). According to the WE are laid down the number of men, vehicles, weapons etc which the unit is authorized for carrying out it's assigned role. The infantry battalions (inf bns) in the Indian Army have a standard organization called the Inf Bn Standard. Other types of inf bns according to their assigned role are called by various modifications to the Inf Bn Standard like Inf Bn CI, Inf Bn Mountains, Parachute Inf Bn, Para Commando Bn and even (till 1975) Camel Mounted Bn. Till the RR came into the picture, the infantry battalions tasked for CI ops were on the Inf Bn CI. They had four companies and retained their battalion heavy weapons since they were dual tasked. The RR on the other hand has an organization structure tailor made for CI ops. They have six infantry companies and do not have the heavy battalion weapons which the Inf Bn CI carry although RR troops do train on them. Thus they do not incur the costs of a heavier unit. Also unlike regular army units which were rotated out of the valley regularly, the RR concept was to rotate personnel after fixed periods of deputation. Currently this is for two years. The RR units are permanently located in "sectors", with each sector being the equivalent of a brigade with three battalions. To create a distinct identity, the RR has its own dress, special insignia and flag logistics.

The RR units come under four CI Force HQs. Victor Force looks after Anantnag and Pulwana districts in the south Kashmir valley, Kilo Force looks after Kupwara and Baramulla districts in the north Kashmir valley. Both these forces come under the operational control of the 15 Corps. The Delta Force looks after the Doda district and the Romeo Force after Poonch and Rajouri. These two forces come under the operational control of the 16 Corps. Each force is headed by a GOC-in-C with the rank of a Major General. In terms of their location and use, each of the units and sectors was seen as being interchangeable with a regular, equivalent army formation. GOC Victor Force in some instances would have 2 sector HQs and a regular infantry brigade in his charge. On the other hand when 8 Mountain Division moved to Kashmir, it came with 2 brigades which were then augmented by adding a sector of the RR apart from a couple of independent mountain brigades to it.

After the government gave the go-ahead to setup the RR, the army decided to milk its existing units by 10-20% of their personnel to set up it up quickly. The officers and men came on deputation from all branches of the army including the Infantry, Army Service Corps, EME, Artillery, Armoured Corps. The infantry provides 50%, services 10% and other arms 40% of the troops. In fact the army mothballed a few armoured regiments and transferred their manpower to the RR.

Each regimental center was given the task of raising 1-2 battalions in one year time. During this period, the units were raised and sent to the Northern Command where they got another 4 to 6 weeks to consolidate. All of them went through a structured 8 week course in special CI schools. They were then given another month to stabilize and then sent to the more dormant sectors of Kashmir and to the Punjab. To provide some experience base, 6 RR battalions were exchanged for 6 Assam Rifles units.

In raising the Rashtriya Rifles to full strength, the Army also had to dig into its war-wastage reserves, with the best available vehicles, weapons and radio sets going to the RR. In fact the RR units were even the first to receive bullet-proof jackets and patkas. With manpower drawn from all its arms and services, the Army has had to deal with serious shortages in many of its conventional units, for Rashtriya Rifles battalions are maintained at full authorized strength. However once the teething problems were overcome the RR proved it was worth the trouble.

Evolution

The initial RR units performed well despite certain inherent weaknesses in their class and composition. They were raised on All India/All Class basis with troops from all over the Army. The logic being that since the units were going to fight an insurgency, there should be no scope for vested interests in accusing a battalion of bias based on a class or regional attributes. Unfortunately, this setup created problems in the field. The initial RR units were like transit camps, with troops coming and going at regular intervals. There was little camaraderie and cohesion among troops. There were also numerous problems of administration and even of indiscipline. COs of infantry battalions who were asked to provide manpower generally used to use that as a chance to get rid of troúble makers. If the initial battalions performed well in hostile conditions, it was mainly due to the professional competence of officers who were asked to lead them.

Keeping this in mind, a decision was taken to alter the basic composition of the RR battalions. Instead of its units comprising of troops from all over the Army, two RR battalions were made an integral part of each of the infantry regiments and other arms. Now not only are majority of troops of the two RR battalions drawn from the other units of the Regiment, but their Commanding Officer or the 2IC, is from the same regiment. This ensures not only functional cohesion but also the regimental esprit-de-corps. This experiment has produced excellent results even while the units were deployed in the most difficult areas.

Table 1: RR Sector locations

Sector 1	Anantnag
Sector 2	Kulgam
Sector 3	Kangan
Sector 4	Doda
Sector 5	Baramulla
Sector 6	Poonch

Sector 7	Kupwara
Sector 8	Kupwara
Sector 9	Kistwar
Sector 10	Baramulla
Sector 11	Banihal
Sector 12	Badgam

Table 2: Some known RR battalion affiliations

Battalion	Affiliation
4 RR	Bihar
7 RR	Punjab
10 RR	Rajput
11 RR	Dogra
12 RR	Grenadiers
13 RR	Kumaon
15 RR	1 GR
17 RR	Maratha
21 RR	Guards
22 RR	Punjab
32 RR	3 GR
36 RR	Garhwal Rifles

Another change that was made was to have the Union Home Ministry (MHA) - instead of the Ministry of Defence - take over the burden of funding the RR. Although this was a good step, in reality it existed on paper. In 1997, the MHA owed the Army Rs.950 crores for the RR. The budgetary outlay for the force was Rs.263 crore in 1998-99. This was upped to Rs.375 crore in the revised estimates for that year and the outlay for 1999-2000 was Rs.587 crores. Clearly if the funding were to come from the correct source in time, the army could use it for its modernization programmes.

One unforeseen consequence of the RR being a CI force is that it has led to command & control problems with other police organisations. The latter started arguing that the RR was in effect now a central police organisation (CPO), just like the BSF and the CRPF under the MHA. While BSF units deployed on the border are under the operational command of the Army, the BSF argued it believes that the application of the same structure in the matter of internal security duties would be inappropriate. There is scope for even further reorientation of the RR to make them more effective. Tackling insurgency and terrorism is heavily dependent on intelligence gathering, frequent shifting of units engaged in the conflict should be avoided. There have been occasions when a unit was moved from South Kashmir to the LOC and then back to South Kashmir - all within six months. Also it is common knowledge that even now the best of the officers and jawans, with the right experience and training, are not spared by the regiments for duty with RR battalions. While combating low intensity conflicts, most actions are either at the platoon or the section level and it is important to have the best trained and seasoned 'junior leaders' leading the men into the fray. In a lot of places, they are pitted against highly motivated & trained mercenaries, who are guided by locals familiar with the terrain and topography.

Further it might not be a bad idea to modify two full fledged units of each of the regiments for the RR role for a period of two or three years instead of troops from different units of a regiment teaming up to form the core of the RR battalions. This will ensure greater cohesion since most men and officers would have known each other for a long period. In case of a full-fledged war, the same units on CI role can be used for rear area security.

The army did have a system earlier where regular infantry battalions were raised on a reduced counter-insurgency establishment. These modified infantry battalions were used in the 1971 war with minimal reorganization. This system avoids the current hybrid composition of the RR battalions. Care is needed to ensure that troops of other arms/regiments/units deputed to a RR battalion are properly assimilated and dont feel left out. In one case, the accused in a serious act of indiscipline who was not from the parent regiment, put down discrimination against men like him for his actions.

The RR In Action

The initial RR battalions deployed in the terrorist-infested areas of Tarn Taran in Punjab and Anantnag in Jammu & Kashmir proved to be extremely effective. In Punjab, the deployment of the Army and RR units did contribute to the turnaround in the situation. Since then the RR has been increasingly fighting the low-intensity war on behalf of the army in Kashmir. Casualty figures indicate that from 3 out of 44 army casualties in 1991 being from the RR, the figure has gone up to 82 out of 150 in 1996. Up to February '97, 17 RR officers (including 1 Colonel, 4 Lt. Colonels and 7 Majors), 13 JCOs and 169 ORs have made the supreme sacrifice. The officer to OR casualty ratio for the RR (at 1:9.94 till February 1997) is almost double the average for the army in the Kargil and 1971 war (at 1:20).

Lt. Col. Shanti Swarup Rana, of the 13 Rashtriya Rifles, was one such officer. Born on 17 September 1949 in village Baila of Hoshiarpur District of Punjab, he initially joined the Army in the Corps of Signals and was later selected for the Army Cadet College, Dehra Dun. After completing his training, he was commissioned into 3 Bihar on 11 July 1977. A veteran of Operation Rhino, Operation Pawan and Operation Rakshak he became 2IC of the 13 Rashtriya Rifles, after being promoted to the rank of Lt. Col. in 1994. On 02 November 1996, Lt. Col. Rana was entrusted with the task of destroying two terrorist camps in the Haphruda forest of Kupwara District in Jammu & Kashmir. Lt. Col. Rana spotted four well-fortified hideouts stocked heavily with arms & ammunition including 800 kg of explosives. In a gallant & swift strike he, with his troops, crawled towards the bunker and threw hand grenades and destroyed the hideouts.

One more hideout came to notice. During the action that followed, the terrorists resorted to heavy firing from their well fortified bunkers. Lt. Col. Rana organized his troops, crawled towards the bunker and threw hand grenades inside. Two foreign mercenaries came out firing heavily. Lt. Col. Rana killed them both instantaneously. Meanwhile the terrorists seriously injured Lt. Col. Rana in heavy firing from another location. In spite of this, the gallant officer kept on boosting the morale of his soldiers. When one more terrorist advanced towards the soldiers, Lt. Col. Rana, without caring for his own life, charged and killed him in a face-to-face encounter. In this action, the gallant officer suffered more injuries and made the supreme sacrifice. Lt. Col. Rana thereby displayed indomitable courage, patriotism and gallantry of the highest order for which he was awarded the Ashok Chakra (posthumous).

Major Padmanabha Sri Kumar was killed in an encounter with militants in the Poonch sector of Jammu & Kashmir in December 1997. His fellow officers recount the incident. "He killed 7 dreaded Hizbul Mujahideen militants and walked out of the ambush unscathed. But when one of his men was trapped and injured, he walked back into enemy fire with guns blazing all around him to rescue the injured soldier. Major Sri Kumar was seriously injured in the rescue attempt when a volley of enemy bullets hit his chest. The injured soldier survived. But Major Sri Kumar made the supreme sacrifice of his life for the nation".

Sepoy Mechanda Ganapathy Chittiyappa, was decorated with the Sena Medal for Gallantry for taking on a group of terrorists and killing one of them. On 18 April 1998, Sepoy M.G. Chittiyappa was the leading scout in an operation at the village of Guldandadhar in Doda district of Jammu & Kashmir. He spotted a group of Pakistani terrorists in the area. Undeterred & unmindful of the shower of enemy bullets, he closed in and killed one of them. The rest escaped.

Yet another hero from the RR is one of its decorated Tracker Dog 'Rex'. Rex was a recipient of GOC-in-C Commendation Card for his outstanding & exemplary performance against militants. The 9A 92 Rex, a golden Labrador was born on 25 February 1993 at RVC Centre & School Meerut. After a year's training, he was posted to 14 Army Dog Unit under Delta Force and assigned the areas adjoining the town of Bhaderwah, to help troops in trailing &

tracking militants. In March 1995, operating with troops of 25 RR in jungles of Badrot, South of Bhaderwah, he tracked a militant injured in an encounter for over 3 km in the thick of militant fire. In a chase that lasted for over four hours, he managed to recover one AK 56 rifles and an haversack containing 92 rounds. Recently, in April 1998, out on a patrol in area Gulgandhar, security forces killed two dreaded militants and badly injured one, who managed to escape. Picking up the scent of his blood, 'Rex' went hot on the trail and moved speedily & stealthily over strenuous undulating mountains. After tracking over 2 km, he succeeded in tracing out the body of the militant in a hideout where he had succumbed to his injuries. Let out on yet another 'trial' with the QRT of CO 25 RR in Daraba near Rajouri, Rex suffered an unfortunate fall and sustained serious intestinal injuries. He was evacuated to the nearest Army Veterinary Hospital where he developed acute gastroentrities and finally succumbed on 22 September 1999.

By the time the RR celebrated its 8th anniversary it had become the most decorated organization in the Army. They had more that 500 gallantry awards to their credit. In fact 25% of the units had already been awarded the unit citation by the Chief of Army Staff for their distinguished performances. By that time the RR had already accounted for 1516 terrorists killed, 3932 apprehended and another 458 surrendered.

Table 3: Casualty figures indicate the fight is more & more the RRs.

Year	RR	Army	Security Forces	Terrorists
1991	3	44	185	614
1992	0	50	177	873
1993	10	88	216	1328
1994	26	139	220	1667
1995	86	186	258	1377
1996	82	150	241	1329
1997		153	227	1329

By September 1997 by the combined efforts of the Army, RR, and other paramilitary forces, the situation in Kashmir had stabalized to the extent that the army decided to de-induct 13 battalions (12,000 troops) including two brigades from the Kashmir valley over a two-year period. In fact up to Spring '99, the army had already withdrawn nine battalions (8000 troops) including a brigade from the Kashmir valley without replacements. The last batch of 4 battalions (about 4000 troops) along with a brigade HQ commenced de-inducting in April 1999 and was supposed to complete by mid-summer 1999. Despite all this the army was still contributing about 58 battalions to the CI ops - 36 in Kashmir and 22 in the Jammu region.

KARGIL AND BEYOND

In the spring of 1999, the Pakistani Army intruded into the Kargil heights. To deal with the situation, the army had to withdraw its battalions from CI ops in J&K. The units de-inducted included the battle hardened 8 Mountain Division which has been involved in CI ops for quite some years and which moved to Kashmir from Nagaland. During this period, the RR held the fort with the help of other paramilitary forces. Apart from that, RR units actively contributed to operations in the Kargil heights where they fought shoulder-to-shoulder with jawans of the Sikh, Naga, Granadiers, JAK Rifles and the Para Regiments at heights of 16,000 feet and above.

Naik Mekh Bahadur Gurung of Garhi-Dakra, Dehra Dun was one of them. Naik Gurung lost his life on 22 May 1999, while part of the first recce patrol team that had gone to check on the intruders. Before being shot himself, Naik Mekh shot down at least one of the mercenaries. Lance Naik Balaji Baburao Male of the 5 RR was killed in action in the Kargil sector. L/Nk Male originally joined the 109 Engineer regiment before he was drafted into the RR. With more and more troops being called into action, Lance Naik Male's battalion was also pressed into service in the Kargil sector to bolster the infantry units fighting the enemy from across the border. On

Sunday, 04 July 1999, L/Nk Male's unit was called out to conduct cordon & search operations in the same sector following reports of increased insurgent activity. L/Nk Male was detailed to defuse an improvised explosive device (IED) when fate struck. Something went wrong and the explosion took away another soldier, killed in the line of duty.

The 28 RR saw action in the Mushkoh Pandrass sector. Especially during the period after the Tiger Hill fell, when the Mushkoh sub-sector became the focus of attention. Lance Naik Sukhjeet Singh,was part of an Army column when he was seriously wounded in enemy shelling but did not leave his position and refused to be evacuated 'till his last breath. Rifleman Pradeep Kumar of the same unit laid down his life on 09 July 1999. The next day, the unit lost Rifleman Jagjit Singh to artillery shelling. After Kargil all the RR units involved reverted back to the valley.

It needs to be pointed out that the RR units who held the fort in Jammu & Kashmir while the army fought it out in Kargil were the unsung heroes of the battle. Keeping the road and lines of communications open, fighting the terrorists, taking land mine blasts, that was their job. During this period, 26 RR units were deployed in the valley and three to guard the Banihal/Jawahar tunnel area. The sectors in the not so important areas - like Sector 9 in Kisthwar- were withdrawn and the focus was on the lines of communication and the valley.

The withdrawal of the 58 army units from the CI grid, and the changes that were made, really disturbed it and stirred things up again. They had been replaced by 14 CPRF and 6 BSF battalions. However the replacements were new to the area and also did not make up for the numbers withdrawn. A vast area like Doda for example had to do with only 8 units during Kargil from the 1996 peak of 20 units. Kisthwar and Banderwah area which was under Sector 9 was handed over to the CRPF. The end result of all this was that the insurgents had a field day. Despite the army's extreme reluctance it had to redeploy its units for CI duty. In fact even the

6 Mountain Division - inducted into the Valley during the Kargil conflict - had to be deployed on mopping-up operations in the higher reaches of north and south Kashmir. The setback was estimated to take at least a year to rectify.

Keeping this in mind, after the Kargil battle, the Government decided to immediately raise 12 more battalions of the RR and 20 more battalions of the Assam Rifles. Also sanctioned were the force headquarters Kilo and Romeo. The Kilo seems to be the current focus of attention with the maximum number of sectors and units under it. Apart from the direct increase in its own strength, the raising of the Assam Rifles battalions will allow the RR battalions deployed in the North-East to move to Kashmir. It was also decided in the post-Kargil scenario, that counter-insurgency operations will be undertaken now mainly by the Rashtriya Rifles in J&K and Assam Rifles in the NE, supplemented by other paramilitary forces such as the BSF and CRPF. The Army is to be used only in extreme situations. However it it to be seen how far this can be really implemented keeping in view the fact that about 100 army units are still involved in CI ops. Either way the Rashtriya Rifles has a job to do and do it they will.

Table 4: RR Battalion wise current approximate known area of operations. The focus seems to be on the Kilo Force.

Battalion	Approx Area of Operations	Battalion	Approx Area of Operations
1 RR	Pulwana	19 RR	Kupwara
2 RR	Srinagar	20 RR	Banihal
3 RR	Anantnag	21 RR	Kupwara
4 RR	Doda	22 RR	Sopore
5 RR	Ganderbal	23 RR	Kupwara
6 RR	Kupwara	24 RR	Kupwara
7 RR	Anantnag	25 RR	Surankote
8 RR	Doda	26 RR	Kishthwar
9 RR	Anantnag	27 RR	Poonch

10 RR	Doda	28 RR	Baramulla
11 RR	Doda	29 RR	Baramulla
12 RR	Doda	30 RR	Sopore
13 RR	Pattan	31 RR	Kistwar
14 RR	Bandipore	32 RR	Kupwara
15 RR	Bandipore	33 RR	Bandipore
16 RR	Poonch	34 RR	Badgam
17 RR	Poonch	35 RR	Badgam
18 RR	Kupwara	36 RR	Anantnag

Origin of ITBP-The " Himveers" and National security

Indo-Tibetan Border Police was conceived on October 24, 1962.ITBP was initially raised under the CRPF Act, however in 1992, the parliament enacted the ITBPF Act and rules there under were framed in 1994(you may access same under relevant menu).

The " Himveers" and National security

ITBP is a multi-dimensional force. Presently Battalions of ITBP deployed on Border Guarding Duties from Karakoram Pass in Ladakh to Diphu La in Arunachal Pradesh covering 3488 KM of India China Border are manning Border Out Posts at an altitude ranging from 9000' to 18500' in the Western, Middle & Eastern Sector of India China Border. ITBP is basically a mountain trained Force and most of the officers & men are professionally trained Mountaineers and Skiers,. They have scaled more than 140 Himalayan peaks including Mt. Everest three times (Recent successful expedition in May, 2006), besides ITBP batallions are also deployed on CI OPS / IS / VIP security duties at Chamba - Doda border, in VA/Startegic locations and with VIPs in Delhi and VIPs in Srinagar J&K.

The border posts manned by ITBP are exposed to high velocity storms, snow blizzards, avalanches, and landslides, besides the hazards of high altitude and extreme cold, where temperature dips up to minus 40 degree Celsius. ITBP conducts Long Range and Short Range patrols to keep an effective vigil on inaccessible and unmanned areas on the border. To maintain optimum operational efficiency of troops, periodical tactical exercises are conducted independently as well as jointly with Army.

Multifarious Facets of the Force

New challenging role that has emerged for ITBP is disaster management. Being the first responder for natural Disaster in Hamalayas, ITBP was the first to establish 06 (Now 08) Regional Response Centres in HP, Uttaranchal and North East and carried out numerous rescue and relief operations in various disaster situations, which took place in our areas of responsibility as well as other parts of the country. ITBP has already trained 1032 personnel in Disaster Management including 98 personnel in Radiological and Chemical/ biological emergencies.

ITBP has established a National Centre for Training in Search, Rescue & Disaster response at Bhanu, Haryana which is imparting training to personnel of ITBP and other Paramilitary / State Police Forces. there is also a training center for the Dogs at Basic Training center situated at Bhanu. The center is known as NICD.

Presently ITBP Commando's are providing security to Embassy of India Kabul, Consulate General of India, Jalalabad and Khandar in Afghanistan since November, 2002. Besides this 02 Coys of ITBP are providing security to BRO personnel for their Delaram – Zaranj road construction project in Afghanistan since July 2004.

ITBP has also excelled in UN peace keeping operation. The Force personnel have been deployed for peacekeeping operations in Angola, Namibia, Cambodia, Bosnia & Herzegovina, Mozambique and Kosovo. Presently 01 coy of ITBP is deployed in United Nation Mission in Congo since November, 2005. A National Centre for UNCIVPOL training has been setup at ITBP Camp, Tigri, New Delhi for providing systematic training to Indian Police Officers for deployment in UN Mission.

ITBP is also providing security to the pilgrims during Annual Kailash Mansarovar Yatra from 1981. ITBP provides communication, security and medical cover to the yatries from Gunji to Lipulekh Pass and back to Gunji in co-ordination with MEA and Kumaon Mandal vikas Nigam.

FUNCTIONS AND TASKS

Functions & Tasks of the force proves its mettle as a multi-dimensional force.

1. Vigil on the northern borders, detection and prevention of border violations, and promotion of the sense of security among the local populace.
2. Check illegal immigration, trans-border smuggling and crimes.
3. Security to sensitive installations, banks and protected persons.
4. Restore and preserve order in any area in the event of disturbance.

In border vigil task ITBP mans forward border posts at altitudes ranging from 9000' to 18000'. Most of the forward posts remain cut off by the surface route during winter months. The border posts are exposed to the fury and violence of the nature like snow blizzards, avalanches, landslides, besides the hazards of high altitude and extreme cold where temperature normally remains below minus 40 degrees Celsius.

The force, besides guarding the border, is heavily engaged in fighting terrorism in the State of Jammu & Kashmir, where it has displayed exemplary nerve and gallantry.

The "Himveers", as the personnel are affectionately called, also provide security cover to installations and to VIPs in Delhi.

Each year ITBP personnel are deployed to UN Peace Keeping Missions in Kosovo, Angola & Western Sahara and Sierra Leone.

SPECIAL SECURITY BUREAU

The Special Security Bureau (SSB) was set up in the early 1963 in the wake of Indo China conflict of 1962 to build people's morale and inculcate a spirit of resistance in the border population against threats of subversion, infiltration and sabotage from across the border. However, the charter of duty of SSB has since been amended and it has been given the border guarding responsibilities along the Indo-Nepal Border. The SSB now functions in five border states covering a stretch of 1,751 km of International Border in 20 districts along Indo-Nepal Border. The SSB has two Frontier HQs at Patna and Lucknow, six Sector HQs at Ranikhet, Bahraich, Gorakhpur, Muzaffarpur, Purnia and Ranidanga. Out of 24 SSB areas to be relocated along Indo-Nepal border, 16 have already been relocated and started functioning. Orders for the relocation of eight more areas have been issued.

Since its deployment on Indo-Nepal border, contrabands worth Rs. 3.5 crore, narcotics worth Rs. 56.72 lakh, Indian fake currency amounting to Rs. 65,000, some illegal Indian currency and small arms and live cartridges have been seized. 18 suspected Nepali militants, 103 smugglers and 16 anti-national elements were apprehended. Besides, 37 couriers of smugglers, four fake currency racketeers, five suspected Pak ISI agents and 81 militants active in bordering districts of Darchula and Baitadi of Nepal (opposite Pithoragarh district, Uttranchal) and 28 madarssas suspected to be indulging in subversive activities were identified. The organization is gearing up in its new role of a Border Guarding Force. A comprehensive modernization plan for induction of sophisticated weaponry and equipment costing to Rs.189.16 crore is being drawn up for the force.

The Special Services Bureau (SSB), which has been assigned the task of policing the volatile Indo-Bhutan border, is likely to get a few more battalions. The proposal is part of Delhi's strategy to improve management of the country's borders. A source in the Union home ministry said as many as 12 new battalions could be added to the SSB. "This expansion is required for various reasons. Firstly, the SSB has the unenviable task of guarding both the Indo-Nepal and Indo-Bhutan borders. Both the borders are sensitive and frequented by militants and smugglers," the source said. The SSB's role in guarding the 370-km Indo-Bhutan border assumes more importance in view of the ongoing operation by the Bhutan Royal

Army to flush out militants of the Northeast from the Himalayan kingdom. Though it is almost certain that all the camps will be dismantled, it will be a challenging task to prevent further attempts by the militants to sneak into the jungles and re-establish their bases.

The present strength of the SSB is about 30,000, which makes it the third largest paramilitary organisation in the country. Once its expansion is completed, the manpower will increase to over 40,000. An official said the proposed addition of new battalions was part of the overall modifications being planned to tackle militancy in the region. The Union Home Ministry is planning to assign the task of combating militants to the Assam Rifles and the CRPF (Central Reserve Police Force), while the BSF (Border Security Force) and the SSB will be asked to focus on the frontiers. Created under the Cabinet Secretariat in 1963 and brought under the Union home ministry only two years ago, the SSB is supposed to have expertise in gathering intelligence, which distinguishes it from other paramilitary units.

It was initially deployed in the areas near the Indo-China border, where it trained the local populace in handling arms and ammunition. Union Minister of State for Home in Charge of the Northeast, Swami Chinmayanand, said the process of recruitment to the proposed new battalions of the SSB would begin shortly. "The decks have been cleared and the process will be initiated soon," he said. The minister indicated that once the operation by the Royal Bhutan Army was over, Delhi would do an "evaluation" of the security requirements along the border. "It is necessary to ascertain the kind of infrastructure that will be required to check illegal activities. This includes an estimate of the number of outposts that need to be set up and identification of the strategic points where these should be located," he said.

ASSAM RIFLES

The Force Profile as on date is as follows:

HQ DGAR located at Shillong.

Two HQ IGAR operationally deployed.

Nine Sector HQs operationally deployed.

46 Battalions of Assam Rifles.

Role and Tasks: Conduct counter insurgency operations in the north-east and other areas where deemed necessary, under control of the army.

During peace and 'proxy war', ensure security of the indo-china and indo-myanmar borders.

During war, rear area security in the TBA.

Act as penultimate interventionist force of the central government in internal security situation, under the control of army; when the situation goes beyond the control of central paramilitary operations.

Organization Structure: HQ DGAR The Force is commanded by an officer of the rank of Lieutenant General of the Army. The highest HQ of the force known as the HQ Directorate General of Assam Rifles is located at Shillong. Assam Rifles is a region specific force with its operational role in the North East and therefore the HQ DGAR is also located in the East. The HQs of all other Central Para Military Forces are located at Delhi.

HQ IGAR HQ Inspector General Assam Rifles comes next in chain of command after HQ DGAR. HQ IGAR is commanded by an officer of the rank of Major General from the Army. HQ IGAR in turn exercises command and control over the sector HQs.

Sector HQs The Sector HQs are commanded by Army Officers of the rank of Brigadiers from the Army. The Sector HQ exercises direct command and control over the Assam Rifles Battalions deployed in its area of responsibility.

Maintenance Group Assam Rifles (MGAR)

The Maintenance Groups located at various location provide the requisite administrative support to the Assam Rifles formations and battalions deployed in the field. The MGsAR are commanded by officers of the rank of Lt Col from the Army.

Workshops The workshops are co-located with the MGsAR to provide repair and recovery cover to the field formations. These workshops further provide detachments to the Sector HQs to provide repair and recovery cover as far forward as possible to the Battalions.

Para Military Forces first came to be employed on the Indian sub-continent, some time in the mid-19th century, essentially to consolidate and extend the annexation of the northeastern and the northwestern portions of the Indian landmass, with the least expense to the treasury. The then sovereign authorities found it increasingly difficult to garrison newly conquered territories; lying at great distances from the Presidency towns; with the regular troops. This was mainly owing to the exorbitant outlays involved. Paucity of readily available units was another reason. The problem was solved by raising special local units, such as the Punjab Irregular Frontier Force in the Punjab. In the northeast, the Assam Rifles (AR), initially named the Cachar Levys, came into being. Assam Rifles is the oldest para military force in India; rather the only para-military force in the strictest sense of the term. Its primary role as of now is to keep a vigil on a portion of India's northeastern International Border (IB). It also has the role of maintaining law and order in the tribal areas of Assam; a role that is now being abrogated to the police forces of the States and Union Territories that have emerged in northeastern India.

The AR traces its genesis back to 1835, when it was raised as a semi-military force known as the Cachar Levy with a complement of only 750. The role of this Force, as it was then conceived, was to maintain law and order in the Lushai Hills, and more generally to safeguard British interests; like tea gardens and other developmental work in relation to the opening up of the Assam area from the depredations of the head-hunting tribes which found great outdoor relief in raiding neighbouring settlements just for adventure and the fun of it. The Force was extensively used for extending administrative control over remote tribal areas in very difficult conditions with only rudimentary administrative back-up and at nominal pecuniary cost; however, it bore all odds with exemplary fortitude and stoicism - characteristics which still underlie the ethos of the Force to date.

Small townships, such as Aizawl, Lungleh, Kohima, Mokokchung, Tuensang, Haflong, Cherrapunji and Tura gradually mushroomed around its outposts. These are bustling population centres now. Variously designated and reorganised from time to time, as the Assam Frontier Police (1883), the Assam Military Police (1891) and Eastern Bengal and Assam Military Police (1913), it came to be known by its present name of the Assam Rifles in 1917 in recognition of its contribution to the war effort during the Great War.

The Force performed very commendably in the World Wars. In WW I it provided 23 officers and 3,174 soldiers to the various British Indian Army Gurkha Regiments, a process, which over the years resulted, into permanent affiliations of the battalions of AR to different groups of the Gurkhas. They fought shoulder to shoulder alongside regular army troops in the Middle East and acquitted themselves creditably, bagging as many as 76 decorations in the bargain. Later on, men were provided to the army columns engaged on punitive expeditions into the erstwhile Assam Hill Districts and North Eastern Frontier Agency (NEFA) and also some in trans-border reprisal missions into Burma. It was used for restoration of law and order in Patna in 1917 and also against the Moplah rebels in 1924. WW II saw it functioning as an element of the much-fabled, hush-hush and ghost-like "V" Force, on reconnaissance and harassment missions behind Japanese lines in Burma. Many of its sub units fought alongside regular British and Indian troops in the fiercely contested battles of the Burma Front from Ukhrul to Kohima. One platoon was even para-dropped behind the Japanese on the Sittang River. Though only five battalion strong then, it soldiered on valiantly to tally up a staggering total of 48 battle gallantry decorations/ medals. Some of its units did a historic and yeoman service in the management, evacuation and control of refugees staggering out on long, arduous and miserable treks in the dense jungles of Burma/ NEFA in the face of the Japanese onslaught.

The AR along with the Church, have managed to transform pre-historic animalistic societies of the northeast from the stone-age to space-age in three or four generations. Their humane and tactful handling of the inhabitants of our far-flung regions and tribal areas; be it during the initial era of pacification, or in the immediate post-Independence period of political turmoil, instability, ethnic tribal aspirations and resultant disturbed conditions; the AR troops have managed to win the hearts and minds of the populace in a good natured and large-hearted manner. It is, therefore, not for nothing, that the famous and erudite anthropologist and naturalist, Verrier Elwin has bestowed on them a singularly significant sobriquet of sorts: "The Friends Of The Hill People"! This is what he has said of them in tribute:

"The custodians of law and order, the pioneers of every advance into the interior, the guardians of our borders and the friends of the hill people. Modestly, and without fuss, they have faced every hardship and difficulty, and thousands of villagers in the wildest of areas think of them with affection and gratitude."

The AR operations are characterised by their total lack of any unfavourable post-operation fall-out whatsoever. They rely heavily on real-time intelligence and very swift reactions against pinpointed targets and specific individuals. They are loath to the ham-handed ways of the other forces, including the army, which only go to firm up the resolve of the dissidents and those gone astray, apart from antagonising the general public. They are past masters at roughing it out, and of course, very adept at improvisation, make do and living off the land with good grace. They know the border areas of their deployment like the palms of their hands. Experts in water crossing expedients, braving the elements and long cross-country marches on a self contained basis, they lend themselves excellently to their role as "the sentinels of the North East" as Major General DK Palit, VrC, FRGS (Retd) refers to them in his definitive regimental history of this remarkable Force. The AR units communicate on a very reliable, quick-response, secure and efficient static radio grid. Their MT drivers are experts in winding up and down narrow hill tracks in all kinds of weather conditions. It speaks volumes of their savvy in daily technical chores that, despite the step-motherly treatment meted out to them, they manage to keep the large vehicle fleet in a good roadworthy condition. These soldiers are quite skilled at elementary civil engineering tasks like construction of living quarters and road building including bridging. The troops are very mature, hardy, weather beaten, courageous, and know how to get on with the job at hand. They have the added advantage of conversing in the local lingo - a definite asset in a counter insurgency environment. This capability of the AR is further augmented by the presence of the locally recruited lads in units. Properly handled, these boys are real treasures in different situations such as in disturbed areas. Contrary to a misconception, the AR ethos is, in fact, one of accountability and honesty; sincerity and sagacity; the 'do or die' kind. Despite all these substantial positive attributes, it generally takes committed and sympathetic leadership to bring out the best in the men. They cannot be taken for granted for they can see through commanders in no time. Army officers have generally earned a good reputation for themselves. Names like Sushil Kumar, Father Lazarus, OP Bhandari, Sidhiman Rai, Kukreti, Jas Ram, RS Dayal and Krishan Pal are legends. One or two of these officers are even revered as demi-Gods, and this is no hyperbole!

Till Independence, the AR formed an integral part of the civil police under the Inspector General of Police, Assam. At that time, the units were commanded by civilians/police officers, though only those with a military background were preferred. This arrangement was not found to be particularly satisfactory, as it did not provide the desired degree of military captaincy particularly on mobile missions. This lead to the army providing officers on a volunteer basis. For over a hundred years now, the Indian Army has been providing the higher echelon leadership in the AR. On the transfer of power, Colonel Sidhiman Rai MC was appointed the first Indian IG AR. Since then, army officers have led the AR at different rungs of command. Prior to 1965, this Force was under the Ministry of External Affairs which was looking after the tribal areas till then. It was transferred to the Ministry of Home Affairs when the latter took over this responsibility.

From a nominal complement of only five battalions in 1947, it grew to 17 by 1960, to 21 by 1968 and to a substantial 31 as of now. The force is in the process of adding a further 12 rifle battalions post-Kargil. In addition, the Force has several range HQs, a training centre, and a number of logistics units under the HQ DG AR, Shillong. The Assam Rifles Public School, a brainchild of Lt Gen Sushil Kumar, the then DG AR, is a much sought after educational institute in the northeast.

Most of the AR units are under the operational control of the army. Their battle potential is as good as that of the regular infantry battalions. AR battalions are adept in counter insurgency operations, where their performance has been better than that of the Army/ Rashtriya Rifles. They are especially proficient in the un-orthodox type of small-scale missions to seek and destroy/apprehend hostiles. The study of one such mission, code named *Operation "Zebra"*, successfully launched and executed by 19 AR, was included in the curriculum of training of army infantry battalions being inducted for counter insurgency operations.

Organisation, leadership, equipment and training of the Force is generally on the Army pattern, however, each battalion has a unique Peace Establishment (PE). It is mostly officered by army officers who are being provided by the army on the same basis as it does for its own units. There is a fair number of ex-ECOs as also departmental promotees as well. The AR battalions have been permanently affiliated to various Infantry Regiments (mainly Gorkha regiments) for the purpose of providing officers from the regimental panels. AR commissioned JCOs lead at the sub-sub unit level. They can be easily rated above the army infantry JCOs. They have a lot of pride in the Force and their battalions; physically they are very fit, they exhibit a lot of initiative and a yen for independent command. The AR draws its rank and file from the hill tribes of northern/northeastern India, though a sprinkling of people from all corners of India is to be found down to the section level. Gorkhas, both Nepalese and domiciled, constitute approximately 40 per cent, followed by Garhwalis, Kumaonis and Dogras/

Himachalis. A large number of Malayalis, generally serving in the signals/cypher/medical sub-units, have also found their way into the Force. Be that as it may, the predominant culture is Gorkhali, and *Khas-kura* is the unofficial lingua franca. AR battalions, also have on their rolls, a fair number of "ministerial staff" or plain civilians, including ladies, in the finance branches and integral hospitals. The rank and file of the units under the operational control of the army are subject to the Army Act, those not, can be dealt with only under the provisions of the Civil Services rules even when operationally deployed. The age of retirement of men is 57 years but this is proving a strain after prolonged and continuous deployment of the AR in remote, far flung, backward, inhospitable and under-developed tribal border areas.

Some notable achievements and landmark events concerning the AR are:

1. In the disastrous 1950 earthquake in Upper Assam, 2 AR *jawans* rendered immediate and invaluable help in the reconstruction, resettlement and rehabilitation of the victims.
2. In 1959, it was the forward elements of this Force that received His Holiness The Dalai Lama and his entourage fleeing into India, and ensured their safe passage up to Misamari.
3. The initial onslaught of the Chinese in 1962 was borne by delaying elements of the AR. They gave a good account of themselves in this delaying role to enable the army to take up whatever defences that it was able to manage in the event.
4. The AR filled the void in toto in Nagaland and Manipur after the army formations deployed there were pulled out for operations in the west during the 1965 Indo-Pak War. They conducted counter insurgency operations and were in addition responsible for the general law and order situation. The AR deployment was further stretched as they were to stand in for the army along the Indo-Tibetan border and the International Border with the erstwhile East Pakistan in

Tripura. Rather thin on the ground, as indeed they undoubtedly were, they fulfilled their assignments with the usual élan and fortitude.

5. Similarly, the AR relieved the army for operations in the 1971 Bangladesh War. This time, their brief encompassed not only Nagaland and Manipur but also Mizoram and Tripura, where active counter insurgency operations were in full swing.
6. The 22nd, 23rd and 26th AR Battalions were committed for Op Pawan in Sri Lanka from December 1988 to February 1990. They were under the direct operational control of the army. Adept in the counter insurgency type operations undertaken there, they were on home ground and as such came out with colours flying very high!.
7. Two battalions of AR, the 7th and the 26th, have operated in the Srinagar Valley with great success. Their catches were more than those of the adjoining army units and formation commanders rated their performance very high.

At present the Force is deployed primarily in the northeast. It is helping out the civil administration in the maintenance of law and order, assisting the army in counter insurgency duties, and the general welfare of the locals and development of the inaccessible areas. It has proved itself as more than a match at least, if definitely not a rival for vying for honours and awards of army units engaged in counter insurgency and border surveillance roles. It can, therefore, be safely argued that, there exists a strong case for independent and more substantial role for this extraordinary Force, in the realm of the strategic defence of the Nation.

For example, to start with, the DG AR could be entrusted with operational duties as well. He could be directly responsible to the Army's Eastern Command for CI Ops in the northeast particularly in the troubled states of Nagaland, Mizoram, Tripura, Manipur, and Arunachal. Army formations should be pulled out from these areas, because they hardly provide any tangible benefits in a CI environment when the AR is placed under their command. In fact, they contribute in no uncertain way in fettering the AR troops and their typical *modus operandi*, not to speak of kindling a smouldering heart-burning as far as sharing the booty of gallantry awards goes. Some of the Army brass tries to steal their thunder and belittle the achievements of AR units. They are impatient for results and quick fixes, conveniently forgetting in their over exuberance that, quick fixes in a CI environment are few and far between. They should remember that, there are no short-term military solutions to a CI situation. Therefore, let it be stated once and for all time to come that, the army battalions, which are inducted for only fleeting tours of duty, can never aspire to be even a patch on the AR units which remain static in their areas of responsibilities for ages, and accrue innumerable operational advantages at the cutting edge of combat as a result of this.

Operations cannot be divorced from logistics, therefore, it goes without saying, that in order to shoulder this enhanced responsibility, the Force will have to be provided the requisite, integral and dedicated administrative backup, a sizeable portion of which is being provided by the Army on a book debit basis as of now. Later, suitably augmented with supporting arms, the AR could also be held responsible for guarding the entire northeastern border contiguous to the Tibetan Autonomous Region of China. New raisings of AR battalions in sufficient numbers, on War Equipment Tables (WETs) similar to the infantry battalions on Modification 'M', will be required. The existing ones will have to be reorganised. Additional raisings will have to cater for training, rest and refitting within the Force. As of now, hardly any collective training worth its name is practicable in the continuous deployment for operations scenario. Any training the troops can manage is of the on-the-job type. This is not at all a happy arrangement. As far as rest and recuperation, and the welfare of their families goes, the picture is even more grim. Troops are prone to bouts of loneliness and battle fatigue after such a prolonged deployment in remote war-torn regions. About time they got a break. The Force will require some dedicated heli-borne air reconnaissance, lift and mobility for quick reactions and re-supply in the mountainous northeast, which even in this age, has only, a rather primitive overland communications infrastructure.

In their proposed new and enhanced commitment, the AR ranges need to be deployed in three predominant tiers. The first one on the International Border in forward defended localities and border outposts/piquets/Early Warning Elements. The second tier, about fifteen to twenty kilometres in depth along routes of ingress of the anti-national elements and enemy approaches, for interception, apprehension and annihilation. The last one has to be sited in and around important population centres/towns.

This deployment will lend itself eminently to the proposed roles as it caters to step-by-step detection, discovery and planned destruction of intruders of any kind, be it the hostiles or the enemy. For effective command and control in this deployment, the DG AR will per force be required to function out of a tactical headquarters located at Dimapur, during active operations. IG HQs will have to be situated in each state. A few additional Range HQs will be imperative in the interest of methodical monitoring of the fluid and continuously changing battle situations that will invariably develop at short notice. Ranges should be closely integrated with not more than four to six battalions in each. These units should be rotated periodically within the range for rejuvenation thereby precluding the possibility of their going to seed and preventing over fraternisation with the local populace.

The AR has a proud record of devotion to duty and exemplary service. Nothing denotes it better then perhaps the honours and accolades bestowed on its rank and file. They have gone on to win as many as 534 army awards (including three Ashok Chakras Class 1, 28 Kirti Chakras, 94 Shaurya Chakras, and 5 Vir Chakras) after Independence! Civil/Police awards total a staggering 1997 (including 3 President's Police medals, and 117 President's Medals for Meritorious Service) 604 of them have also given the supreme sacrifice in the service to the Nation.

CENTRAL INDUSTRIAL SECURITY FORCE

It was established in its current form on June 15, 1983. Presently there are 90,000 personnel working in it.

Central Reserve Police Force: Presently there are 165,000 personnel in 200 battalions. The CRPF's primary role lies in assisting the State/Union Territories in police operations to maintain law and order and contain insurgency. It came into existence as the Crown Representative's Police on July 27, 1939. After Indian Independence, it became the Central Reserve Police Force on enactment of the CRPF Act on December 28, 1949.

CIVIL DEFENCE

The Civil Defence Policy of the Government till the declaration of emergency in 1962 was confined to making the States and Union Territories conscious of the need of Civil Defence measures and to ask them to keep ready Civil Defence Paper Plans for major cities & towns under the then Emergency Relief Organisation (ERO) Scheme. Two major incidents gave reason to the development of Civil Defence in India; the 1962 Indo-China and the 1965 Indo-Pak conflicts. This led to a considerable rethinking about the policy & scope of Civil Defence and as a result the Civil Defence Policy as it exists today, was evolved and Civil Defence legislation was enacted in the Parliament in 1968. In the 1971 Indo-Pak War, the Civil Defence acquitted itself commendably.

Civil Defence aims at saving lives, minimising damage to the property and maintaining continuity of industrial production in the event of an hostile attack. The Civil Defence Act of 1968, is though applicable throughout the country, but the organisation is only raised in such areas & zones which are tactically and strategically considered vulnerable from enemy attack points of view. At the moment Civil Defence activities are restricted to 135 categorised towns spread over 32 States/Union Territories. To meet the early warning communication requirement for an impending hostile attack, a reliable and flexible network, both on telephone lines and radio/wireless, have been established in most of the categorised Civil Defence Towns. Communication facilities, on telephone lines & radio, has also been planned and established in most of the Civil Defence towns for the purpose of command, control, coordination & liaison and also for mutual aid and cooperation.

Civil Defence is primarily organised on a voluntary basis except for a small nucleus of paid staff and establishment which is augmented during emergencies. The present target of Civil Defence volunteers is 394,000 personnel in 135 towns in 32 states. Apart from carrying out training and demonstration of Civil Defence measures during peacetime, Civil Defence volunteers are also deployed, on voluntary basis, in various constructive activities including assistance to the administration, relief & rescue work during natural calamities like floods, earthquakes, cyclones, droughts, etc. by the administration of the State Governments/Union Territories of their own. Civil Defence Training is conducted in the country on a three-tier concept, i.e. Local/Town level, at State level and National level. The National Civil Defence College at Nagpur, a subordinate training establishment of the Ministry, conducts various courses in civil defence and disaster relief management.

Civil Defence Capabilities of the Indian State

Few discussions of the implications of nuclear weapons in the India-Pakistan context make any mention of the civil defence capabilities of either state. It is generally assumed that the civil defence services in both countries will be rapidly overwhelmed by a nuclear attack and would be as good as useless. This may well be true – we have yet to find out - however, in India's case, the state has had enormous experience in dealing with some of the most catastrophic natural disasters known to man. While these may not approach the magnitude of a nuclear attack, they provide an interesting insight into the strengths and weaknesses of the Indian disaster management apparatus.

India maintains and trains a sizeable civil defence force and has laid down a reasonably comprehensive set of procedures and regulations governing civil defence operations in the event of war. While many of India's state governments do not implement these plans in peacetime, the fact that these plans exist and are periodically reviewed cannot be ignored. Moreover, as will be shown, the plans lay emphasis on rapid emergency measures rather than on a well-developed peacetime infrastructure.

In addition to the civil defence organization, India spends considerable money on a reserve body called the Home Guards and on the National Cadet Corps. These organizations do receive a modicum of civil defence training and are expected to reinforce and assist the regular emergency services in the event of war. India's huge police and paramilitary forces also have considerable experience in disaster management and would be a very valuable asset. The question as to how this set up will perform in the event of a nuclear war, however, remains unanswered.

The Development of Civil Defence in India

India's first steps in creating civil defence organization came at the start of the Second World War. Between the years 1939 and 1941, a cell in India's Home Department was established to deal with the subject of Civil Defence/Air Raid Precautions. A Lieutenant -Colonel of the Indian Army was placed in charge of this cell with effect from October 1939. This officer was given the status of a Deputy Secretary to the Government of India and his duties included extensive touring to advise and help Provincial Governments in preparing Civil Defence plans. Another officer was later appointed to act as a liaison between General Headquarters and the Home Department and to assist with technical advice on Air Raid Precautions matters.

It was not until June 1941, however, that an army Major was appointed as Deputy Assistant Director General - Indian Medical Service in order to deal with the medical aspects of civil defence. It can be seen from this that civil defence was not taken particularly seriously by the Indian government. Despite these developments, virtually no civil defence plans or organization existed on the ground.

It took the start of the war in Europe for civil defence to receive more attention in India and in July 1941, a decision was taken to create a full-fledged Civil Defence Department. In September 1941, India's first Director General of Civil Defence was posted to the Home Department. The Civil Defence Department came into being on 24 October 1941 when Dr. E. Raghavendra Rao - the first Civil Defence Member of the Governor General 's Executive Council - arrived after training in England. The Air Raid Precautions cell in the Home Department was transferred to the new Civil Defence Department and was expanded.

Throughout 1942, the Indian Civil Defence Department expanded at a rapid pace as the threat of Japanese attack intensified. In close cooperation with the Provincial Governments - who were responsible for the implementation of the individual plans - a series of plans were drawn up to cope with the perceived threats. As the main Japanese threat came from the North-East, most of the civil defence efforts were concentrated in this area. The Civil Defence Department was responsible form planning , advice and provision of equipment while the provincial government was responsible for the distribution of civil defence instructions and on raising of fire-fighting and rescue units. The Civil Defence Department and the Provincial Governments did some remarkable work, but, civil defence activities in India were not particularly extensive or comprehensive. Compared to what existed before the war substantial progress had been made, but, compared to the massive civil defence efforts of, say, the United Kingdom, India's measures were woefully inadequate.

As the threat of Japanese attack faded, the Civil Defence Department was steadily wound down. In 1946 the Department was liquidated. A small cell - a mere shadow of the wartime organization continued to exist in the Home Department, but for all intents and purposes, India's civil defence organization ceased to exist. After independence, in 1948, the Emergency Relief Scheme existed as a cell in the Ministry of Home Affairs. This cell concerned itself with fire-fighting and fire-prevention and eventually led to the establishment of the National Fire Services College and the Central

Emergency Relief Training Institute - now called the National Civil Defence College - at Nagpur in 1956-57. The formal initiation of civil defence in India started in 1953 when a civil defence plan was drafted. However, this failed to get accepted and was drastically revised. While the Civil Defence and Fire Service Colleges continued to run courses, for the first 15 years of Indian independence, there was no civil defence organization in existence on the ground. The Chinese invasion of 1962 changed all this.

As part of the massive rethinking and reorganization of India's national security policy, the British civil defence expert, General Irwin, was invited to draft the blueprint of a national civil defence plan and to give practical advice on how to meet both conventional and unconventional attacks. Two manuals were compiled and circulated to all state governments for the preparation of comprehensive civil defence plans in selected high priority towns which were categorized on the basis of their importance.

The Defence of India Act 1962 gave the State and Union Territory governments with all the powers necessary for the implementation of the measures outlined in General Irwin's manuals. These two manuals - ' The Master Plan for Civil Defence in India' and 'General Principles of Civil Defence' - form the structural basis for India's Civil Defence Organization to the present day. As regards the implementation of these plans, it was officially stated in the Indian Parliament in 1963, that while certain recommendations were implemented immediately, other measures regarding civil defence were to be kept on paper, to be implemented when needed. To this end, a comprehensive plan of operation was drawn up and directives issued to the State and Union Territory governments to make their own civil defence plans and to keep them, even if just on paper, in a state of readiness for their successful implementation in an emergency.

Over time, certain states have drafted a number of other emergency plans to cope with natural disasters such as cyclones and earthquakes as well as man-made calamities such as chemical and nuclear accidents. These plans tend to be kept in a higher state of readiness than the civil defence plans since the civil defence plan allows for the mobilization of resources in a phased manner to meet a threat for which there is considerable prior warning. In the case of natural disasters, this warning is not available.The 1965 and 1971 wars provided some experience for the Indian Civil Defence Organization. Despite this, no major changes have been recommended and the civil defence organization in India continues as envisaged in the Irwin Plan of 1962.

Strength, Organization and Structural Foundations

In 1995, the Indian Civil Defence Organization had a sanctioned strength of 676,000 volunteers in addition to a small (strength unknown) nucleus of professional staff which is to be augmented in an emergency. However, only 376,000 have actually been raised and of these, only 330,000 are fully trained. The civil defence staff and volunteers are a distinct and separately organized group from the other Indian emergency services - i.e. fire departments and paramedics. At present, civil defence units are raised and stationed in categorized civil defence towns. These towns are graded on both their vulnerability and on their strategic importance - a practice dating back to the Second World War. At present, there are 110 categorized towns spread over 24 states and union territories. This means that civil defence personnel and expenditure are concentrated in the areas where they are needed most. This is particularly important since the regular civil defence forces receive only Rs. 65 million from the central government. The Central Government handles all matters regarding equipment and communications. All the central government ministries have civil defence cells which would be activated in wartime.

In addition to these volunteers, the Indian Civil Defence Organization relies heavily on the Home Guards and the National Cadet Corps. These two organizations are funded and, in the case of the NCC, trained separately from the civil defence volunteers. The Home Guards have a sanctioned strength of 573,793 and has a current raised strength of 418,493. Unlike the Civil Defence

Organization, the Home Guards are spread across the country and extend into the rural as well as the urban areas. The Home Guards were created as an auxiliary to India's vast police and paramilitary forces and have an important role in the maintenance of law and order as well as internal security. In peacetime, the Home Guards assist communities in emergencies as epidemics, fires and floods, while their role in wartime extends to civil defence work as well as assisting the army in maintaining rear area security. The Home Guards have a budget of Rs.280 million - considerably higher than the Civil Defence Organization. The organization, since it is more geographically widespread, provides a veneer of civil defence cover to rural areas as well as reinforcing the civil defence units in the 110 categorized civil defence towns. Their training, as will be discussed later, prepares them for rescue and fire-fighting work. There is also provision for raising auxiliary Home Guards from the ex-soldiers population of India in case of extreme necessity - as in the case of the 1965 India-Pakistan war.

The National Cadet Corps are another important source of manpower for civil defence. Their training will be discussed in some more detail later, but since the 1980s, 32 NCC officers and cadets are trained as civil defence instructors at the National Civil Defence College each year. The National Cadet Corps Act of 1948 states that NCC cadets have no military service liability. This means that they cannot be deployed on duties where they have to be armed - unless special legislation is passed. This, however, does not exempt them from civil defence work. On 9th. September 1965 - during the 1965 India-Pakistan war - the Indian Central Government drew up a list of duties which were to be performed by NCC personnel over the age of 17. These included the following:

(a) Passive Air Defence - including rescue work, first air, casualty evacuation fire fighting and removal of debris
(b) Manning of Civil Defence Posts - including civil defence patrols and look outs
(c) Maintenance of essential services - including motor transport, pioneer and engineering and water and power supply

(d) Traffic Control

(e) Manning Static Signal Installations

(f) Administration and running of evacuation camps

With these duties assigned to them, the NCC forms a very useful reinforcement for the Civil Defence Organization. This is even more obvious when it is realised that the NCC has 420,000 cadets in its Senior Division - made up of university students over the age of 17. The central and state governments contribute to the expenditure on the NCC in the ratio of 2:1. The budget for the NCC comes, in part from the Ministry of Defence - not the Home Ministry in the case of the Home Guards and Civil Defence Organization. It should be stated that the army regards the NCC as a waste of money. In addition to these organizations, the Indian government controls the Central Industrial Security Force and the Crisis Management Group of the Atomic Energy Regulatory Board. These two organizations, while not specifically created for the task of civil defence, could provide vital equipment, training and skilled personnel when operating in an environment of either radioactive or chemical contamination. As regards funding, the Indian central government maintains a sizeable calamity relief fund for use in the case of a natural disaster. This would provide a valuable source of reconstruction funds for post-war recovery. In fact, it can be said that the published expenditure on civil defence - Rs. 65 million - represents a relatively small fraction of the expenditure on a disaster relief/civil defence infrastructure. While little evidence of civil defence activities can be seen in peacetime, the extensive pool of manpower, combined with plans and an organizational set up, gives India to field a civil defence organization in wartime that is far better organized, larger and more capable than would first be apparent from the rather pathetic peacetime infrastructure.

THE CIVIL DEFENCE SET-UP - CENTRAL AND STATE RESPONSIBILITIES

The Indian Ministry of Home Affairs has, under its direct control, a Directorate of Civil Defence headed by a Director

General - usually a senior police officer. He advise the Home Ministry on all matters relating to the Civil Defence Organization and the Home Guards as well as regular fire-fighting units. The central government has the responsibility for coordinating civil defence activities in States and Union Territories. This is done to ensure that civil defence personnel have a uniformly high standard of training and that plans are kept up to date. The principal role of the central government is that of supervision and coordination - laying down principles and policies on air raid shelters and on protection in general.

The civil defence set-up at the centre drafts all emergency plans for all states and provides for the provision of equipment and training where necessary. In order to effectively carry out its assigned task, the central Directorate of Civil Defence maintains close contact with other government ministries for expertise on various subjects.

For example, the Ministry of Urban Development provides technical advice on the construction of air raid shelters while the Ministries of Communications and Surface Transport provide communications equipment and transport for civil defence units. Other ministries provide advice on evacuation, bomb disposal and on health and welfare. Each of these ministries has a small civil defence cell.

The Ministries of Defence and Railways are responsible for civil defence on properties owned or managed by them. These include ordnance factories and army cantonments as well as railway stations. These two ministries receive their advice and instructions from the Central Directorate of Civil Defence. The main functions of the Central Civil Defence Organization can be summarized as follows:

(1) To coordinate work among the various ministries of the Indian government - including the State governments
(2) To lay down general policy for Civil Defence in India
(3) To prepare and keep ready in peace times, plans for training of personnel and organization of Civil Defence services

(4) To determine the manpower requirements of the organization by assessing the existing resources and preparing plans to remedy the deficiencies

(5) To ensure uniformity of practice and procedure and to indicate the action which should be taken in any towns as and when an emergency arises

(6) To build up stockpiles of essential civil defence equipment

(7) To prepare draft civil defence legislation, plans and literature on evacuation, welfare, precautionary and protective measures for the protection of life and property.

It can thus be seen that the central government of India plays only a advisory, planning and coordination role in Civil Defence Matters. The real responsibility for the implementation of civil defence measures in the event of war falls to the State and District administrations in the States and Union Territories. The officials manning these tiers of government are in the forefront of any emergency. They are responsible for all rescue and rehabilitation measures in the event of either war or natural disaster. They have considerable experience in the latter - not so much in the former.

Each State and Union Territory government has, under the overall control of its Inspector General of Police, a Director General of Home Guards and Civil Defence. As in the case of the central government, he is a senior police officer and is responsible for controlling fire departments as well. It must, however, be pointed out, that many of the urban fire fighting units in India are under the control of Municipal Corporations and as such are not always equipped to the standard established by the DG - Home Guards & Civil Defence. Fire-fighting regulations are also routinely ignored.

The local governments are responsible for fire-fighting, maintenance of municipal roads, water supply, conservation etc. The Public Works Department is responsible for the provision of shelters, sandbags, trenches, salvage, repairs and demolition. The other state government branches - health, labour, railways etc. - assist in their various fields, as in the case of the central government. All State governments have plans for civil defence against attacks - both conventional and unconventional - as per the recommendations of General Irwin. Most of these plans are kept on paper, to be activated only in times of war- involving mobilization of manpower and resources.

The State governments rely heavily on the central government for the provision of equipment. However, their record in dealing with natural disasters is quite impressive - even when disasters strike suddenly. Moreover, in addition to their civil defence plans, most states have disaster management plans and schemes which are usually kept in a considerably higher state of readiness as they are needed almost annually. The Commissioner, District Magistrate and Sub-Divisional Officer are the ultimate authority for Civil Defence in the Division, District and Sub-Division respectively. The District Magistrate functions as the Controller of Civil Defence, but in certain cases there may be a need to a separate and autonomous Civil Defence Controller to give additional assistance to the local authorities.

The Civil Defence Controller nominates various departmental heads of the district as the commanders of the various civil defence services. For example, the Chief Medical Officer functions as the head of the casualty service and the Executive Engineer - Public Works Department (Building & Roads) as head of the Rescue and Demolition Service. The Civil Defence Controller - the District Magistrate in most cases - coordinates the activities of all these departments in respect of planning, enrolment, training and provision of equipment. In times of need, regular meetings are held to ensure the readiness of the various civil defence units.

The civil defence of a city or town is organized on the basis of its population as well as on its vulnerability. Any city/town having a population of more than 300,000 is divided into one or more zones of 2-300,000 people each. Each zone is further divided into two or three Divisions - each with 100,000 people - which are in turn divided into Warden Post Areas - with 10-12,000 people. These are further subdivided into Sectors - with a population of 2-3,000. Each Sector has one House Fire Party per 500 people.

The civil defence structure of a town having a population of more than 300,000 looks like this:

Zone (2-300,000 persons)

|

Division Division Division

|

Warden Posts - 1 per 10-12,000 people

|

Sectors - 1 per 2-3,000 people

|

House Fire Parties - 1 per 500 people

Civil Defence Services in India can be broken down into three basic categories:

(1) Volunteer Services - provided by the public e.g Air Raid Wardens

(2) Control & Depot Services - provided by Home Guards, NCC etc. e.g Rescue Units

(3) Special Services - provided by other Departments e.g Engineering

In peacetime - the volunteer units are not active - the various government departments responsible for these tasks pay little attention to them. In times of crisis, coordination and mobilization are absolutely essential for India's civil defence plans. The service categories listed above are themselves broken down into the basic civil defence services that form the backbone of any civil defence structure.

The civil defence authorities in India are required to make provision for both control and sub-control centres. These are located in the various civil defence zones and towns and are to coordinate all civil defence efforts between them. The Indian government believes that one sub-control centre can deal with 40-50 Wardens posts. These control centres are to be protected against both blast and fragmentation effects of high-explosive bombs. This standard of construction also gives significant protection against limited atomic strikes as well.

As would be expected, the control centres would have good communications links to the various wardens posts and the civil defence emergency services. In addition to this, the control centres are responsible for the Air Raid Warning system. This includes both the standard air raid sirens - including factory sirens - as well as a more direct warning system based on telephone links. Air raid wardens also assist by using whistles and flags to warn their areas of responsibility.

A reliable and flexible early warning network based on both telephone lines and on radio/wireless has been established in categorized civil defence towns. Most states have communications networks for use in the event of a natural disaster - cyclones and floods in particular. The Indian Department of Telecommunications would be responsible for most emergency broadcasts. Agencies like All India Radio will play an essential role in any civil defence situation in the Indian context. As in the Second World War, the backbone of the civil defence effort will be borne by the Air Raid Wardens. These are unpaid volunteers in peacetime and would be responsible for all civil defence efforts in their sectors. The warden is responsible for advising local people on civil defence, organizing self-help parties for fire fighting and rescue and reporting all damage to the control centres. Each civil defence division is sanctioned 114 wardens, including special advisors from government departments.

The civil defence emergency services - casualty, rescue, fire-fighting and welfare - are all under the direction of the control and sub-control centres. These services rely heavily on other government agencies for the manpower, equipment and expertise for their embodiment and successful operation.

The casualty service relies heavily on the emergency hospital organization for its operation. This involves the use of ambulance trains to evacuate casualties in vulnerable areas to hospitals in safer zones. The Director of Health Services in each state is responsible for the various hospitals in the state - government, local, charitable, private and railway hospitals. All of these come under the emergency hospital organization and will be used in the event of an emergency. This ensures that all medical and paramedical personnel and equipment is used as efficiently as possible. The importance of this cannot be underestimated since in peacetime, the Indian health system, while extensive, is extremely inefficient and badly coordinated. It is likely that medical personnel and equipment will be requisitioned for areas lacking adequate resources.

As part of the overall casualty service, there are provision for mobile and static first aid posts as well as mobile surgical units. The mobile surgical units are to be allocated on a scale of one per civil defence zone, with a 25% reserve of manpower and equipment. The first aid posts are to be provided on a scale of ten per division - one per Warden Post. Ambulances, which come under the control of the staff officer of the first aid parties, are to be provided on a scale of 2 per 5 first aid posts and 1 per first aid party. This plan relies heavily on the mobilization of manpower and vehicles for the provision of first aid personnel and vans for use as ambulances.

Rescue units - eight men per unit - are provided on a scale of one per 25,000 people. Drawn from men in the Home Guards and National Cadet Corps - as well as from police, paramilitary forces and the Public Works Department - the rescue units are under the overall control of the District Executive Engineer. Advice is also provided by specialists from various government departments - both from state and central governments. Equipment and vehicles are supposed to be earmarked for use by the rescue units - again, this relies heavily on mobilization of resources.

As can be imagined, fire fighting teams are the single most important element in civil defence work. The regular Indian fire departments are woefully undermanned and, in a few cases, poorly trained and inadequately equipped. In wartime, they are to augmented by auxiliary fire-fighting units - manned by Home Guards and equipped with trailer pumps towed by trucks. These are to be provided on a scale of one per 25,000 population. There are also provisions for small house fire-parties, under the control of air raid wardens. These, equipped with stirrup pumps and buckets, are unlikely to be of any use in the event of a nuclear attack. However, they would provide an extremely valuable asset in the event of conventional air attack.

All states are also required to make provisions for a self-contained Civil Defence Mobile Force. It was recognized that State civil defence units would have to reinforce each other and to this end, the concept of the mobile civil defence forces came into being. The Civil Defence Mobile Force is to consist of separate civil defence battalions, each battalion having four companies with 200 personnel each. Each company would have the following four platoons and would operate semi-independently:

(a) Company Headquarters

(b) Rescue Platoon

(c) Medical Platoon

(d) Fire-Fighting Platoon

It is not known if any states maintain fully operational mobile civil defence battalions, however, the Central government maintained (maintains?) a Mobile Civil Emergency Force. This force, based at Delhi and Calcutta and under the direct control of the Home Ministry was well equipped and trained for all aspects of civil defence work. This force was used extensively for emergency relief operations during the 1977 cyclone in Andhra Pradesh and its performance was found to be more than satisfactory. In peacetime, the Delhi unit was used as a training school, conducting courses on rescue, fire-fighting and casualty clearance. However, in 1988, it was reported that the Delhi unit was being wound up - perhaps because of the significant improvements in emergency services in the national capital and its surrounding states.

As far as the individual states are concerned, there is a nucleus of civil defence instructors and experts under the control of the state police and fire services. These have in the past been used for rescue operations beyond the ability of the regular emergency services. They are apparently well trained and reasonably well equipped - including protective masks and clothing for chemical attacks/disasters. It is not clear, however, as to how many personnel are available for immediate use nor are any clear details available about their organization - it is unlikely to be above company/battalion strength.

Civil Defence emergency services are stationed at civil defence depots. These depots, to be based at each sub-control centre, house first-aid, ambulance, rescue and fire-fighting services as well as mobile surgical units and canteens. The depots are to be located at least one kilometre away from any likely target - this would assist in minimizing damage, even in the event of a limited nuclear attack. The depots are also to provide all the emergency units with air-raid shelters - for personnel, vehicles and stores - indicating at least some awareness of the risk of loss in the event of attack.

As far as air-raid shelters are concerned, the Indian Civil Defence Act of 1968, makes provision for any Indian police officer or civil defence official to order the construction of an air raid shelter wherever and whenever necessary. The Crisis Management Group of the Atomic Energy Regulatory Board constructed a number of shelters for use in the event of a nuclear accident , designed to be blast and fallout proofed. All military installations have underground command centres and major fuel and ammunition stores at airbases are buried deep underground. The Indian civil defence plans place great emphasis on the construction of emergency air raid shelters. Particular emphasis is given to trench shelters - both covered and uncovered. While these would provide very little protection against blast effects, the trench shelter offers very considerable protection against the effects of nuclear fallout and radiation.

The Civil Defence Act also gives some indication regarding evacuation. Either the State or Central Government may order any area to be evacuated. Guidelines are also provided regarding the accommodation of evacuated persons and their welfare. The Welfare Service deals with the feeding, accommodation and evacuation of the population. A fully equipped welfare unit is to be set up at each civil defence division - with feeding, information, housing and emergency clothing facilities. All states have evacuation plans of some kind and some have become quite adept at emergency evacuation of even extremely remote areas. The government of the impoverished state of Andhra Pradesh, for example, was able to evacuate over 260,000 people over the course of a few days in November 1996. This was done to avoid a sudden cyclone - much more could be expected to be done with adequate warning and from urban centres well served with road and rail links- like the various state capitals.

The Indian central government maintains a substantial buffer stock of foodgrain - between fifteen and twenty-two million tonnes - and has had considerable experience in providing emergency supplies of drinking water. Thanks to India's very considerable experience with natural disaster management, both central and state governments have considerable practical expertise in dealing with relief efforts, including the provision of food, water, shelter and medical care. This expertise would be invaluable in the event of an attack - nuclear or conventional (or chemical- Bhopal provided practical experience).

With regards to vital industries, India's defence planners have based their war assessments on a war lasting roughly two months. As a result, the Indian government maintains a stock of imported raw materials - those required by vital industries - for about six months. The Indian military industries stockpile vital components - both imported and locally produced - for several months based on a high usage rate.

The existing civil defence structure, therefore, relies heavily on auxiliary units for the provision of emergency services. The officials responsible for this task are already in place - though not acting in their civil defence capacities. These officials, at both the central and state government level are supposed to have some training in their assigned civil defence tasks. This also applies to the Home Guards, NCC cadets and policemen who will provide manpower for the civil defence emergency units.

TRAINING, PLANNING AND EQUIPMENT

The training of civil defence personnel takes place at the national, state and district level, reflecting the nature of the organization. The National Civil Defence College at Nagpur conducts courses for all probationers in the Indian Police Service and the Indian Administrative Service. The two week long training course includes basic disaster management as well as civil defence against nuclear, chemical and biological threats. The National Civil Defence College also trains civil defence instructors for the state governments as well as over thirty NCC officers and NCOs each year. Over 28,000 personnel have been trained at the college since 1957. Most personnel trained at this institute have shown themselves to be reasonably competent in times of crisis. In fact, it is now accepted that the training standard and quality of civil defence officers and volunteers is of an acceptable standard, even if their morale is not. As is the case throughout the Indian services, civil defence personnel are woefully underpaid.

The central government also trains key fire fighting personnel for the central forces as well as the state fire fighting services. The National Fire Service College - also located at Nagpur - trains the fire officers from all the Indian states as well as from foreign countries. Almost 11,000 fire officers have been trained since 1957. These in turn provide advice and training to the state fire services. The College is the only one of its kind in South/South-East Asia and provides reasonably comprehensive training. At the state level, each state has a combined training institute for the training of the Home Guards as well as Civil Defence volunteers. These institutes provide a nucleus of instructors who are responsible for the training of the District civil defence volunteers and Home Guards. One civil defence instructor per four Home Guard companies is assigned to train the Home Guards in civil defence. The Home Guards receive additional courses in fire-fighting, crowd control and weapons training.

As regards equipment, the Public Works Departments possess almost all equipment necessary for rescue work. The fire departments are usually equipped to a reasonable standard - including aluminized fabric garments and breathing apparatus, which protect against NBC agents to a considerable extent.

The auxiliary fire fighting, rescue and emergency units would be provided with protective gear as and if required.Paper plans to cope with emergencies abound in India - though they are not publicized. However, the moves by the Indian government to create a comprehensive disaster management plan must be viewed positively, even if much of the infrastructure is not in place. This policy, drawn up in consultation with the state governments as well as central ministries and institutions, lays out a comprehensive set of guidelines for dealing with natural calamities, civil strife as well as chemical and nuclear disasters. A crisis management plan has already been implemented for dealing with chemical emergencies at the central, state and district levels. Guidelines have already been sent to the states and the central government is providing assistance for the development of the required infrastructure. While this may seem to be of little relevance, the coordination of skilled personnel now being trained and equipped under this scheme would be invaluable in the event of a chemical attack - as would the protective equipment used by such personnel. Of even greater importance are the emergency plans of the Crisis Management Group of the Atomic Energy Regulatory Board. In addition to the provision of shelters mentioned earlier, the CMG has organized a central stockpile of protective clothing and monitoring equipment which could be airlifted to the scene of an emergency. The CMG has also trained medical and relief workers in the areas around nuclear power plants on how to deal with a nuclear disaster- invaluable in the event of war.

Weaknesses of the Indian Civil Defence Organization

As has been shown, the Indian civil defence authorities have a comprehensive series of plans to cope with emergencies. There are provisions for auxiliary emergency units and for evacuation and medical care. However, the system has a number of inherent weaknesses. What is striking about the Indian civil defence plans is their reliance on the Home Guards, police and NCC to provide manpower for the emergency units. The problems with this scheme are twofold: how well trained are these units and how fast can they be mobilized? Elements of the National Cadet Corps do receive training in civil defence - instructors at the National Civil Defence College and others at annual training camps. The NCC has, during the 1965 and 1971 wars, been used for civil defence duties. In 1971, over 100,000 cadets volunteered for civil defence duties. The performance of the NCC units in both wars was considered reasonably good and they earned considerable praise. It is not known how well they would perform in any future war, but their previous performance gives cause for some optimism. With regard to the Home Guard units, they have, even in peacetime, been used to augment both the police and regular fire brigades. Their performance in any future war would depend on how much time was available for refresher training in new civil defence techniques. Also, Home Guard officers are specifically tasked with civil defence.

The mobilization of the manpower for civil defence tasks could well be a very time consuming task. Home Guards are raised in their specific towns and are therefore available at relatively short notice. However, it is not clear whether their equipment would be available as easily, nor is it clear that this equipment would be in a good state of repair. Nonetheless, at least some equipment - especially the fire-fighting and rescue apparatus - is kept to a very high standard as it is often needed by the regular fire-fighting services and the public works departments. The NCC units are based at colleges and universities and as such may be easily mobilized. Additional manpower is available from the State Armed Police Battalions, which are usually available at short notice and have a fair amount of expertise in rescue work - with natural disasters.

Perhaps the biggest hurdle faced by the Indian Civil Defence Organization is public apathy in peacetime. It is extremely difficult to motivate people and governments to allocate either time or money for civil defence tasks. This is why there is a shortfall of 300,000 personnel in the strength of civil defence volunteers. Indian state government, while receiving adequate funding from the central government, tend to cut back on the state's contribution to civil defence units. The worst offender in this regard has been the incredibly corrupt and impoverished state of Bihar where gross mismanagement and a state of utter chaos exists in the state civil defence department. In peacetime, the police officers assigned to civil defence departments are usually officers who are anti-corrupt or who have the courage to stand up to illegal orders. These officers, while reasonably competent, feel frustrated as they are considered to be out of favour with the police high command. In some states, however, these police officers are also in command of the regular fire-fighting units. Here, as in the case of civil defence, inadequate funds are provided, though, with help from Japan and from the Government Insurance Corporation of India, additional funds for the modernization and expansion of state fire services have been recently been forthcoming.

Public apathy is far more difficult to overcome. As soon as an air-raid materializes, there is a clamour for civil defence measures, yet, the public have not taken and do not take civil defence seriously - until war breaks out. It is virtually impossible for the police officers, Home Guards and fire service personnel to encourage the population to take civil defence more seriously in peacetime - it is almost impossible to get Indian civilians to take peacetime fire prevention regulations seriously. The other problems faced by civil emergency units in India are extremely serious. There is a lack of coordination among various agencies and many lack adequate preparation for their assigned tasks. In addition there is a lack of centralised ambulance, accident and trauma services. These make relief operations in peacetime extremely difficult, yet,India copes quite effectively with several natural calamities each year. The civil defence plans provide for rectifying many of these weaknesses in times of war by mobilizing auxiliary units - it remains to be seen if this will work effectively.

CONCLUSIONS

It is not possible for the central and state governments of India to maintain large full-time civil defence forces in peacetime. The existing scheme, while far from perfect, is at least realistic in relying on auxiliary units to provide the bulk of the emergency services. It is also realistic in assuming that much of the required civil defence infrastructure would have to be set up in a short space of time.How will the Indian civil defence structure cope with a nuclear attack ? The answer is not known as such a situation has not yet arisen (fortunately) in India, or in any other country for that matter. However, India's enormous experience in dealing with natural and man-made calamities has provided India's relief officials at both state and central levels with considerable expertise in handling mass rescue and relief operations. The current drafting of a comprehensive disaster management plan will be of great help. Serious questions remain about the ability of the Indian auxiliary forces to mobilize, train and equip quickly enough to operate effectively. The plans look good on paper, but their reliance on mobilizing assets could reduce their potential effectiveness. However, the Home Guard and Civil Defence units are located in or very near to the 110 categorized civil defence towns. This would dramatically reduce response time and also permits concentration of resources at vulnerable areas. Adequate warning would, of course be needed to mobilize all the necessary resources - a warning time of at least 48 hours should suffice to at least prepare emergency personnel and measures. This is not to say that the Indian civil defence agencies will not be hard pressed to cope with a nuclear attack. However, given the available resources and past experience, it is unlikely they would collapse into complete chaos and ineffectiveness.

Bibliography

Azad, Maulana Abul Kalam: *India Wins Freedom*, New Delhi, Orient Longman, 1959.

Bellamy, C.: *Knights in White Armour: The New Art of War and Peace*, London, Random House, 1997.

Bose, S. C., *The Indian Struggle, 1920-1942*, Bombay, Asia Publishing House, 1964.

Chandra, R.: *Judicial System in India*, Lucknow, Print House (India), 1992.

Greer P.: *Transforming Central Government: the Next Steps Initiative*, Buckingham, Open University Press, 1994.

Holsti, K.: *The State, War, and the State of War*, Cambridge, Cambridge Univ. Press, 1996.

Huntington, S.P.: *The Soldier and the State*, N.Y., Vintage Books, 1964.

Keane J.: *Democracy and Civil Liberty*, London, Verso, 1988.

Majumdar, R. C.: *An Advanced History of India*, New York, St. Martin's Press, 1967.

Noorani, A.G. : *Indian Political Trials : 1775-1947*, New Delhi, Oxford University Press, 2005.

Posen, B.R.: *The Sources of Military Doctrine*, Ithaca, 1984, Cornell Univ. Press.

Rosen, P.: *Societies and Military Power: India and its Armies*, Ithaca, Cornell University Press, 1996.

Rosen, P.: *Societies and Military Power: India and its Armies*, Ithaca, Cornell University Press, 1996.

INDEX